2008–2009 Annual Supplement to

THE PIANO BOOK®

BUYING & OWNING A NEW OR USED PIANO

LARRY FINE

BROOKSIDE PRESS • BOSTON, MASSACHUSETTS

Brookside Press
P.O. Box 300168, Jamaica Plain, Massachusetts 02130
(617) 522-7182
(800) 888-4741 (orders: Independent Publishers Group)

info@pianobook.com
www.pianobook.com

Printed in the United States of America

Distributed to the book trade by Independent Publishers Group,
814 North Franklin St., Chicago, IL 60610
(800) 888-4741 or (312) 337-0747

ISBN 978-1929145-23-2 (print edition)
ISBN 978-1929145-24-9 (electronic edition)

NOTICE

Reasonable efforts have been made to secure accurate information for this publication. Due in part to the fact that manufacturers and distributors will not always willingly make this information available, however, some indirect sources have been relied upon.

Neither the author nor publisher make any guarantees with respect to the accuracy of the information contained herein and will not be liable for damages—incidental, consequential, or otherwise—resulting from the use of the information.

INTRODUCTION

Given the long time span between new editions of *The Piano Book,* it's impractical to provide in the book itself the detailed model and price data that piano shoppers increasingly seek. Similarly, updated information about manufacturers and products is needed in a timely manner. This *Annual Supplement to The Piano Book,* published each summer, is designed to fill that information gap. I hope this modest companion volume will effectively extend the "shelf life" of *The Piano Book* as a valuable reference work, and serve as an additional information resource for piano buyers and piano lovers.

Thanks to my research assistant, Barbara Fandrich, for her many hours spent communicating with manufacturers by phone and email, inputting data, and rewriting copy, tasks that were often frustrating, but which she nevertheless handled quickly, cordially, and with careful attention to detail.

Larry Fine

June 2008

CONTENTS

MANUFACTURER and PRODUCT UPDATE 5

    Trends 5

    Summary of Brands and Ratings 11

    Brand Listings 20

MODEL and PRICING GUIDE 117

For more assistance:

- New Piano Pricing Guide Service
- Phone Consultation with the Author

See www.pianobook.com

MANUFACTURER and PRODUCT UPDATE

This section contains brief descriptions of most brands of new piano distributed nationwide in the United States. The articles contain (often verbatim) material from the fourth edition of *The Piano Book* where still relevant and accurate, accumulated changes from past *Supplements*, and new material gleaned from interviews with manufacturers, distributors, dealers, technicians, and other sources. Most manufacturers had an opportunity to see, comment upon, and correct for factual accuracy the descriptions of their products.

The articles are written as complete, standalone pieces of writing, rather than as an accumulation of changes that must be integrated by the reader into the main reviews in *The Piano Book*. To keep the size manageable, however, much historical and technical information was abbreviated or omitted, including information on older, discontinued models and on problems or defects that have long since been rectified. Although the information in this *Supplement* will usually be sufficient to help guide you in purchasing a new piano, you may wish, at your leisure, to peruse *The Piano Book* for additional commentary on the brands you are considering. Just be aware that, particularly where it conflicts with information in this *Supplement*, *The Piano Book* may no longer be accurate. In most cases, brands included in *The Piano Book* but not in the *Supplement* are either out of business or no longer being distributed in the United States.

As in *The Piano Book*, the articles here are a bit quirky—that is, they vary in their length and in the thoroughness with which they treat their subjects. Some companies have more interesting history, some instruments have more unusual technical features, some brands have more controversial issues associated with them, and some manufacturers were more helpful than others in providing access to interesting material. The comments are more descriptive than evaluative, preferring the perspective of the piano technician to the vague, flowery (and, in my opinion, unhelpful) descriptions of piano tone sometimes found in instrument reviews. For a "road map" depicting how I think the piano industry views the different brands relative to one another, see the "Summary of Brands and Ratings" on page 11.

Be sure to read *The Piano Book* for basic information on buying a piano, understanding technical features, and negotiating the best deal.

Trends

Pianos made in China continue to dominate the North American market. By some estimates, more than one-third of all new pianos sold in the U.S. are made in China. As recently as 2001, most pianos from China, though technically acceptable, were not musically desirable. Over the past few years, however, the musical qualities have taken a big leap forward. The jury is still out as to whether these pianos will hold up over the long term and in demanding climates and situations. Reports suggest less consistency than with pianos from most other countries, and the need for thorough pre-sale preparation by the dealer (and sometimes the dealer needs to weed out the bad ones and return them to the factory), but otherwise few major problems. Prices are so low, however, that for many entry-level buyers, and even for some mid-level buyers, these pianos are an excellent value despite their short track record. Certainly as short-term investments, and in milder climates and less demanding situations, they should be fine.

The first piano factory in China is said to have been established in 1895 in Shanghai (perhaps by the British?). During the 1950s, the Communists consolidated the country's piano manufacturing into four government-owned factories: Shanghai, Beijing, and Dongbei (means "northeast") in the northern part of the country, and Guangzhou Pearl River in the south. Piano making, though industrial, remained primitive well into the 1990s. In that decade, the government of China began to open the country's economy to foreign investment, first only to partnerships with the government, later to completely private concerns.

As the economy has opened up, the rising Chinese middle and upper classes have created a sharp increase in demand for pianos. Tempted by the enormous potential Chinese domestic market, as well as by the lure of cheap goods for the West, foreign interests have built new piano factories in China, bought existing factories, or contracted with existing factories for the manufacture of pianos. The government has also poured money into its own factories to accommodate the growing demand and to make the factories more competitive.

Except for the government involvement, the piano-making scene in China today is reminiscent of that in the United States a hundred years ago: Hundreds of small firms assemble pianos from parts or subassemblies obtained from dozens of suppliers and sell them on a mostly regional basis. The government factories and a few large foreign ones sell nationally. Most of the pianos sold in the Chinese domestic market are still primitive by Western standards. Primarily where foreign technical assistance or investment has been involved has the quality markedly improved, and only those pianos are good enough to be sold in the West.

Although the government factories have long had a monopoly on sales in China through piano dealers, that hold is gradually being eroded, and the government entities are experiencing great competitive pressure from all the smaller players. Combined with the inefficiencies and debt inherent in government operations, the current competitive situation is probably making the government think twice about continuing to subsidize the piano industry. Already, one of its factories, Dongbei, has been privatized through its sale to Gibson Guitar Corporation, parent of Baldwin Piano Company.

For the first half of this decade, most sales of Chinese pianos in the United States were based on the idea of luring customers into the store to buy the least expensive piano possible. Dealers that staked their business on this approach often lost it. A growing trend now is to manufacture and sell somewhat higher-priced pianos that have added value in the form of better components, often imported from Europe and the U.S., but still taking advantage of the low cost of Chinese labor. The best ones are not just a collection of parts, however, but also have improved designs developed with foreign technical assistance, and sufficient oversight to make sure the designs are properly executed.

The oversight is especially important. Chinese piano manufacturers have been quite aggressive at acquiring piano-making knowledge, and are happy to use their alliances with Western distributors to that end. However, the distributors frequently complain that agreements as to technical specifications, quality, and exclusivity of relationship are routinely disregarded by their Chinese business partners. Once the Western inspectors leave the factory, the Chinese managers do whatever they feel is in their own best interest, which often amounts to maximizing production at the expense of quality. The distributors have gradually discovered that the only way to overcome this problem is to own the factory themselves, to maintain a constant presence at the factory, or to constitute such a large percentage of the Chinese company's business that they (the Westerners) can control production. Alternatively, a Western company can examine all the pianos in its home country before sending them on to dealers, but this is less satisfactory than stopping problems at the source. Western distributors of Korean pianos used to complain of a similar problem with Korean piano factory managers during the height of that country's piano industry in the 1980s and '90s. As in Korea, the situation in China is gradually improving as the Chinese become accustomed to Western ways of doing business.

For the consumer, there are two lessons to take from this. First, although the average quality is quite reasonable, depending on how well the distributor handles the quality-control issue, and how well the dealer examines and prepares the pianos, you may find a fair amount of variation among Chinese-made pianos as you shop (this is in addition to whatever variation naturally exists between brands). Therefore, it may be in your best interest to hire a piano technician to examine one of these pianos before purchase. Second, statements by salespeople as to particular specifications or exclusivity of relationship ("Of all the brands that ZYX Piano Company makes, this is the only one with a graduated calibrator") should not be relied upon as true in every case, even though such statements may be made in good faith. Buy what you can see with your eyes and hear with your ears.

There has been an explosion of different brand names under which Chinese-made pianos are being marketed, there now being about a dozen Chinese manufacturers making pianos for export to the U.S. Piano shoppers should keep in mind, however, that cosmetics aside, if two brands of piano originate in the same factory, they are often very similar, sometimes identical. (Exceptions to this are usually noted in the brand reviews.)

On the other end of the price spectrum, European piano makers seem to be in a race to redesign their pianos for better sound projection and sustain, à la Steinway. While the European piano market is languishing, the U.S. market for high-end pianos, relatively speaking, is thriving, and for a number of companies, Steinway is the principal competitor. Considering how tradition-bound these companies are, this degree of activity is unusual. Some of the redesigns—new models from Seiler, Schimmel, and Bösendorfer come to mind—have been terrific musical successes. My only worry is that the palette of available piano tonal qualities is becoming smaller and more homogeneous as the old-world sounds pass away.

Changes in China and in Europe, and their far-reaching consequences, are causing a paradigm shift in the piano industry that is making it more difficult to give advice to piano shoppers. (A paradigm is a theoretical framework from which generalizations are formulated.) For many years, the paradigm for piano quality has been an international pecking order with pianos from Russia and China (and, more recently, Indonesia) at the bottom, followed by Korea, Japan, Eastern Europe, and finally Western Europe (mostly Germany) at the top, with pianos from the United States scattered here and there depending on the brand. While this pecking order has never been foolproof, it has served its purpose as a generalization well enough for use by a generation of piano buyers.

Now these distinctions are being blurred by globalization. Unable to escape the high cost of doing business at home, some Western European manufacturers are developing satellite operations and more affordable second product lines in Eastern Europe and third product lines in China. Some makers of high-end instruments are also quietly beginning to source parts and subassemblies from Asia and elsewhere. To the extent they can afford it, they are also investing in high-tech equipment to reduce the expense and inconsistency of hand labor, even while continuing to tout their status as makers of "hand-made" instruments. Some Korean and Chinese manufacturers, on the other hand, are importing parts and technology from Germany and Japan, producing instruments that when well prepared by the dealer rival the performance qualities of far more expensive pianos from Japan and, occasionally, Europe. The most we can say is that their longevity is unknown, an argument that, while true, becomes weaker with each passing year. In addition, global alliances are sure to bring new products to the market that are more hybridized than anything we've seen before. Although the old paradigm still has validity, the number of nonconforming situations is increasing, all of which will cause temporary confusion in the marketplace until such time as a new paradigm emerges.

At the same time that quality differences between low-end and high-end instruments are becoming narrower, price differences are greater than they've ever been, bringing issues of "value" into greater prominence. Pianos from Western Europe have become frightfully expensive due to high labor costs and the rapid appreciation of the euro against the dollar. Eastern European quality in some cases now closely approaches that of Western Europe, but at a price comparable to that of Japan. Some of the better pianos from China, Korea, and Indonesia have specifications equal to almost anything from Japan, and workmanship nearly as good, at a fraction of the price. Caught in the middle, the Japanese are gradually being squeezed out of the piano market despite their perennially good quality.

Another consequence of globalization has been the diminishing number of independent suppliers of parts and materials (actions, hammers, pinblocks, soundboards, keys, plates, etc.) to the piano industry. (Actually, the enormous Chinese piano industry has numerous parts suppliers, but most of these supply parts only for pianos sold in the domestic Chinese market, not internationally.) At one time there were large differences in quality between suppliers, but globalization has reduced and sometimes eliminated those differences. For example, as recently as a few years ago, Detoa (Czech) actions were markedly inferior to Renner (German) actions, and Chinese-made actions were terrible. Now there is at most only a small difference in quality between Detoa and Renner, virtually all Chinese actions are acceptable, and one Chinese supplier, Ningbo Orient, is producing very good-looking knockoffs of Renner actions.

At the same time, many manufacturers continue to use a "recipe" approach to differentiating differently priced piano lines: Choose an action (Renner, Detoa, Orient), combine it with a hammer (Renner, Abel, Imadegawa), add a pinblock (Delignit, Dehonit, Bolduc), and so forth, to produce a piano at a particular price. But with fewer suppliers to choose from, and less difference between them, the implied difference in quality at different price points is threatening to become more a matter of image than actuality.

The above notwithstanding, differences still do exist. The most important is that between performance-grade pianos on the one hand (Groups 1 and 2 in *The Piano Book* rating system) and consumer-grade pianos on the other (Groups 3, 4, and 5). There have been some fairly successful attempts by makers to bridge this gap (e.g., some high-end Japanese pianos), but for the most part, the two different types of manufacturers still live in two different worlds. The difference between the two worlds is less than it used to be, but still exists in the form of selection, drying, and use of wood; final regulation and voicing; and attention to technical and cosmetic detail; in other words, the difference is more than just the "recipe."

Theoretically, it would be possible for, say, a Chinese company to duplicate the finest pianos. But the market for these instruments is small, and some have unique and idiosyncratic designs that are not amenable to mass production. Therefore, it is always likely to be more of a niche market entered into by those whose profit-seeking is mixed with a love for the instrument and perhaps a desire to carry on a family business. At this point in time, such businesses are more likely to be Western than Asian, but who knows . . . that may one day change.

As I mentioned, globalization means more than just Chinese pianos, and in general it should not be feared. A German company making pianos or parts in a Czech or Polish factory it owns or controls is not much different from an Ohio company sourcing parts from a factory over the border in Kentucky. These days, among the countries of Europe, there is enough of a commonality of business practices, laws, culture, and attitudes toward quality that geographic differences carry little meaning, except as to labor costs, where the savings may be great. (In fact, it's not unusual for an Eastern European piano manufacturer to make parts for its Western European competitors.) When a Japanese or Korean piano maker sets up shop in China or Indonesia, it tends to transplant the entire culture of its home factory to the new one, including machinery, managers, and quality standards. After a short period of start-up issues, the quality will usually be comparable to what is produced at home.

The phenomenon of Western makers of high-end pianos sourcing parts in China may be inevitable, but it does trouble me a little more than the other manifestations of globalization. I'm especially concerned about action parts, which get tremendous use and abuse over the life of the piano and are especially sensitive to microscopic imperfections, climate changes, and so forth. Piano makers are seeking out alternatives because of the high price of Renner parts from Germany and the danger of relying too heavily on one supplier. This certainly makes sense for lower-cost pianos. But when a customer is laying out tens of thousands of dollars for a high-end piano, he or she expects that the manufacturer will use only the most time-tested components. I don't want to be alarmist about this because I know that several manufacturers have tested the Chinese parts and are convinced they are as good as the genuine Renner parts. However, experience has shown, especially with regard to action parts, that there are a myriad of opportunities for things to go wrong, and some may be ones that do not show up in tests other than the test of time. In fact, some may not show up as "problems" at all, but rather as a subtle difference in musical expressiveness or as slightly greater wear and tear over the long term. The risk is theoretical at this point, as no substantial issues have been reported with these parts to date. But purchasers of high-end European and American pianos probably do not expect Chinese-made components in their instruments, and the pianos are certainly not advertised that way. My feeling is that customers should be notified in an appropriate way of substantial "alternative" content in high-end pianos so they can make a risk/benefit analysis according to their own values. (Renner has begun to inscribe its name and logo on every part it makes so dealers and customers can positively identify them. It will be a few years, however, before these new parts make their way into the marketplace in sufficient quantity to be a reliable guide.)

SUMMARY OF BRANDS AND RATINGS

People absorb information in different ways. Just reading product descriptions will usually not be enough to orient a newcomer to the piano market; rather, a simple, visual summary is also needed. The charts and commentary that follow are intended to provide that summary in the form of a "road map" to how the brands compare to one another in quality. This chart is much simpler than the one in the fourth edition of *The Piano Book*. Although that one contains a great deal more information, readers too often skip the explanations and end up misunderstanding or misusing the chart. This one, on the other hand, though more up-to-date, is simple to the point of being simplistic; I've added commentary to provide some additional context.

The ratings take into account musical design, workmanship, durability, quality control, and the perceived dependability of the company in honoring the warranty. For the purposes of this simple chart, many generalizations have had to be made, as there can be great differences in quality even within a single model line. For a few newer brands, mostly from China, about which I have yet had little feedback, I have estimated the quality based on what I know about the maker, materials, specifications, and so on. However, where I have not felt comfortable even estimating, I have omitted a brand. No negative inference should be drawn from this.

It has never been my intention to set myself up as the ultimate judge of pianos, nor are these ratings about my own personal taste in piano tone or touch. Rather, through my contacts with dozens of piano technicians, dealers, and other industry personnel, and from thirty years of involvement with the piano industry, I have made a good-faith effort to find a consensus of informed opinion to the extent it may exist. Of course, a perfect consensus rarely exists, so I must sometimes use my own judgment to determine how much weight to give different opinions and to decide where the thread of "truth" lies on any given matter. Needless to say, the ratings and commentary are anecdotal and subjective in nature, not scientific, and I cannot guarantee they accurately represent the typical or average opinion about any brand. One thing I *can* guarantee is that the ratings will be controversial. While most knowledgeable people in the industry are likely to agree with the rating system's structure in the broadest sense, they will disagree endlessly about the details. I, myself, change my mind about the details quite frequently, so you should consider this only an approximation intended to start you on your own path of discovery, not something set in stone.

Please use common sense when comparing one brand with another. Compare verticals to verticals and grands to grands, and compare only similar sizes with one another.

Pianos can be divided into two types, largely according to the intention of the manufacturer. One type is built to a high standard, or even to the highest standard possible, and the price charged is whatever it takes to build such a piano and bring it to market. I call this type of piano "Performance Grade." The other type is built to be sold at a particular price, and adjustments (compromises) to materials, workmanship, and method and location of production are made to meet that price. I call this type "Consumer Grade." Both types of piano are necessary, of course, as not everyone needs or can afford the best possible piano.

Each type can be further subdivided into two groups, creating a four-group structure. Groups 1 and 3 represent the highest quality within the two types of piano. Groups 2 and 4 represent a slightly lower quality within each type, but at a lower cost, and are often a better value as a result. So if you are buying for quality, you will generally look at Groups 1 and 3. If you looking for the best value for the money, you will generally look at Groups 2 and 4. (In *The Piano Book*, there is a fifth group, consisting of pianos that are not good enough even to be recommended. That group, thank goodness, is currently empty.) This is not a perfect scheme for describing the piano market, and there are some brands and models that do not neatly fit the above description, but it is close enough that you are not likely to be seriously misled.

I have also subdivided each of the four groups into several subgroups, each containing one or more brands that can be recommended about equally. **Within each subgroup, the brands are listed in alphabetical order and no other inference should be made from this order.** It's important to understand that just because two brands are listed together does not mean they are similar in their characteristics. For example, one brand could have an excellent musical design but questionable quality control. Another could have a so-so musical design but terrific quality control. On balance, though different, they might be recommended about equally. Of course, depending on whether musical design or quality control is more important to you, you might place the brands in a different order, another reason why a generic list such as this must be considered only a rough calculation.

Don't get too hung up on small differences. The distinction between one group and the next (especially between Groups 1 and 2) can be subtle, and the difference between adjacent subgroups can be miniscule, even questionable. Furthermore, the preparation of the piano by the dealer can be far more important to the quality of the product you receive than many of the distinctions shown on the chart. When it comes to dealer prep, it really is possible (to some extent, anyway) to turn "a sow's ear into a silk purse." Look for a dealer known for providing thorough and competent make-ready and you won't have to worry so much about what group your piano is in!

Prices shown below are the approximate lowest and highest typical selling prices of new pianos in the least expensive style and finish.

Group 1: Highest quality performance pianos

These pianos are for those who want the best and can afford it. They utilize the very best materials, and the manufacturing process emphasizes much hand labor and refinement of details. Advanced designs are painstakingly executed, putting quality considerations far ahead of cost and production output. They are suitable for the most advanced and demanding professional and artistic uses. Most of the pianos in this group are made in the U.S. and Western Europe. *Comparison with automobiles: think Rolls-Royce, Bentley, Mercedes-Benz.*

Verticals:	$18,000 to $40,000
Grands 5' to 7':	$40,000 to $90,000

Group 1A: Bechstein, C. (Concert Series)
Blüthner
Bösendorfer
Fazioli
Steingraeber & Söhne
Steinway & Sons (Hamburg)

Group 1B: Förster, August
Grotrian
Sauter

Group 1C: Kawai, Shigeru
Steinway & Sons (New York)

Commentary on Group 1: It was easier to arrive at a consensus on Group 1A than on any other subgroup in this rating system. So celebrated are the pianos in this subgroup that dealers eagerly nominated their competitors for the list. These pianos have everything, and the attention to detail can only be called fanatical. Some of the names in this group are well known and expected, but one that is not is Steingraeber & Söhne. I was aware of this brand, but was surprised at how many others with even passing acquaintance with it named it without hesitation. Note that Steinway & Sons (Hamburg) is not routinely available in North America; I include it for informational purposes only.

The pianos in Group 1B are also fabulous, and very "fussy," but there was little doubt that they were second to the pianos in Group 1A, either because their workmanship is not quite as fussy as the first group, or because their musical designs are considered slightly less desirable, or perhaps because they're not as well known. However, preference throughout Group 1 is highly dependent on musical taste, and the brands in Group 1B definitely have their devoted following. Sauter pianos, relatively new to Group 1, are beautifully crafted and sound terrific, but the company tends to maintain a low profile in the U.S. and the tone is not as distinctively European as the others, so it's easy to overlook.

As for Group 1C, Shigeru Kawai, another newcomer to Group 1, is the first piano from Japan to make the grade. It is beginning to gain acceptance in universities and other venues as one of the great instruments of the day.

Steinway & Sons (New York), at its best, has one of the finest sounds of any piano in Group 1, but relative to the others in this group, there is less attention to detail in a number of areas of production and musical preparation. It's a testament to the amazing piano designs of this venerable brand, and the integrity of its sound-body construction, that the instruments can potentially sound and play as well as they do. The pianos vary, but if you bother the salespeople until they get their technicians to prep them, you can find some really nice ones.

A brand for which I have not had enough feedback to place accurately, but which would probably fall in Group 1, is Feurich.

Group 2: High-performance pianos

These instruments are built to a standard favoring high-performance design features, materials, and workmanship. They are suitable for home, institutional, and some professional and artistic uses. Greater hand labor is put into refining touch and tone during manufacture, although perhaps not quite as much as some in Group 1. Cost considerations, virtually absent for Group 1 instruments, may affect decisions regarding materials and production methods to a limited extent. For a variety of reasons, these pianos have not received as much critical acclaim as those in Group 1. Although the difference in quality between the two groups is small—and for many buyers will be undetectable—the price difference is substantial, making these pianos a great value for those who can settle for "almost the best." Most pianos in this group are made in the U.S. and in Eastern and Western Europe. *Comparison with automobiles: think BMW, Saab, Volvo, Audi, Lexus.*

| Verticals: | $8,000 to $22,000 |
| Grands 5' to 7': | $25,000 to $55,000 |

Group 2A: Estonia
Mason & Hamlin
Schimmel (Konzert series)

Group 2B: Bechstein (Academy series)
Haessler
Schimmel (Classic series)

14

Schulze Pollmann
Seiler
Steinberg, Wilh.
Walter, Charles R.
Yamaha ("S" series)

Group 2C: Baldwin (grands)
Bohemia
Hoffmann, W.
Irmler
Kemble
Petrof
Vogel

Commentary on Group 2: Although the best pianos must of course be of the highest technical competence, part of what many buyers of luxury goods also seek (whether they admit it or not) is association with things that will enhance the way they view themselves or how others view them—in other words, image. That is, for these buyers and with these goods, "image" is not just some superfluous gimmickry added to fool the public (as it sometimes is with goods of lower quality), but rather is actually perceived and sought out by the public as part of the product's quality. I say this without judgment; it's simply human nature. This is as true for high-quality pianos as for any other luxury items. Image is cultivated by manufacturers through the company's name and history, printed literature and advertising, artist endorsements, and use in high-profile places and situations, among other things. Although I believe that most of the pianos in Group 1 have at least slightly greater refinement in design, workmanship, or performance than most in Group 2, part of what separates the two groups in my mind is that to one extent or another most in Group 1 have broken the "image barrier" for luxury goods, while those in Group 2— some arguably of nearly equal technical competence—have not.

Group 2A contains three brands that are close runners-up for Group 1. In fact, many people would place them in Group 1 based on their performance. But for each there is some factor that seems to me to dictate conservatism.

Estonia, formerly at the bottom of Group 2, has become so much more advanced over the last five years that it is virtually a different instrument. Likewise Schimmel, in its most recent series of redesigns, has elevated itself to a new level of perfection. In both cases, however, I feel these advances have not yet been sufficiently recognized by the piano community in general to deserve placement on a par with the pianos in Group 1. As for Mason & Hamlin, the company's extensive worldwide sourcing of quality, lower-cost parts seems more consistent with the manufacturing philosophy of Group 2 than Group 1, even though the results to date have been excellent.

I found it difficult to further subdivide Group 2, and sensed little agreement among my contacts about how it should be done. I believe the instruments in Group 2B, each in its own way, have just a little more finesse than those in Group 2C. Don't be fooled, though, by the fact that Group 2C pianos are at the bottom of Group 2. They are still wonderful instruments, and some of the best values in the piano world.

Group 3: Better quality consumer-grade pianos

These instruments give roughly equal weight to economy and performance. The dominant pianos in this group are by Japan-based companies manufacturing in Japan, China, Taiwan, and Indonesia. They are mass produced but with attention to detail, and are consistent, predictably uniform instruments with few defects, suitable for both home and institutional use. For decades they have been legendary for their high quality-control standards and commitment to excellent warranty service. Also in this group are the higher-level pianos made by Korea-based companies in Korea or Indonesia, with more variation in quality, but enhanced by some advanced design features; and some of the best pianos from China. *Comparison with automobiles: think Honda, Toyota, Subaru (Group 3A); upper-level Kia, Hyundai (Groups 3B and 3C).*

Verticals:	$3,500 to $12,000
Grands 5' to 7':	$9,000 to $36,000

Group 3A: Boston (Kawai with Steinway)
Kawai (verticals and RX series grands)
Perzina (verticals)
Pramberger, J.P. (Samick)
Weber, Albert (Young Chang)
Yamaha (verticals and C series grands)
Young Chang (Platinum Edition)

Group 3B: Essex (Young Chang/Korea with Steinway)
Kawai (GM and GE series grands)
Knabe, Wm. (Samick)
Weber (Sovereign series) (Young Chang)
Yamaha (GB and GC grands)
Young Chang (Professional Artist series)

Group 3C: Brodmann (grands)
Kohler & Campbell (Millennium series) (Samick)
Pramberger (Samick)
Story & Clark (Signature series) (Samick)

Commentary on Group 3: Group 3A consists of most pianos made by the Japanese-based companies Yamaha and Kawai and the highest-level Korean-made pianos of Young Chang and Samick. The latter are built to advanced designs, and when expertly prepared by a technician, can play as well as some pianos in higher categories. However, quality control is a little more variable than with pianos from Japan. Also in this category are Perzina verticals, one of the few brands made in China thus far to make it out of Group 4. They have excellent tone and action, and have been out in the field without problems long enough for me to feel comfortable recommending them.

Group 3B consists of the smaller Kawai and Yamaha grand models with simpler case construction and features, mid-level Korean-made models from Young Chang, and mid- to upper-level pianos from Samick (Wm. Knabe) made in either Korea or Indonesia.

Group 3C are mid-level Samick pianos made in Korea or Indonesia (Kohler & Campbell Millennium), upper-level pianos entirely from Indonesia (Pramberger), and Brodmann grands, the only grands from China thus far to make it to Group 3. The same comments made about Korean pianos in Group 3A also apply to the Korean and Indonesia pianos in Groups 3B and 3C.

Group 4: Medium quality consumer-grade pianos

Most of these instruments are somewhat more oriented toward economy than performance. In general, quality control is not as perfect as many in Group 3, so the pianos may need a little more attention by the dealer both before and after the sale. For some upper-level Chinese brands, the quality control and features might normally make the piano a candidate for a higher-level group, but their track record is short, so as a precaution, I am leaving them in this group for the time being. These pianos are suitable at least for average home and lighter institutional use, and sometimes more. Students with smaller models of some of these brands may wish to upgrade to a larger or better instrument after a number of years. Pianos in this group are made in China, or in Indonesia by Korean-based companies. *Comparison with automobiles: think Kia, Hyundai (and Chinese-made cars).*

Verticals: $3,000 to $7,000
Grands 5' to 7': $7,000 to $17,000

Group 4A: Brodmann (verticals)
Ebel, Carl (Perzina)
Hailun
Heintzman
May Berlin
Palatino (AXL)
Perzina (grands)
Steigerman (Premium series) (Hailun)
Steinberg, Gerh. (Perzina)

Group 4B: Everett (grands) (Dongbei)
Hallet, Davis (grands) (Dongbei)
Nordiska (grands) (Dongbei)
Weinbach (grands) (Dongbei/Petrof)

Group 4C: Cristofori (Pearl River)
Essex (Pearl River or Young Chang/China with Steinway)
Kohler & Campbell (except Millennium series) (Samick)
Miller, Henry F. (Pearl River)
Pearl River
Remington (Samick)
Ritmüller (Pearl River)
Samick
Story & Clark (Heritage series) (Samick)
Weber (Legend series) (Young Chang)
Young Chang (Gold series)

Group 4D: Cable, Hobart M. (Sejung)
Everett (verticals) (Dongbei)
Falcone (Sejung)
Gulbransen (Sejung)
Hallet, Davis (verticals) (Dongbei)
Hardman, Peck (Beijing)
Meister, Otto (Beijing)
Nordiska (verticals) (Dongbei)
Steck, Geo. (Sejung)
Steigerman (Beijing)
Suzuki (Artfield)
Wyman (Beijing)

Commentary on Group 4: Many of the Group 4 piano brands are new or rapidly improving. I have tried as best I can to estimate their relative quality positions, preferring to err slightly on the low side rather than overstate their quality. I expect the future will bring many changes to this list.

Group 4A consists of the best of the Chinese pianos that have not already graduated to Group 3. Some of these actually have the performance characteristics of higher-grade instruments and may eventually migrate upward on this chart as their track record and reputation warrant. The pianos in this subgroup (and also pianos from China that have graduated to Group 3) are distinguished from those in lower subgroups by superiority in a combination of design, materials, and execution. Most use a large amount of parts and material imported from Europe or North America. They also excel in the oversight given them by the sponsoring company (where applicable). My contacts generally gave cautious praise to these brands, recognizing that they provide tremendous value for the money, but were not yet ready to abandon better-known, established, more expensive brands from other parts of the world in favor of them.

Group 4B consists of the grand pianos from Dongbei, distributed in the U.S. under a variety of names by several distributors. These pianos don't have the finesse of the ones in Group 4A, but are clearly distinguished from most other Chinese grands by the excellence of their design. When properly prepared by the dealer, they perform exceptionally well. Most of these brands are quite similar to one another; however, there is some dispute among the distributors as to the degree of the differences and how consistently they are applied. Weinbach is a deluxe piano from Dongbei with a Petrof keyboard and action. Though it has been grouped with the other Dongbei grands, it's possible it belongs in Group 4A.

Group 4C consists of the large, middle ground of Chinese pianos—those from the Young Chang and Pearl River factories—and the lower-level pianos from the Samick factory in Indonesia. These pianos are not likely to win awards for anything in particular, but with proper dealer make-ready and some follow-up home service, they should be fine for casual home use and sometimes more.

Group 4D pianos are a little less advanced in design or execution than those in higher categories. The smaller sizes of grands and verticals in particular are for those buyers for whom low price or furniture are the most important considerations. With thorough dealer prep, good after-sale service, and realistic expectations, these brands can be successfully purchased by buyers with simpler needs.

BRAND LISTINGS

ALTENBURG, OTTO

Wyman Piano Company
P.O. Box 218802
Nashville, Tennessee 37221

908-351-2000
george.benson@wymanpiano.com
www.altenburgpiano.com

Pianos made by: Beijing Hsinghai Piano Group, Ltd., Beijing, China

This is the house brand of Altenburg Piano House, a New Jersey piano retailer in business for over 150 years, at one time as a manufacturer. This brand is sold via the Internet and through other dealers in addition to the company's own stores. For many years Otto Altenburg pianos have been made by Samick in Korea or Indonesia, though sometimes to musical and cabinet designs different from Samick's own. More recently, Altenburg has engaged the Beijing Hsinghai Piano Group in China to make a new line of pianos, some of which are special to Altenburg with individually hitched strings. The Beijing models are the ones shown in the Pricing Guide section of this *Supplement*. Grand models up to 5' 3" use a laminated soundboard, larger models use solid spruce.

Warranty: Twelve years, parts and labor, transferable to future owners within the warranty period.

ASTIN-WEIGHT

Astin-Weight Piano Makers
P.O. Box 65281
Salt Lake City, Utah 84165

801-487-0641
gr8pianos@networld.com
www.astin-weight.com

Astin-Weight pianos have been made in Salt Lake City since 1959. Due to storm damage at the factory, the company continues to engage in limited production from several temporary locations.

Astin-Weight vertical pianos, 50" in height, are unusual from a technical standpoint because they have no backposts, instead relying on a massive full-perimeter plate; and also because the soundboard takes up the entire back of the piano, behind the pinblock, resulting in a much larger volume of sound than a conventional piano (see *The Piano Book* for an illustration of this feature). Many of the cabinet finishes are simple, hand-rubbed oil finishes. The 41" console has been discontinued.

The Astin-Weight 5' 9" grand is produced in very limited quantities. It has an unusual symmetrical shape and is hinged on the treble side instead of the bass. The company says this shape allows for much longer strings and soundboard area.

Warranty: Twenty-five years, parts and labor.

BALDWIN

including D.H. Baldwin, Hamilton, Howard, Chickering, Wurlitzer, ConcertMaster

Baldwin Piano Company
309 Plus Park Blvd.
Nashville, Tennessee 37217

615-871-4500
800-876-2976
800-444-2766 (24/7 consumer hotline)
www.baldwinpiano.com

Pianos made by: Baldwin Piano Company, a division of Gibson Guitar Corporation, Trumann, Arkansas; Baldwin Dongbei (Yingkou) Piano and Musical Instrument Co., Ltd., Yingkou, Liaoning Province, China; Baldwin (Zhongshan) Piano and Musical Instrument Co., Ltd., Zhongshan, Guangdong Province, China

Baldwin Piano & Organ Co. was established in Cincinnati in 1862 as a retail enterprise and began manufacturing its own line of pianos in 1890. Throughout most of the twentieth century, the company was considered one of the most successful and financially stable piano makers in the United States. Beginning in the 1980s, however, the quality declined, especially as a result of the relocation of action manufacturing to Mexico. A combination of foreign competition and management problems led to bankruptcy in 2000. The company was purchased out of bankruptcy in 2001 by Gibson Guitar Corporation. Baldwin manufactures in Trumann, Arkansas, and in two factories that it owns in China, where it also maintains a major presence in the Chinese domestic piano market.

[Note: As this issue of the *Annual Supplement* goes to press, Baldwin is completely revamping its product line, moving nearly all production of vertical pianos to China, and moving production of pianos formerly made at the Sejung factory in China to its own Dongbei and Zhongshan China facilities. Baldwin grands and custom grands, and an enhanced version of the model 6000 vertical, will continue to be made in Arkansas, with a concentration on the custom grands. Only the Baldwin brand name will be used on Baldwin acoustic piano products sold in the U.S. Use of the Hamilton, D.H. Baldwin, Howard, Wurlitzer, and Chickering names in the U.S. will be discontinued. Certain Baldwin vertical models formerly made in the U.S. will be redeveloped in China and made at Baldwin's Zhongshan facility. This has already been done for the 52" model 6000 vertical, and the model 243 and the 2000 series are in the development stage and due by the end of 2008. In addition, the vertical pianos most recently made under the Hamilton name by Dongbei (which are Dongbei's stock designs, not Baldwin designs) will be a second, lower-cost piano line sold in the U.S. under the Baldwin brand name. All Baldwin pianos made in China will be visually distinguished from those made in the U.S. by a small "c" over the "i" in Baldwin on the fallboard (in addition, of course, to the internal musical design differences). Because everything is in flux, complete information is not available, but the Baldwin Web site contains information on currently available new and old models. For the time being, we are repeating below model information from last year, with changes noted that we are aware of. This is still useful information, since many of these pianos are still on dealer's showroom floors. Prices are included in the Model and Pricing Guide section of this *Supplement* only for current Baldwin grands and new Baldwin vertical models for which prices had been set at press time.]

Baldwin verticals come in four sizes: 43½", 45", 48", and 52". The 43½" console comes in two basic models, the series 660 "Classic" console and the series 2000 "Acrosonic." They both use the same back and action, but the Acrosonic has fancier cabinet features and hardware. The 45" studio, long known as the "Hamilton," also comes in two levels of cabinetry. Model 243 is the institutional school studio version (one of the most popular school pianos in history) and the series 5000 models are the fancy furniture styles. They are otherwise identical. Model 248, a 48" upright introduced in 1997, and the model 6000 "Concert Upright," both with some interesting technical features, round out the vertical piano line. A Custom Vertical program includes the limited edition Gibson studio, each one signed by guitarist Les Paul; the Elvis Presley Signature model, authorized by the Presley estate; and a B.B. King model (also available as a grand).

All Baldwin verticals share certain technical features, including a 19-ply maple pinblock, a solid spruce soundboard, and a full-size, direct blow action (even the consoles). The action, now made in China, has been redesigned with a Schwander-type hammer-butt return spring and other changes, and is now known as the Stealth™ action (to signify that it is quieter than the previous action). It can be recognized by its visually striking black and deep blue colors. In addition, vertical pianos with the new action have model numbers ending in "E."

Baldwin also makes a line of vertical pianos under the name "D.H. Baldwin." Those in the trade may recall this as a name Baldwin used on a line of pianos made in Korea. The new D.H. Baldwin line, however, is made in Arkansas (and as mentioned above, is being discontinued) and is based on the regular Baldwin 43½" vertical scale. The company says these new models are essentially like their higher-priced cousins musically, but with scaled-down cabinetry. Also made in Arkansas (and being discontinued) are pianos with a variety of minor brand names Baldwin owns and uses at dealer request, such as Ivers & Pond, Cable, J&C Fischer, and others. These are essentially the same as the D.H. Baldwin pianos.

Baldwin grands include the model M1 (5' 2"), R1 (5' 8"), L1 (6' 3"), SF-10E (7'), and SD-10 (9'). Model 225E is the model M1 in French Provincial styling; model 226E is the model R1 in French Provincial styling; and model 227E is the model R1 with round, fluted, tapered legs. Baldwin has a Custom Grand Finishes program, allowing customers to completely custom-design the appearance of their own grand piano. A new "Exotic Collection" includes twenty wild, dramatic, exotic, fun, or elegant designs, from a tied-dyed design with a happy face to a striped zebra to a tropical sunset.

Baldwin grands use a strong, one-piece rim construction, the inner rim entirely of maple and the outer rim of maple and poplar. Soundboards are of tapered solid spruce. The pinblock, for many years known for its extreme density, has been changed from forty-one highly compressed laminations to eleven normal laminations of maple. The grands also use the patented Accu-just™ hitch pin system (illustrated in *The Piano Book*), in which the downbearing pressure of each string on the bridge can be individually adjusted. This mainly allows for more efficient and uniform construction of grand bridges, but may also occasionally be useful in servicing the piano. The 7' and 9' models use special treble termination pieces to provide more precise termination of each treble string. As of 2008, all Baldwin grands come with Renner action and Renner hammers. Each piano also comes with an adjustable artist bench. Baldwin maintains a long roster of well-known concert artists, musicians, and composers who endorse and use its concert grand.

A "Howard" line of grands, made in Arkansas, is being discontinued. Currently, the Howard line consists of two models, 5' 2" and 5' 8". They are based on regular Baldwin scales, but made with lower-cost materials and components.

Baldwin also has several lower-cost lines of piano that were made in China by Sejung to Baldwin's specifications and then recently moved to Baldwin's Dongbei, China facility. The first of these is the "Hamilton." This is not to be confused with the famous Hamilton model studio piano that says "Baldwin" on the fallboard; rather, this new line says "Hamilton" on the fallboard. (As mentioned earlier, however, the verticals in this line will henceforth be imported into the U.S. under the

Baldwin brand name as a lower-cost alternative to the regular Baldwin verticals to be made at Zhongshan, China.)

In the 1980s, Baldwin acquired the Wurlitzer and Chickering names, and for many years sold a Wurlitzer line of pianos made in Korea. Like the Hamiltons, Wurtlizer pianos were more recently made in China by Sejung. However, whereas the Hamilton pianos were made with Sejung-designed scales and plates, the Wurlitzer pianos were made with Baldwin-designed sand-cast plates based on old Chickering scale designs. The pianos, all grands, came in six sizes from 4' 7" to 9'. Wurlitzer will no longer be imported into the U.S.

After Baldwin filed for bankruptcy and until some time after being purchased by Gibson, piano production at Baldwin's Arkansas factories came to a near standstill for a time and a great deal of piano-making talent and know-how was lost to layoffs—at least temporarily. Over the past few years, Baldwin has been very gradually resuming production. Baldwin grands still have great designs and specifications, but as can be expected, quality has been uneven while the factory has been gaining experience. For protection and peace of mind, I would advise hiring an independent technician to inspect a Baldwin piano before purchasing it.

Warranty: Baldwin and D.H. Baldwin verticals—25 years on parts, 10 years on labor. Baldwin grands—lifetime on parts, 10 years on labor. Howard, Hamilton, and Wurlitzer pianos—10 years on parts and labor.

A note to current Baldwin owners: When Gibson acquired Baldwin out of bankruptcy, it acquired only its assets, not its liabilities. Therefore, the company is not required to honor warranty claims for pianos purchased prior to the acquisition date. Pianos purchased by the consumer from an authorized dealer on or after November 9, 2001 are eligible for warranty coverage, even if the dealer purchased the piano before that date. Warranty coverage for pianos purchased by the consumer before November 9, 2001 will only be considered on a case-by-case basis.

ConcertMaster

Please read "Electronic Player Piano Systems and Hybrid Acoustic/Digital Pianos" on pages 160–161 of *The Piano Book*.

ConcertMaster is an electronic player piano system available only on new Baldwin, Chickering, and Wurlitzer grand and vertical pianos. (ConcertMaster CD is a simplified version that can be installed on any brand of piano, new or old, by a Baldwin dealer.) Sometimes ConcertMaster is installed at the Baldwin factory, sometimes at the local Baldwin dealership. The system comes with a floppy disk drive, a CD drive, and a 1.2-gigabyte hard drive pre-loaded with twenty hours of music. Baldwin says the floppy disk drive can read just about any type of standard MIDI music software on the market, including such software made for other player piano systems. The CD drive can read the QRS CDs containing analog audio accompaniment. The hard drive has a capacity of nearly 10,000 songs, which can be organized into ninety-nine different libraries containing up to ninety-nine songs each. ConcertMaster also reads video discs and can be integrated into whole-house audio and video systems. It comes with a 128-voice General MIDI sound card and two amplified speakers, and can be operated via either a stationary controller or a wireless remote. The operating system is software upgradeable. A new optional feature provides piano accompaniment to a number of popular music CDs available on the general market. When a customer plays one of the CDs, ConcertMaster links the accompaniment, located on the system's hard drive, to the CD and plays them together.

A "Performance Option" adds single or multi-track recording capabilities to ConcertMaster, as well as features found on many digital keyboards, including velocity sensitivity and assignable split point. This option includes a record strip that uses light beams to determine key velocity. There is also an optional stop rail to silence the acoustic piano sound and allow you to listen via headphones to the instrumental sounds from the sound card.

Warranty: ConcertMaster—Two years, parts and labor, to the original purchaser.

BECHSTEIN, C.
including W. Hoffmann

Bechstein America, LLC
207 West 58th Street
New York, New York 10019

212-581-5550
info@bechstein-america.com
www.bechstein.de

Pianos made by: C. Bechstein Pianoforte Fabrik GmbH, Berlin and Seifhennersdorf, Germany; and C. Bechstein Europe Ltd. (former Bohemia Piano Ltd.), Jihlava, Czech Republic

Bechstein was founded in 1853 by Carl Bechstein, a young German piano maker who, in the exploding world of piano technology of his day, had visions of building an instrument that the tradition-bound piano-making shops of Berlin were not interested in. Through fine workmanship and the endorsement of famous pianists, Bechstein soon became one of the leading piano makers in Europe, producing over five thousand pianos annually by 1900. The two world wars and the Depression virtually destroyed the company, but it was rebuilt successfully. In 1963 it was acquired by Baldwin, and in 1986 Baldwin sold it to Karl Schulze, a leading West

German piano retailer and master piano technician, who undertook a complete technical and financial reorganization of the company. In the early 1990s, Bechstein acquired the names and factories of Euterpe, W. Hoffmann, and Zimmermann. Pianos with these names are currently being sold in Europe, but only W. Hoffmann is sold in North America. All Bechstein pianos are manufactured in Seifhennersdorf, Germany. Bechstein also co-owns a plant in China, where it makes less expensive pianos for sale in other parts of the world.

Several years ago, Bechstein and Korean piano maker Samick each acquired a small financial interest in the other and agreed to cooperate in technical matters, marketing, and distribution. Pursuant to that agreement, SMC, Samick's North American distributor, also distributed Bechstein pianos. The distribution agreement has terminated, and Bechstein is now distributing through its own North American subsidiary, Bechstein-America LLC, based in New York.

All Bechstein pianos use Abel or Renner hammers, solid European spruce soundboards, and beech or beech and mahogany for grand rims and some structural parts. American maple pinblocks are used in the most expensive grand and vertical pianos, Delignit in the others. Three pedals are standard on all pianos, the grands with sostenuto and the verticals with practice pedal (sostenuto optional). Over the past few years, all Bechstein grands have been redesigned with a capo bar (eliminating the agraffes in the treble), higher tension scale, and front and rear duplex scales for better tonal projection and tonal color. Also, unlike older Bechsteins, which had an open pinblock design, in the redesigned grands the plate covers the pinblock area. For better tuning control, the higher-level pianos are without tuning pin bushings.

Bechstein pianos are available in two levels of quality. The regular verticals and partially redesigned versions of the old grand models are known as the "Academy Series" and say only "Bechstein" on the fallboard. A series of designer verticals that recently received the Chicago Design Award, the Concert 8 vertical, and the fully redesigned grands (models D, C, B, M/P, and L) are called the "Concert Series" and say "C. Bechstein" on the fallboard. (The 51½" Concert 8 vertical is one of my all-time favorite vertical pianos.) The company says both lines are made in Germany, though for cost effectiveness some parts and components may originate at the Bohemia Piano Company in the Czech Republic.

The differences between the two lines appear to be primarily in tonal philosophy and cabinetry. C. Bechstein grands were designed with a higher tension scale for better projection and with various components that the company believed would result in the greatest usable palette of tonal color (tapered soundboard, vertically laminated bridges, hornbeam hammer shanks, solid keybed, thicker rim, and hammers with walnut moldings and AAA felt). The grand soundboard is installed after the inner and outer rims are joined. The ribs are tapered after being glued to the soundboard, and the heavy-duty rim posts are dovetailed and embedded into the rim.

The Academy Series grands have an untapered soundboard, solid beech bridge with beech cap, maple hammer shanks, expansion-type keybed, and hammers with mahogany moldings and AA felt. The same quality wood and strings are used in both. The rim parts are joined, and the soundboard and ribs installed, in a more efficient, less time-consuming manner than with the C. Bechstein. C. Bechstein keys still use leather key bushings, whereas the Academy Series keys use the more conventional cloth bushings. Bone keytops are an option on the C. Bechstein pianos and genuine ebony sharps are used on both series.

Bechstein uses its own action it calls "Silver Line" in the Academy Series, and one called "Gold Line," with slightly tighter tolerances, in the Concert Series. As part of its global strategy the company uses multiple suppliers for nearly all parts and as such, action parts for the Gold Line come from Renner in Europe and for the Silver Line from China. Bechstein says that whatever the origin, all parts are inspected and reworked as necessary to conform to the company's rigid standards. Both actions appear to be well made, and both are of the Renner design and have the smooth, responsive touch characteristic of that design. Of course, the parts from Renner are more time-tested than the others.

The C. Bechstein cabinetry is much sleeker and more sophisticated than the plain Academy Series, though both cabinets are finished to the same standards. The C. Bechstein plates receive the royal hand-rubbed finish; the Academy Series plates are just spray finished in the conventional manner.

C. Bechstein grands are impeccably made in Europe with the customary brighter tone that Europeans prefer, and may need considerable voicing to suit the American musical taste. (However, several of my informants had high praise for the wide dynamic range, tonal color, and responsive action of the recently-redesigned 7' 8" model C grand.) The company maintains that since voicing is a matter of overall piano design, their pianos are voiced at the factory to their tonal standard and should not be altered. Some customers may still prefer the slightly warmer sound of the Academy Series grands, which are also about half the price.

In 2006 Bechstein purchased a controlling interest in the Czech piano maker, Bohemia, and integrated it into a new entity called C. Bechstein Europe Ltd. Bechstein engineers oversee production of the Bechstein-designed W. Hoffmann line of pianos at the Bohemia facility. This is a mid-priced line intended to compete with other mid-priced pianos from Eastern Europe. Currently it consists of one grand and two vertical models, with more to come in the near future.

Warranty: Five years, parts and labor, to original purchaser.

BEIJING HSINGHAI

Beijing Hsinghai Piano Group, Ltd., part of the Beijing Hsinghai Musical Instruments Co., has been producing pianos in Beijing, China since 1949. It manufactures more than fifty thousand vertical and grand pianos annually, mostly for domestic Chinese consumption. In 2005 the company consolidated its three older plants into a new 1.2 million square foot facility. The pianos are available throughout the world under the "Otto Meister" and "Hsinghai" (or "Xinghai") labels, as well as under various other labels as joint ventures with other manufacturers and distributors, including Steigerman, Wyman, and Altenburg. Kawai also has a joint venture with Beijing, though the pianos (formerly under the name "Linden") are distributed only in Canada and Europe.

BERGMANN — See "Young Chang"

BLÜTHNER
including Haessler, Irmler, Breitmann

Blüthner USA LLC
5660 W. Grand River
Lansing, Michigan 48906

517-886-6000
800-954-3200
info@bluthnerpiano.com
www.bluthnerpiano.com

In Canada, contact Blüthner Agency, Canada at 416-236-8870
www.bluethner.ca

Pianos made by: Julius Blüthner Pianofortefabrik GmbH, Leipzig, Germany

Blüthner has been making pianos of the highest quality in Leipzig, in the eastern part of Germany, since 1853 and, though nationalized in 1972, has remained under the management of the Blüthner family to this day. Until 1900, Blüthner was Europe's largest piano factory. During World War II, the factory was bombed, but after the war the East German government allowed the Blüthner family and workers to rebuild it because the Blüthner piano was considered a national treasure (and because the Soviet Union needed quality pianos). With the liberation of Eastern Europe, Blüthner is again privately owned by the Blüthner family.

Blüthner pianos have beech rims (grands), solid spruce soundboards, Delignit pinblocks, Renner actions, Abel hammers, and polyester finishes. Pianos for export have three pedals, including sostenuto on the grands, and celeste (practice) on the verticals. Blüthner builds about 100 verticals a year in four sizes and 500 grands a year in six sizes.

In addition to numerous specialized furniture styles and finishes, Blüthner has two recently issued special editions. In honor of the company's 150th anniversary, Blüthner introduced a Jubilee model with a commemorative cast-iron plate in the style of the special-edition pianos of a century ago. It is available in several sizes, in any style or finish. A "Julius Blüthner" edition, in honor of this fifth-generation company's founder, and available in most grand sizes, features a very fancy, elaborately carved music desk in the styling designed by the founder; brass inlays in the lid; and round Victorian legs; among other embellishments.

Blüthner pianos incorporate several unique technical features. With aliquot stringing, the notes in the highest treble section (about the top two octaves) have four strings each instead of three. The extra string is raised slightly above the others and vibrates only sympathetically. The effect, heard mainly in medium to forte playing, is similar to that of a duplex scale, adding tonal color to the treble and aiding the singing tone. Another feature concerns the angled hammers, which may at first look odd, though the reason may not be readily apparent. It turns out that the angled hammers are actually cut at an angle to match the string line and mounted straight on the shanks instead of being cut straight and mounted at an angle like other brands. The company says that the effect is to more evenly distribute the force of the blow across both the strings and the hammers, and to make a firmer connection with the backchecks, which are also positioned in a straight line. Visually, the effect is an even, rather than a staggered, hammer line.

In what is perhaps a world's first, Blüthner has designed and built a piano for left-handed pianists. This is a completely backward piano, with the treble keys, hammers, and strings on the left and the bass on the right. When it was introduced, a pianist gave a concert on it after only a couple of hours of practice! It is currently available in the 6' 10" and 9' 2" sizes by special order (price not available).

With voicing, Blüthner pianos have a very full sound that is warm, romantic, and lyrical, generally deeper and darker than some of its German counterparts. Sustain is good, but at a low level of volume, giving the tone a refined, delicate character. The action is a little light, but responsive. The pianos are built of superb materials, and are favorably priced compared to some of their competitors.

In the 1990s a "Haessler" line of pianos was added to the Blüthner line. (Haessler is a Blüthner family name.) Created to compete better in the American market, Haessler pianos have more conventional technical and cosmetic features than Blüthner pianos and cost about 25 percent less. For example, the grands are loop-strung instead of single-strung, there is no aliquot stringing, and the hammers are cut and mounted in the conventional way. Case and plate cosmetics are simpler. The pianos are made in the Blüthner factory in Germany to similar high quality standards.

Blüthner has temporarily discontinued the Irmler and Breitmann piano lines.

Warranty: Blüthner and Haessler—Ten years, parts and labor, to original purchaser.

BOHEMIA

German American Trading, Inc.
P.O. Box 17789
Tampa, Florida 33682

813-961-8405
germanamer@msn.com

Pianos made by: C. Bechstein Europe Ltd. (former Bohemia Piano Ltd.), Jihlava, Czech Republic

The factory that makes Bohemia pianos began production in 1871, after World War II becoming part of the Czech state-owned enterprise that included the better-known Petrof. Privatized in 1993, Bohemia now makes 1,500 verticals and 400 grands per year. Originally it exported to the U.S. under the name Rieger-Kloss, a name now used only in other markets. The name Bohemia is derived from the original term used by the ancient Romans for the part of Europe that is now the Czech Republic.

In 2006, C. Bechstein purchased a controlling interest in Bohemia Piano Ltd. and integrated it into a new entity called C. Bechstein Europe. The existing Bohemia dealer network will continue as usual. C. Bechstein now provides Bohemia with technical assistance and support, and the two companies collaborate in the manufacture of certain components. (Bechstein also makes the W. Hoffmann line of pianos there. See "Bechstein, C.") The components for Bohemia pianos are made in the Czech Republic or elsewhere in Europe. Model numbers with "BR" have Renner parts on Bohemia action frames; otherwise they have Czech actions. The pianos have either Abel or Renner hammers. All pianos come with a leather upholstered adjustable artist bench, and the grands have a slow-close fallboard. Bohemia pianos play very well, with a nice, bright singing treble tone.

Note that models 113, 121, 150, and 170 have been discontinued in 2008. Some have been replaced with newer models of a similar size.

Warranty: Five years, parts and labor, to the original purchaser.

BÖSENDORFER

Bösendorfer USA
1771 Post Road East, Suite 239
Westport, Connecticut 06880

203-520-1801
usinfo@bosendorfer.com
www.bosendorfer.com

Pianos made by: L. Bösendorfer Klavierfabrik GmbH, Vienna, Austria

Bösendorfer was founded in 1828 in Vienna, Austria by Ignaz Bösendorfer. The young piano maker rose to fame when Franz Liszt endorsed his concert grand after being unable to destroy it in playing as he did every other piano set before him. Ignaz died in 1858 and the company was taken over by his son, Ludwig. Under Ludwig's direction, the firm greatly prospered and the pianos became even more famous throughout Europe and the world. Ludwig, having no direct descendants, sold the firm to his friend, Carl Hutterstrasser, in 1909. Carl's sons, Wolfgang and Alexander, became partners in 1931. Bösendorfer was sold to Kimball International, a U.S. manufacturer of low- and medium-priced pianos, in 1966. In 2002 Kimball, having exited the piano business, sold Bösendorfer to the BAWAG-P.S.K. Group, Austria's third largest banking group, which sold the company to Yamaha in 2008. Bösendorfer manufactures fewer than five hundred pianos a year, with close to half sold in the U.S.

Bösendorfer makes a 52" upright and seven models of grand piano, from 5' 8" to the 9' 6" Imperial Concert Grand, one of the world's largest pianos. The company also makes a slightly less expensive version of the 6' 7" and 7' grands known as the Conservatory Series (CS). Conservatory Series grands are like the regular grands except that the case and plate receive a satin finish instead of high-polish, and the pianos are loop-strung instead of single-strung. All Bösendorfer grand pianos have three pedals, the middle pedal being a sostenuto.

One of the most distinctive features of the grands is that a couple of models have more than eighty-eight keys. The 7' 4" model has 92 keys and the 9' 6" model has 97 keys. The lowest strings vibrate so slowly that it's actually possible to hear the individual "ticks" of the vibration. Piano technicians say that it is next to impossible to tune these strings by ear, although electronic tuning aids can help accomplish this. Of course, these notes are rarely used, but their presence, and the presence of the extra long bridge and larger soundboard to accommodate them, adds extra power, resonance, and clarity to the lower regular notes of the piano. In order not to confuse pianists, who rely on the normal keyboard configuration for spatial orientation while playing, the keys for these extra notes are usually covered with a black ivorine material.

The rim of the Bösendorfer grand is built quite differently from that of all other grands. Instead of veneers bent around a form, the rim is made in solid sections and jointed together. It is also made of spruce instead of the maple or beech normally used for this purpose. Spruce is better at transmitting sound than reflecting it, and this, along with the scale design, may be why Bösendorfers tend to have a more delicate treble and a bass that features the fundamental tone more than the higher harmonics. Although the stereotype that Bösendorfers are "better for Mozart than Rachmaninoff" may be an exaggeration (as evidenced by the number of performing artists who successfully use the piano in concert for a wide variety of music), the piano's not so "in your face" sound is certainly ideally suited for the classical repertoire in addition to whatever else it can do. In recent years, Bösendorfer has made some refinements to its designs to increase tonal projection. The relatively newer 6' 1", 7' 4", and 9' 2" models have been designed specifically to appeal to pianists looking for a more familiar sound. In all models, however, the distinctive Bösendorfer difference is still readily apparent.

During the past few years, Bösendorfer has introduced a number of interesting instruments in new cabinet styles. These include a Porsche-designed modern piano in aluminum and polished ebony (or special-ordered in any standard Porsche finish color); Victorian-styled pianos "Liszt" and "Vienna"; and a model called "Yacht" in a decorative veneer finish with brass inlay that can be ordered without casters to be bolted to the deck of a ship! "Edge" is a modern piano designed by a group of industrial designers and was the winner of a design competition. "Mozart" commemorates the 250th anniversary of the composer's birth and is limited to twenty-seven individually numbered instruments, one for each Mozart piano concerto. Its case has subtle modifications, including gold leaf trim, round legs and lyre posts, and a carved music desk.

Bösendorfer's SE Reproducer (player piano) system, out of production for a number of years, has been replaced by an all-new design called "CEUS" (Create Emotions with Unique Sound) with updated electronics and solenoids. The visual display is discreetly located on the fallboard and is wireless, so the fallboard can be removed for servicing the piano without the need to disconnect wires. Player controls for recording, playback, and data transfer are by means of a combination of keystrokes on the sharp keys, pedal movements, and fallboard touch sensors. Optical sensors measure key and hammer movement at an extremely high sampling rate for maximum accuracy and sensitivity to musical nuance. Bösendorfer has a library of recordings for CEUS, and the system will also play standard MIDI piano files. CEUS is available in every Bösendorfer grand model and adds about $60,000 (list) to the price of the piano. Retrofitting of CEUS into previously sold Bösendorfers is available at the factory. A CEUS "Master" keyboard is an optional MIDI controller that contains a complete key and action set from a Bösendorfer model 280 concert grand.

Perhaps the world's most expensive piano inch for inch, Bösendorfer grands make an eloquent case for their prices. They are distinctive in both appearance and sound, and are considered to be among the finest pianos in the world.

Warranty: Ten years, parts and labor, transferable to future owners within the warranty period.

BOSTON

Steinway & Sons, Inc.
Steinway Place
Long Island City, New York 11105

718-721-7711
800-842-5397
boston@steinway.com
www.steinway.com

Pianos made by: Kawai Musical Instrument Mfg. Co., Ltd., Hamamatsu, Japan and
    Karawan, Indonesia

In 1992 Steinway launched its Boston line of pianos, designed by Steinway & Sons and built by Kawai. Steinway's stated purpose in creating this line was to supply Steinway dealers with a quality, mid-priced piano containing some Steinway-like design features for those customers "who were not yet ready for a Steinway." In choosing to have a piano of its own design made in Japan, Steinway sought to take advantage of the efficient high-technology manufacturing methods of the Japanese while utilizing its own design skills to make a more musical piano than is usually available from that part of the world. Sold only through select Steinway dealers, Boston pianos are currently available in three sizes of vertical piano and five sizes of grand. All are made in Japan, except the model 118S, which is made in Kawai's Indonesian factory.

Boston pianos are used by a number of prestigious music schools and festivals, including Aspen, Tanglewood, Brevard, Ravinia, and Bowdoin.

The most obvious grand piano design feature, visually (and one of the biggest differences from the Kawai), is the Boston's wide tail. Steinway says this allows the bridges to be positioned closer to the more lively central part of the soundboard, smoothing out the break between bass and treble. This, plus a thinner tapered soundboard and other scaling differences, may give the Boston grands a longer sustain though less initial power. The wide-tail design may also endow some of the grands with the soundboard size normally associated with a slightly larger piano. The verticals are said to have a greater overstringing angle for the same purpose. Over the last few years, the Boston verticals have been redesigned for greater tuning stability and musical refinement.

A number of features in the Boston piano are similar to those in the Steinway, including vertically laminated bridges for better tonal transmission, duplex scaling for additional tonal color, rosette-shaped hammer flanges to preserve hammer spacing, and radial rim bracing for greater structural stability. The Boston grand action is said to incorporate some of the latest refinements of the Steinway action. Cabinet detailing on the Boston grands is similar to that on the Steinway. Boston hammers are made differently from both Kawai and Steinway hammers, and voicers in the Kawai factory receive special instructions on voicing them. All Boston grand models come with a sostenuto pedal; the verticals have a practice pedal.

Boston grands also have certain things in common with Kawai RX series grands: the composition of their rims, pinblocks, and bridges; tuning pins, hardware, and grand leg and lyre assemblies; radial rim bracing and a sostenuto pedal; and the level of quality control in their manufacture. The same workers build the two brands in the same factories. One important way they differ is that Kawai uses carbon-fiber reinforced ABS Styran plastic for most of its action parts, whereas Boston uses only traditional wooden parts. Although similarly priced at the wholesale level, Kawai pianos tend to be a little less expensive to the retail customer than comparably sized Bostons due to the larger discounts typically given by Kawai dealers.

Steinway guarantees full trade-in value for a Boston piano at any time a purchaser wishes to upgrade to a Steinway grand.

Piano technicians are favorably inclined toward Boston pianos. Some find Boston pianos to have a little better sustain and more tonal color than Kawai pianos, though otherwise similar in quality. When comparing the two brands, I would advise making a decision based primarily on one's own musical perceptions of tone and touch, as well as the trade-up guarantee, if applicable.

Warranty: Ten years, parts and labor, to the original purchaser.

BREITMANN — See "Blüthner"

BRODMANN

Piano Marketing Group, LLC
752 East 21st Street
Ferdinand, Indiana 47532

812-630-0978
gary.trafton@brodmann-pianos.com
www.brodmann-pianos.com

Company Headquarters: Joseph Brodmann Piano Group, Viktorgasse 14, 1040 Vienna, Austria. Phone: +43-1-890-3203; christian.hoeferl@brodmann-pianos.com

Joseph Brodmann was a well-known piano maker in Vienna in the late eighteenth and early nineteenth centuries. Ignatz Bösendorfer apprenticed in Brodmann's workshop and eventually took it over, producing the first Bösendorfer pianos there. Today's Brodmann is a new company, headquartered in Vienna, started by two former Bösendorfer executives in 2004, pursuing a direction they say was planned as a possible second line for Bösendorfer a number of years ago, but never acted upon.

Brodmann says its mission is to produce a piano with high-end performance characteristics at an affordable price by using European components in key areas, through strict quality control, and by manufacturing in countries with favorable labor rates.

There are two lines of Brodmann pianos in production. The "Professional Edition" (formerly with the model initials BU and BG, now with the prefix PE), is made in Yichang, Hubei Province, China, by a manufacturer affiliated with Parsons Music, a major retailer in Hong Kong and China. The scales and designs of these pianos are exclusive to Brodmann. The pianos are designed in Vienna and use European components in critical areas of sound production, such as Strunz soundboards, Abel hammers, Röslau strings, and Langer-designed actions (Renner in the model 228, a Chinese action in the verticals). Brodmann has its own employees from Europe in the factory for quality control purposes. I've received positive feedback about these Brodmann pianos from many sources, the grands to a somewhat greater degree than the verticals.

The second line of vertical and grand pianos, called the "Vienna Edition," is made in two small factories in Vienna in limited quantities. The verticals are made in a factory that specializes in stunning cabinetry and exotic wood veneers, such as Bubinga, Pyramid Mahogany, African Pommele, and Brazilian Rosewood. The grand pianos are built in Brodmann's own small facility. The Vienna Edition has the same high-quality components as the Professional Edition, but with Renner actions. The Vienna Edition is brand new at press time and prices are not yet available.

Warranty: Ten years, parts and labor, transferable to future owners within the warranty period.

CABLE, HOBART M. — See "Sejung"

CABLE-NELSON — See "Yamaha"

CHASE, A.B.

Musical Properties, Inc.
823 South Sixth Street, Suite 100
Las Vegas, Nevada 89101

702-425-8540

Pianos made by: Dongbei Piano Company, Ltd., Yingkou, Liaoning Province, China

A.B. Chase is an old American piano name formerly owned by Aeolian Pianos, which went out of business in 1985. Since 2001, the brand has been used by a different distributor on pianos from the Dongbei Piano Company in China (see "Dongbei").

CHICKERING — See "Baldwin"

CONCERTMASTER — See "Baldwin"

CONOVER CABLE — See "Samick"

CRISTOFORI

Jordan Kitt's Music
9520 Baltimore Avenue
College Park, Maryland 20740
800-466-9510 x1267
(Chris Syllaba)

Schmitt Music
2400 Freeway Blvd.
Brooklyn Center, Minnesota 55430
800-920-9540 x5075
(Wayne Reinhardt)

info@cristoforipianos.com
www.cristoforipianos.com

Pianos made by: Guangzhou Pearl River Piano Group Ltd., Guangzhou, Guangdong Province, China

Originally issued under the name "Opus II," the Cristofori piano is a joint venture between Jordan Kitt's Music and Schmitt Music, which own and operate a combined twenty-five piano dealerships throughout the country. At present, Cristofori pianos are sold only in their stores. (Cristofori was, of course, the inventor of the piano.)

In mid-2007, Cristofori began sourcing its acoustic pianos from Pearl River, switching from its former supplier Sejung. The Cristofori pianos are differentiated from Pearl River's regular pianos by upgraded feature specifications such as the use of Mapes' highest quality strings from the U.S., premium solid Siberian spruce soundboards in the larger grands and taller verticals (instead of laminated soundboards), a different selection of cabinetry, and an upgraded warranty. U.S. technicians in the factory inspect every Cristofori piano prior to crating and shipping.

The "Vivace" brand of pianos, formerly made by Sejung for Jordan Kitt's stores has been discontinued.

Warranty: Twelve-year full, transferable, warranty on parts and labor.

DISKLAVIER

including Silent Piano (formerly MIDIPiano) — See also "Yamaha"

Yamaha Corporation of America
P.O. Box 6600
Buena Park, California 90622

714-522-9011
800-854-1569
infostation@yamaha.com
www.yamaha.com

Pianos made by: Yamaha Corporation, Hamamatsu, Japan and other locations

Please read "Electronic Player Piano Systems and Hybrid Acoustic/Digital Pianos" on pages 160–161 of *The Piano Book*.

Disklaviers are regular Yamaha pianos that have been outfitted with an electronic player piano mechanism. These mechanisms are installed only in new Yamahas and only at the factory. They cannot be retrofitted into older Yamahas or any other brand. (There are other systems on the market that do that.)

As with all such systems, the Disklavier consists of a solenoid rail installed in a slot cut in the piano keybed; a processor unit mounted under the piano; and a control box that plays floppy disks and/or CDs, depending on the model, that is either mounted under the keybed at the front of the piano or sits on or near the piano. There is one solenoid for each key and solenoids for the damper and una corda (soft) pedals. When playing Disklavier's specialized software (or other compatible software), one track contains the MIDI signal that drives the piano solenoids, the other tracks provide an instrumental or vocal accompaniment that plays through a stereo system or through amplified speakers that come with the piano. The accompaniment may be in the form of synthesized or sampled sound, or actual recordings of live musicians. Except for playback-only models, Disklavier grands also include an optical record system beneath the keys that records key stroke information in MIDI format. Pedal movement is recorded, and hammer stroke information is also recorded on the larger grand models. This information can be stored for later playback on the same piano, stored on other media, or sent to other MIDI-compatible devices, including if desired, another Disklavier piano. The sophistication of the key, hammer, and pedal sensing will vary depending on which generation of Disklavier (Mark III or IV) is associated with that particular piano model.

Disklavier differs from the popular after-market systems PianoDisc and QRS Pianomation in that Disklavier is not modular. That is, you cannot pick and choose which features you wish to buy. For the most part, whatever Disklavier features come with a particular model of piano is what you get. The features vary a little from one model to another. All grands contain the features of the Mark IV (i.e., fourth generation) Disklavier except the model DGB1, which is playback-only, and the models DGC1B and DC2B, which are Mark III systems. Verticals include the 48" model U1 Disklavier upright (DU1A) and the 48" model YUS1 (DYUS1A), which are also Mark III systems. Disklavier versions of the smaller verticals have been discontinued.

The new features of the Mark IV Disklavier, released in 2004, include the following: An 80-gigabyte hard drive capable of holding all the Disklavier software ever written (and then some); pocket remote control to communicate wirelessly with the Disklavier; built-in Ethernet for connecting to your network and downloading MIDI files; the ability to play much softer as a result of a higher-speed CPU, greater MIDI resolution, and improved solenoids; more sensitive recording capabilities due to the use of grayscale (continuous) hammershank and key sensors; karaoke capability; and an improved speaker system. The performance level of the standard Mark IV Disklavier is the same as formerly found in the Mark III PRO series. The Mark IV PRO provides the highest level of performance in the Disklavier line. The PRO series has a much higher internal recording resolution and a greater dynamic range in playback. There is a tablet remote control available as an option for Mark IV pianos.

In addition to the new features mentioned above, the Mark III and IV Disklaviers have the following features as well, described in greater detail in *The Piano Book*: floppy and CD drives, flash memory (Mark III only), tone generator with hundreds of synthesized or sampled sounds, digital piano sound chip, built-in speakers, 16-track recording capabilities, Silent Mode (silencing the acoustic piano and listening through headphones), Quiet Mode (silencing the acoustic piano and directing the sound to speakers), Quick Escape Action (maintains correct action regulation when using Silent Mode or Quiet Mode), headphones, SmartKey (a teaching device), and CueTIME (a smart accompaniment feature). Note: Models DGC1B and DC2B are Mark III Disklaviers with some limits to their functionality. They do not support Silent Mode, Quiet Mode, or Quick Escape Action, and do not come with headphones or a digital piano sound chip (they use the piano sound in the tone generator).

PianoSmart Audio Synchronization technology is a new feature of all Mark III and Mark IV Disklavier pianos. Yamaha has prepared a piano track in MIDI format on a floppy disk to go along with each of a number of popular audio CDs available on the general market. When the owner plays the floppy and the CD at the same time, PianoSmart links them together, enabling the Disklavier to accurately play along with the CD. One can also record a piano accompaniment to a favorite audio CD. Pop the CD and a blank floppy into a Mark III or Mark IV Disklavier and record yourself playing along. The two will then be linked together for future playback. PianoSmart Video Synchronization on the Mark IV system works the same way. Plug a camcorder into the Disklavier while videotaping a piano performance, and the Disklavier will play the performance back perfectly on the piano whenever you play back the video of the performance through the camcorder. PianoSmart is available as a free software upgrade from Yamaha.

Version 2.0 is the latest operating system for the Mark IV Disklavier. Among other things, this operating system upgrade allows the user to purchase and download music over the Internet directly to the instrument using the pocket remote controller screen without the use of a computer. It also enables Disklavier Radio, a group of streaming MIDI music stations encompassing a variety of music formats to choose from and play on the Disklavier, available on a subscription basis. With this operating system the Disklavier is upgradeable for free over the Internet.

Version 3.0 for the Mark IV system is planned for release during the summer of 2008. New capabilities will include the ability to make audio recordings of the piano and anything coming into the mic input. This new version will make it possible to control the Mark IV with a PC or Macintosh computer through the use of a web browser.

For simple playback, most of the player piano systems on the market are probably equally recommended. The Disklavier, however, has a slight edge on quality control, and its recording system is much more sophisticated than most of the others, especially on the larger grands. For this reason, it is the system of choice for professional applications such as performance and teaching, and much of Yamaha's marketing efforts are directed at that audience.

Two examples are especially noteworthy. Yamaha sponsors regular piano "e-competitions" in which contestants gather in several cities and play on Yamaha Disklavier concert grands. Their performances are transmitted over the Internet to judges located far away who listen to the music reproduced perfectly on other Disklavier pianos, rather than listen to recordings. A similar concept is the technology called "Remote Lesson," recently demonstrated and to debut in the near future, in which a student can take a lesson on one Disklavier, while a teacher located far away teaches and critiques on a second Disklavier connected via the Internet, both communicating with each other in real time via videoconferencing. In

2006, the Disklavier received the Frances Clark Keyboard Pedagogy Award from the Music Teachers National Association. Typically awarded to a music educator who has made significant contributions to the field of keyboard pedagogy, this marks the first time the award has been given to a music product.

Yamaha maintains a large and growing library of music for the Disklavier, including piano solo, piano with recorded "live" accompaniment, piano with digital instrumental accompaniment, and PianoSmart arrangements. The system will also play Standard MIDI files type 0 and 1 and most of its competitors' CDs. (Because competitors frequently change their formats and encryption, the ability to play the format of a particular competitor is not guaranteed.)

Yamaha also makes a line of MIDIPianos, which were renamed Silent Pianos in January 2008. Technically, these are not Disklaviers because they do not use solenoids for playback. They are included here because they are closely related products that have some similar features. As with the Disklaviers there are sensors associated with the keys, hammers, and pedals that record their movement in MIDI format and output the information through a digital piano sound chip to headphones or speakers, or to a computer for editing if desired. With the addition of Yamaha's piano mute rail, the acoustic piano can be silenced and the instrument can be used as a digital piano, though with a real piano action. Silent Pianos don't have disk drives for recording MIDI data, but an optional add-on unit is available with floppy disk drive and tone generator (to create sounds other than piano). A new vertical Silent System, called "SG" is now available. The "SG" system offers nine additional sounds, has the ability to record, and has USB capability to preserve recorded performances.

Warranty: Acoustic Piano—Ten years, parts and labor, to original purchaser. Player piano/Silent Piano system—Five years, parts; one year, labor, to original purchaser.

DONGBEI

Pianos made by: Baldwin Dongbei (Yingkou) Piano and Musical Instrument
   Company, Ltd., Yingkou, Liaoning Province, China

The Dongbei Piano Company in China is owned by Baldwin and makes pianos that are sold in North America by various distributors and under a variety of names, including Baldwin, Nordiska, Everett, and Hallet, Davis & Co., among others (see listing under each name).

Dongbei is Chinese for "northeast." In 1952 Dongbei was formed by splitting off from a government-owned piano factory in Shanghai and establishing a new government-owned factory in the northeastern part of the country. Dongbei began a process of modernization in 1988 when it purchased the designs and manufacturing equipment for a vertical piano model from the Swedish company Nordiska when that company went out of business. The Swedish-designed vertical model 116 was strikingly more advanced than Dongbei's own "Prince" and "Princess" piano lines. At that time, Dongbei made only vertical pianos.

In 1991 Dongbei entered into an agreement with Korean piano maker Daewoo whereby Daewoo would assist Dongbei in improving its vertical piano production. In 1996 that relationship was extended to grand piano design and production. In 1997 Daewoo decided to exit the piano business and Dongbei purchased nearly all of Daewoo's grand piano manufacturing equipment and commenced making grand pianos. Export to the U.S. began in 1994 under the brand name Sagenhaft, at first only with vertical pianos. When export of grand pianos began in 1998, other brand names such as Nordiska, Everett, and Story & Clark began to become available.

Over the past ten years, production for both domestic use and for export has grown enormously. Dongbei has about one million square feet of factory space, employs 2,300 workers, and makes about 21,000 vertical and 7,000 grand pianos per year. More than 25 percent of Dongbei's production is for export to the United States. In early 2007, Gibson Musical Instruments, parent of Baldwin Piano Company, acquired Dongbei Piano and renamed it as Baldwin Dongbei (Yingkou) Piano and Musical Instrument Co., Ltd., thus forming a major piano manufacturing power in China with two plants. (The other plant, Baldwin (Zhongshan) Piano and Musical Instrument Co., Ltd., is located in southern China.) Baldwin has greatly expanded its presence in China over the last five years and the company says it will use the manufacturing capacity of Dongbei toward servicing the Chinese domestic market as well as the world market.

When Daewoo exited the piano business in 1997, some of the technicians and designers sent by Daewoo to advise Dongbei stayed on with Dongbei for many years, designing numerous new piano models during that time. Some of these technicians had trained in both Korea and Germany. In the opinion of many technicians who have examined a variety of pianos from China, the Dongbei grand piano designs are among the best and most successful musically. Dongbei recently upgraded its designs to utilize a focused beam structure that concentrates the piano's structural support toward the nose flange of the plate, a design used by Steinway and others that is thought to increase the tonal projection of the instrument by making the frame more rigid. This design was first brought out under the Nordiska brand name (see "Nordiska"), but may be available to other Dongbei-made brands. You can tell if the Dongbei-made piano you are looking at uses this improved system by looking up at the beam structure of the piano from underneath. If all the beams are more or less parallel to one another, the piano is of the old design. If several of the beams converge toward the front of the instrument, the piano is of the new design.

EBEL, CARL — See "Perzina, Gebr."

ESSEX

Steinway & Sons, Inc.
Steinway Place
Long Island City, New York 11105

718-721-7711
800-842-5397
essex@steinway.com
www.steinway.com

Pianos made by: Young Chang Co., Ltd., Inchon, South Korea and Tianjin, China; and Guangzhou Pearl River Piano Group Ltd., Guangzhou, Guangdong Province, China

Essex pianos are designed by Steinway & Sons engineers and are made in factories in China and Korea by both Young Chang and Pearl River. Steinway first introduced its Essex line of pianos in early 2001 with a limited offering of models made by Young Chang, and the brand kept an unusually low profile in the piano market for a number of years. In 2006, a major relaunch of Essex was held that included a new and very complete line comprising thirty-five grand and thirty-one vertical models and finishes.

Four grand sizes and three vertical scales are made. The 44" model EUP-111 console comes in a variety of furniture styles, and 43" model EUP-108 is a version of the console in continental style. The newly designed 46" model EUP-116 studio is available in 14 different and striking cabinets, designed by Steinway & Sons and renowned furniture designer William Faber. Styles include: Classic, Queen Anne, Italian Provincial, French Provincial, Formal French, English Country, English Traditional, Contemporary, and Sheraton Traditional. These models incorporate various leg designs (including cabriole leg, spoon leg, and canopy-styled tapered leg and arm designs) and hand-carved trim (such as Acanthus leaf designs, tulip trim, vertical bead molding), highly molded top lids, picture frame front panels, and stylized, decorative music desks. The newly designed 48" model EUP-123 upright comes in a traditional style in four finishes along with Empire and French styles.

The Essex grands are available in 5' 1" (EGP-155), 5' 3" (EGP-161), 5' 8" (EGP-173), and 6' (EGP-183) sizes in (depending on model) Classic, Neoclassic, Traditional, Renaissance, and French Provincial styles. They come in a variety of regular and exotic veneers in high polish and satin luster (semi-gloss) finishes.

Like Steinway's Boston line of pianos, the Essex line was designed with a lower tension scale and incorporates many Steinway-designed refinements. Included in these are a wide tail design that allows the bridges to be positioned closer to the more lively central part of the soundboard, smoothing out the break between bass and treble. This, plus a thinner, tapered soundboard and other scaling differences produces a tone with a longer sustain. Other Steinway-designed features include an all-wood action with Steinway geometry, and with rosette-shaped hammer flanges to preserve hammer spacing like those used in Steinway grands; pear-shaped hammers with reinforced shoulders and metal fasteners, vertically laminated bridges with solid maple cap, duplex scale, radial bracing in grands, and staggered backposts in verticals.

At present, Young Chang makes Essex vertical models 108, 111, and 116 in its factory in Tianjin, China, and grand models 161 and 183 in Korea. Guangzhou Pearl River makes vertical model 123 and grand models 155 and 173 in China.

Steinway has put an immense amount of time and effort into the relaunch of Essex. The pianos are new designs by Steinway engineers and not just warmed-over designs of other companies. Steinway has a permanent office in Shanghai, China, and full-time employees inspecting pianos in the Asian factories. I expect that the quality of the Essex pianos will be at the upper end of what these factories are capable of producing. So far, limited feedback from piano technicians confirms this expectation.

Steinway guarantees full trade-in value for an Essex piano toward the purchase of a Steinway grand within ten years.

Warranty: Ten years, parts and labor, to the original purchaser.

ESTONIA

Laul Estonia Piano Factory Ltd.
7 Fillmore Drive
Stony Point, New York 10980

845-947-7763
laulestoniapiano@aol.com
www.estoniapiano.com

Pianos made by: Estonia Klaverivabrik AS, Tallinn, Estonia

Estonia is a small republic in northern Europe on the Baltic Sea, near Scandinavia. For centuries it was under Danish, Swedish, German, and Russian domination, finally gaining its independence in 1918, only to lose it again to the Soviet Union in 1940. It became free again in 1991 with the collapse of the Soviet Union.

Piano making in Estonia goes back over two hundred years under German influence, and from 1850 to 1940 there were nearly twenty piano manufacturers operating in the country. The most famous among them was Ernst Hiis-Ihse, who studied piano making in the Steinway Hamburg and Blüthner factories and established his own company in 1893. His piano designs gained international recognition. In 1950 the

43

Communist-dominated Estonian government consolidated many smaller Estonian piano makers into a factory managed by Hiis, making pianos under the Estonia name for the first time. The instruments became prominent on concert stages throughout the East and, amazingly, more than 7,400 concert grands were made. After Mr. Hiis' death in 1964, however, the quality of the pianos gradually declined, partly due to the fact that high-quality parts and materials were hard to come by during the Communist occupation of the country. After Estonia gained its independence in 1991, the factory struggled to maintain production. In 1994 Estonia pianos were introduced to the U.S. market by Paul Vesterstein, an Estonian American.

In 1994 the company was privatized under the Estonia name, with the managers and employees as owners. During the following years, Indrek Laul, an Estonian with a doctorate in piano performance from the Juilliard School of Music, and a recording artist, gradually bought shares of the company from the stockholders until he became sole owner in 2001. Dr. Laul lives in the United States and represents the company here. In 2005, the Juilliard School named Dr. Laul one of the school's top one hundred graduates at its 100th anniversary celebration. Estonia makes about 350 pianos a year, all grands, mostly for sale in the United States.

Estonia pianos have rims of laminated birch, sand-cast plates, Renner actions and hammers, laminated red beech pinblocks, and European solid spruce soundboards. They come in 5' 6", 6' 3", and 9' sizes. All have three pedals, including sostenuto and come with an adjustable artist bench.

When I reported on Estonia pianos for the fourth edition of *The Piano Book* (2001), it was a good piano with much potential, but as the company was still rebounding from problems suffered during the Communist era, some caution was advised. Since becoming sole owner in 2001, Dr. Laul has made so many improvements to the piano that it is practically a different instrument. Improvements include: rescaling the bass and upgrading bass string making machinery for producing hand-wound bass strings; improving the method of drilling pinblocks; stronger plates and improved plate finishes; thicker inner and outer rims; improved fitting of soundboard to rim; concert-grand quality soundboard spruce on all models; quarter-sawn maple bridge caps; adjustable front and rear duplex scales; wood for legs and keyslips heat-treated to better resist changing climatic conditions; Renner Blue hammers on all models; better quality metal hardware that resists oxidation; suede-covered music desk tray; improved satin finishes; establishing a quality control department headed by Dr. Laul's father (both his father and mother are professional musicians); higher-grade and artistically matched veneers; and establishing a U.S. service center for warranty repairs. All pianos are now accompanied by a quality control certificate signed by a member of the Laul family, and each piano is played and checked by them.

The Estonia factory has recently introduced a new custom line of pianos, offering exotic veneers such as Rosewood, Bubinga, and Pyramid Mahogany, and is willing to finish instruments to fit the desire of each individual customer. The custom line also features a number of different Victorian-style legs and ornamental music desks. For 2008 Estonia has introduced lighter lids for the 190 models, for easier lifting, and provided a new finish of darker ebony satin. New lid pillows add a nice touch, and pianos are available with a combination of nickel and brass parts.

In the short time Estonia pianos have been sold here, they have gathered an unusually loyal and devoted following. Groups of owners of Estonia pianos, completely independent of the company, frequently hold musical get-togethers at different locations around the country. The pianos have a rich, warm, singing tone; are very well constructed and well prepared at the factory; and there is hardly a detail that the company has not examined and impressively perfected. The price has risen over the years, but they are still an unusually good value among higher-end instruments.

Warranty: Ten years, parts and labor, to the original purchaser.

EVERETT

Wrightwood Enterprises, Inc.
717 St. Joseph Drive
St. Joseph, Michigan 49085

616-828-0618
www.everett-piano.com

Pianos made by: Dongbei Piano Company, Ltd., Yingkou, Liaoning Province, China

The Everett Piano Company originated in Boston in 1883 and moved to South Haven, Michigan in 1926. It was acquired by Yamaha in 1973. Until mid-1986, Yamaha made a line of Everett vertical pianos in this factory alongside its U.S.-made Yamaha pianos. When Yamaha moved its U.S. piano manufacturing to Thomaston, Georgia in 1986, it contracted with Baldwin to continue making Everett pianos. The contract terminated in 1989, and Yamaha dropped the line permanently. See the entry for "Everett" in *The Piano Book* for more information about pianos from that era.

The Everett name has been used by Wrightwood Enterprises, Inc. since 1995. The pianos are made in China by the Dongbei Piano Company (see "Dongbei"). The grands have duplex scaling and a bass scale that is custom made for the Everett brand, the company says.

Warranty: Ten years, parts and labor, to the original purchaser

FALCONE — See "Sejung"

FANDRICH & SONS

Fandrich & Sons Pianos
7411 Silvana Terrace Road
Stanwood, Washington 98292

360-652-8980
877-737-1422
fandrich@fandrich.com
www.fandrich.com

Pianos made by: various makers—see text

In the late 1980s, Darrell Fandrich, an engineer, pianist, and piano technician, developed a vertical piano action designed to play like a grand, for which ten patents have issued. You can see an illustration of the Fandrich Vertical Action™, an explanation of how it works, and some history of its development in the third and fourth editions of *The Piano Book* and on the Fandrich & Sons Web site. Since 1994, Darrell and his wife Heather have been installing Renner-made Fandrich actions in selected new pianos, selling them under the Fandrich & Sons label. They also sell some grands (with regular grand actions) under that name.

Over the years, the Fandrichs have installed their actions in over two hundred instruments, including ones from Pearl River, Wilh. Steinberg, Klima, Bohemia, and Feurich. At present, the action is being installed into 49" and 52" Bohemia uprights and 48" Feurich uprights. The converted pianos are available directly from the Fandrichs. The Fandrichs say they are working with factory personnel to train them in completing the actions at the factory, at which time these pianos may also become available from other Bohemia and Feurich dealers.

Playing a piano outfitted with a Fandrich Vertical Action™ is a very interesting experience. The action easily outperforms that of most other vertical pianos on the market, and some grands as well. The Fandrichs have now had years of experience refining and servicing the action, and reports suggest that customers are very satisfied with them.

Fandrich & Sons grand pianos are made in China and "re-manufactured" at the Fandrich & Sons facility in Stanwood, Washington. The company offers three sizes of grand piano, models 165 (5'5"), 185 (6'1") and 203 (6'8"), in two configurations, "S" and "HGS." HGS models feature Renner hammer shanks, Ronsen hammers with Würzen felt, and Arledge bass strings, plus a 40-hour preparation, tuning stabilization, and voicing. The S series pianos retain the original factory hammers and strings, but receive the same extensive preparation as the HGS series. All models also feature redesigned pedal-lyre and trapwork systems, soundboard modifications, and traditional touchweighting. Models 165 and 185 are built by Dongbei (see

"Dongbei") and are available in both the S and HGS configurations. Model 203 is built by Heintzman (see "Heintzman & Co.") and is offered only in the HGS configuration. All Fandrich & Sons pianos come with a Dampp-Chaser de-humidifier system and an adjustable artist bench.

The Fandrichs are passionate about their craft and choose the brands they work with carefully for musical potential. In addition to making standard modifications and refinements to remedy perceived shortcomings in the original Chinese-made instruments, the Fandrichs are inveterate tinkerers always searching for ways to make additional improvements, however subtle. As a result, many who play the pianos find them to be more musical than the price and origin would suggest.

Warranty: Twelve years, parts and labor, to the original purchaser.

Note: Do not confuse the Fandrich & Sons pianos with the 48" Fandrich upright that was once manufacturerd with a Fandrich Vertical Action™ by Darrell Fandrich's brother Delwin Fandrich. That piano has not been made since 1994.

FAZIOLI

Fazioli Pianoforti srl
Via Ronche 47
33077 Sacile (Pn), Italy

+39-0434-72026
info@fazioli.com
www.fazioli.com

In 1978 musician and engineer Paolo Fazioli of Rome, Italy, began designing and building pianos, with the object of making the finest quality instruments possible. Now even the most famous piano makers of Western Europe are recognizing his accomplishment, and artists throughout the world are using the instruments successfully on the concert stage and elsewhere.

As a youth, Fazioli studied music and engineering, receiving advanced degrees in both subjects. He briefly attempted to make a living as a concert pianist, but instead joined his family's furniture company, rising to the position of factory manager in the Rome, Sacile, and Turin factories. But his creative ambitions, combined with his personal search for the perfect piano, finally led him to conclude that he needed to build his own piano. With advice and financial backing from his family, in 1977 Fazioli assembled a group of experts in woodworking, acoustics, and piano technology to study and scientifically analyze every aspect of piano design and construction. The following year, prototypes of his new instruments in hand, he began building pianos commercially in a factory housed at one end of the family's Sacile furniture factory, which is a top supplier of high-end office furniture in Italy.

In 2001, Fazioli built a new expanded, modern piano production facility, and in 2005 opened an adjoining 198-seat concert hall with a stage large enough for a chamber orchestra. Fazioli maintains a regular concert schedule of well-known musicians who perform there. The concert hall is designed so that it can be adjusted acoustically with moveable panels and sound reflectors to optimize the acoustics for performing, recording, or testing, and for different kinds of music, musical ensembles, and size of audience. The hall is used for the research and testing of pianos, and every piano Fazioli makes is tested here. In addition to the research activities in the concert hall, the new factory also contains a research department for ongoing research in musical acoustics in cooperation with a number of educational institutions.

Fazioli builds grands only, about 120 per year, in six sizes from 5' 2" to 10' 2", one of the largest pianos in the world. This model also has the distinction of having four pedals. Three are the usual sustain, sostenuto, and una corda. The fourth is a "soft" pedal that brings the hammers closer to the strings—similar to the function in verticals and some older grands—to soften the sound without altering the tonal quality as the una corda often does. A unique compensating device corrects for the action irregularity that would otherwise occur when the hammers are moved in this manner. The fourth pedal is available as an option on the other models. Fazioli also offers two actions and two pedal lyres as options on all models. Having two actions allows for more voicing possibilities without having to constantly revoice the hammers. A second pedal lyre containing only three pedals can be a welcome alternative for some pianists who might be confused by the presence of a fourth pedal.

All Fazioli pianos have inner and outer rims of maple. Pinblocks are of Delignit, except for the largest two models, which use five-ply maple pinblocks from Bolduc in Canada. The pianos have Renner actions, Kluge keyboards, and either Renner or Abel hammers. The bronze capo d'astro bar is adjustable in the factory for setting the strike point and treble string length, and is also removable for servicing if necessary, and the front and rear duplex scales are tunable. The company says that a critical factor in the sound of its pianos is the scientific selection of its woods, such as the "resonant spruce" obtained from the Val di Fiemme, where Stradivarius reportedly sought woods for his violins. Each piece of wood is said to be carefully tested for certain resonant properties before being used in the pianos.

An incredible level of detail has gone into the design and construction of these pianos. For instance, in one small portion of the soundboard where additional stiffness is required, the grain of the wood runs perpendicular to that of the rest of the soundboard, cleverly disguised so as to be almost unnoticeable. The pianos are impeccably prepared at the factory, including very fine voicing—even perfect tuning of the duplex scales.

Those most familiar with Fazioli pianos describe them as combining both great power and great warmth in a way that causes the music played on them to "make sense" as few other pianos can.

Warranty: Ten years, parts and labor, transferable to future owners within the warranty period.

FEURICH

Unique Pianos
Brian Gatchell
25 South Wickham Rd.
Melbourne, Florida 32904

888-725-6633
321-725-5690
www.feurich.com
www.atlanticmusiccenter.com

Pianos made by: Julius Feurich Pianofortefabrik GmbH, Gunzenhausen, Germany

This German piano manufacturer was founded in Leipzig in 1851 by Julius Feurich. At its height in the early part of the twentieth century, the company employed 360 people, producing 1,200 upright and 600 grand pianos annually. Like many German manufacturers, however, Feurich lost its factory during the Second World War. Following the war, the fourth generation of the Feurich family rebuilt in Langlau in what became West Germany.

In 1991 Bechstein purchased Feurich and closed the Langlau factory, but in 1993 the name was sold back to the Feurich family. For a time, production was contracted out to other German manufacturers, including Schimmel, while the Feurich family marketed and distributed the pianos. In 1995 Feurich opened a new factory in Gunzenhausen, Germany. Under the direction of Julius Feurich, the fifth generation, the company began building its own pianos once again, and is currently building about fifty to sixty instruments per year in two sizes of grand and three sizes of vertical. All pianos and parts are made in Germany. The 49" model 123 vertical is available with a choice of actions, either the traditional Feurich action made by Renner or the Fandrich Vertical Action™, made by Renner under license from the Fandrichs (see "Fandrich & Sons" for more information).

Feurich has a partnership in China to produce pianos for the mainland Chinese market. These pianos are not available elsewhere.

Warranty: Five years, parts and labor, to the original purchaser.

FÖRSTER, AUGUST

German American Trading Co., Inc.
P.O. Box 17789
Tampa, Florida 33682

813-961-8405
germanamer@msn.com
www.august-foerster.de

Pianos made by: August Förster GmbH, Löbau, Germany

The Förster factory was founded by Friedrich August Förster in 1859 in Löbau, Germany, after Förster studied the art of piano building with others. During the years of control by the government of East Germany, the factory was managed by the fourth generation piano maker, Wolfgang Förster, and his daughter, Annekatrin. Since the reunification of Germany and privatization, Wolfgang and his family are once again the owners of the company.

Förster makes about 120 grands a year in four sizes, and 150 verticals a year in two sizes, with a workforce of forty, using a great deal of hand labor. The pianos are very well built structurally and the cabinets elegant. Rims and pinblocks are of beech, soundboards of Siberian spruce, and bridges are of hardrock maple (without graphite). Each string is individually terminated (single-strung). The actions are made by Renner with Renner hammers. A sostenuto pedal is standard on all grand models.

The tone of August Förster grands is quite unique, with a remarkable bass: dark, deep, yet clear. As delivered from the factory, the treble is often quite bright, and for some American tastes might be considered a bit thin. It is a less complex sound, emphasizing clarity. This, however, can be modified somewhat with voicing and a good dealer preparation. The instruments are quite versatile, at home with Mozart or Prokofieff, classical or jazz. The 6' 4" model is often said to have an especially good scale. The concert-quality 7' 2" and 9' 1" models are well balanced tonally and, over the years, have been endorsed by many famous artists. The Renner actions are very responsive and arrive in exacting regulation.

Most of the comments regarding the quality of materials and workmanship of the grands also apply to the verticals. The cabinet of the vertical is of exceptional width, with extra-thick side panels of solid-core stock. Counter bridges are used on the outside of the soundboard to increase its mass. The verticals have a full set of agraffes and all the hardware and handmade wood parts are of elegant quality. The actions are built by Renner. The verticals possess the same warm, rich, deep bass tone as the grands.

Warranty: Ten years, parts and labor, to the original purchaser.

GROTRIAN

Grotrian Piano Company GmbH
P.O. Box 5833
D-38049 Braunschweig, Germany

+49-531-210100
+49-531-2101040 (fax)
contact@grotrian.de
www.grotrian.de

Friedrich Grotrian was born in Schöningen, Germany in 1803, and as a young man lived in Moscow, where he ran a music business and was associated with piano manufacturing. Later in his life, he teamed up with Heinrich Steinweg and Heinrich's son, Theodore, to build pianos in Germany. Heinrich emigrated to the United States about 1850, soon to establish the firm of Steinway & Sons. Theodore followed in 1865, selling his share in the partnership to Friedrich's son, Wilhelm, Friedrich having died in 1860. Thereafter, the firm became known as Grotrian-Steinweg. (In a legal settlement with Steinway & Sons, Grotrian-Steinweg agreed to use only the name Grotrian on pianos sold in North America.)

Even as early as the 1860s, Grotrian pianos were well known and highly respected throughout Europe. Each successive generation of the Grotrian family maintained the company's high standards and furthered the technical development of the instrument. Today the company is owned by the sixth generation of Grotrians. Housed in an up-to-date factory, and using a combination of modern technology and traditional craftsmanship, Grotrian makes about 500 verticals and 100 grands a year.

Grotrian grands have beech rims, solid spruce soundboards, laminated beech pinblocks, Renner actions, and are single-strung. Grotrian prides itself on what it calls its "homogeneous soundboard," in which each piece of wood is specially chosen for its contribution to the tone of the soundboard. The cast-iron plate is attached with screws along the outer edges of the rim, instead of on top of the rim, which the company says allows the soundboard to vibrate more freely. The vertical pianos have a unique star-shaped wooden back structure and a full-perimeter plate.

Grotrian makes five sizes of grand and six sizes of vertical piano. The 43½" "Friedrich Grotrian" vertical is a lower-cost piano with a beech back frame but no back posts, and a simpler cabinet. In 2006 a 6' 10" grand model called "Charis" was introduced.

Grotrian has introduced the Duo Grand Piano, two grand pianos placed side by side with keyboards at opposite ends, as in a duo piano concert, with removable rim parts, connected soundboards, and a common lid (price on request).

The treble of Grotrian pianos has extraordinary sustaining characteristics. It also has a pronounced sound of attack, subtle and delicate. The tenor is darker than many other brands. The bass can be powerful, but without stridency. Overall, Grotrian pianos have a unique, expressive sound and are a pleasure to play. Over the years, many well-known pianists have endorsed or expressed appreciation of Grotrian pianos.

Warranty: Five years, parts and labor, transferable to future owners.

GULBRANSEN

QRS Music Technologies, Inc.
2011 Seward Avenue
Naples, Florida 34109

800-247-6557
www.gulbransen.com

Pianos made by: Sejung Corporation, Qingdao, Shandong Province, China

Founded in 1904, Gulbransen was a well-regarded piano and organ manufacturer of the early twentieth century, and at one time was the world's largest maker of player pianos. An indication of the company's stature and success in its early history is the fact that during World War II, Gulbransen was one of only two piano manufacturers allowed to continue production; along with Steinway & Sons they made pianos for government use. In more modern times, Gulbransen became known for its electronic organs and MIDI products. In 2004 QRS Music Technologies, maker of the Pianomation player piano systems and distributor of Story & Clark pianos, purchased Gulbransen's MIDI products and company name.

Currently, Gulbransen serves as an entry-level line for Story & Clark dealers (see "Story & Clark"), offering two grand and two vertical sizes, made by Sejung in China (see "Sejung"). Gulbransen pianos can be ordered with factory-installed Pianomation systems.

Warranty: Ten years, parts and labor, to the original purchaser.

HAESSLER — See "Blüthner"

HAILUN

Hailun Distribution, LLC
5400 Lawrenceville Hwy., N.W.
Suite A-2
Lilburn, Georgia 30047

770-381-3871
678-898-9931
Aspire@HailunUSA.com
www.hailunusa.com

Pianos made by: Ningbo Hailun Musical Instruments Co. Ltd., Ningbo, Zhejiang Province, China

Ningbo Hailun began making piano parts and components in 1986 under the Ningbo Piano Parts Factory name, and began assembling entire pianos in 1995. Its assembly facility converted to a full-scale piano manufacturing facility in 2000. The company offers a full line of grands and uprights in a designer "Art Case Collection" as well as traditional styles and finishes. In addition to making pianos under the Hailun name, it also makes the Wendl & Lung brand for distribution throughout Europe and a few piano stores in the U.S. The company also makes pianos or components under contract for several other manufacturers and distributors.

The Hailun factory has over 400,000 square feet of production capacity and 800 employees. A 200,000 square foot production expansion project is underway to accommodate distribution in the U.S. market. Additionally, a new cabinet factory is now complete and will begin production in 2008. Since 2001, the company has invested heavily in computer-controlled manufacturing equipment and has hired an impressive group of experts from Japan, Europe, and the United States to help it reach the highest quality standards.

Hailun is a little different from most of the other Chinese companies selling pianos in the United States: its founder and owner, Mr. Chen Hailun, is an entrepreneur in the Western style, and deeply involved in every aspect of the business. Originally a maker of molds for industrial use, Mr. Chen got into the piano business when piano manufacturers started to use his services to make piano parts. In 1998 he bought out the government's position in his company to better control quality and hiring decisions. He seeks out the best workers by paying considerably higher wages than other piano makers in China, he says, and assists in the training of future piano technicians through an association with a local university. His greatest aspiration, Mr. Chen says, is to be like Yamaha.

Over the years, much of Mr. Chen's technical efforts have gone into maximizing the precision and stability of the pianos and parts his company makes. This is evidenced by the substantial investment in computer-controlled machinery used for precision cutting; the design of keys, keybed, and other parts to resist warping; and the fact that grand piano actions are actually interchangeable between instruments of the same model (this requires an usually high level of precision). The pianos themselves exhibit good quality control and intelligence in design. In terms of materials, the company uses maple in grand piano rims and the cast-iron plates are made by the wet-sand method, both features indicative of higher quality and arguably necessary for the best sound. This precision, stability, and quality of materials, combined with the work of experienced design consultants, have resulted in pianos that perform and service better than most other pianos from China, and may compare favorably with some mid-priced pianos from other parts of the world.

Warranty: Fifteen years, parts and labor, transferable to future owners within the warranty period; except for actions parts, cast-iron plate, and metal case hardware, which are warranted for the lifetime of the original purchaser. Freight charges paid by owner.

HALLET, DAVIS & CO.

North American Music, Inc.
11 Kay Fries Drive
Stony Point, New York 10980

800-782-2694
www.namusic.com

Pianos made by: Dongbei Piano Company, Ltd., Yingkou, Liaoning Province, China

This famous old American piano brand name dates back to at least 1843 and changed hands many times over the years. It eventually became part of the Aeolian group of piano brands, and instruments bearing the name were manufactured at Aeolian's Memphis plant before that company went out of business in 1985. For a time, Hallet & Davis pianos were made by Samick in Korea. At the present time, most Hallet, Davis & Co. pianos are made in China by the Dongbei Piano Company (see "Dongbei"). In general, they are similar to pianos built by Dongbei under other names for several other distributors. However, the distributor says that pianos in the "Imperial Collection" (model numbers ending in "I") use higher-quality imported veneers provided to Dongbei by the distributor.

HAMILTON — See "Baldwin"

HARDMAN, PECK & CO.

Hardman Pianos
11 Kay Fries Drive
Stony Point, New York 10980

800-782-2694
info@hardmanpiano.com
www.hardmanpiano.com

Pianos made by: Beijing Hsinghai Piano Group, Ltd., Beijing, China; and Dongbei Piano Company, Ltd., Yingkou, Liaoning Province, China

Hardman, Peck & Co. was an old American piano company whose roots can be traced back to 1842. In the early twentieth century it was absorbed into the Aeolian Corporation, which went out of business in 1985. Until 2007 most Hardman, Peck & Co. pianos were made in China by the Dongbei Piano Co. (see "Dongbei"), and were similar to those built by Dongbei under other names for several other distributors. Now the pianos are being made by the Beijing Hsinghai Piano Group (see "Beijing Hsinghai"), except for three vertical models—the 44" Classic Continental, 44" Decorator Console, and 45" Decorator Studio—which are still made by Dongbei.

HAZELTON BROS. — See "Samick"

HEINTZMAN & CO.

including Gerhard Heintzman

Heintzman Distributor Ltd.
210-2106 Main Street
Vancouver, British Columbia
Canada V5T 3C5

604-801-5393
info@hzmpiano.com
www.hzmpiano.com

Pianos made by: Heintzman Piano Company, Ltd., Beijing, China

Heintzman & Co. Ltd. was founded by Theodore August Heintzman in Toronto in 1866. By 1900, Heintzman was one of Toronto's larger manufacturing concerns, building 3,000 pianos per year and selling them throughout Canada and abroad through a network of company stores and other distributors. The pianos received high praise and won prizes at exhibitions. Even today, technicians frequently encounter old Heintzman pianos built in the early part of the twentieth century and consider them to be of high quality. In the latter decades of the century, Heintzman, like other North American brands, struggled to compete with cheaper foreign imports. The factory finally closed its doors in 1986 and relocated to China. (Some pianos continued to be sold in Canada under the Heintzman and Gerhard Heintzman names for a few years thereafter). At first the company was a joint venture with the Beijing Hsinghai Piano Group (see "Beijing Hsinghai"), but when the Chinese government began allowing foreign ownership of manufacturing concerns, the Canadian partner bought back majority ownership and took control.

The new company, known as Heintzman Piano Company, Ltd., is Canadian owned and managed and has a private, independent factory dedicated to producing Heintzman brand pianos. Heintzman makes pianos to the original Canadian Heintzman designs and scales utilizing some of the equipment from Canada. James Moffat, who was plant manager of the Canadian Heintzman factory for forty years, has been retained as a consultant and visits the factory in China several times a year. The company even utilizes some components from Canada, such as Bolduc soundboards, in grands and larger verticals. The factory makes about 5,000 pianos per year.

The smallest vertical made under the Heintzman name is 43½" tall, but pianos for export to North America typically start at 47½" and contain a mixture of Chinese and imported parts such as pinblocks and treble strings from Germany and Mapes bass strings from the U.S. Verticals 48½" and above use Renner Blue hammers, and the largest two sizes have Canadian Bolduc solid Eastern white spruce soundboards. All verticals have a middle pedal that operates a bass sustain mechanism, as well as a "Silent Switch" that operates a mute bar for silent practice.

The grands, 5' 6", 6' 2", 6' 8", and 9' in size, also use German pinblocks and strings, Mapes bass strings, Renner Blue hammers, and Canadian Bolduc soundboards. The 9' concert grand comes with a full Renner action and Kluge keys from Germany. A Renner action is a higher-priced option on the other models. All grands come with a sostenuto pedal. A 6' 2" model patterned on the old Heintzman model D was introduced in 2007. Heintzman has in development a 5' 1" grand to be introduced by early 2009.

Heintzman Piano Company also makes the "Gerhard Heintzman" brand, intended to compete with less expensive Chinese-made pianos. Most of the pianos in this line are smaller than in the Heintzman line. This brand uses less expensive materials and components than the Heintzman, including Japanese hammers and a laminated spruce soundboard.

Warranty: Heintzman and Gerhard Heintzman—Ten years, parts and labor, from the factory, transferable to future owners within the warranty period.

HOFFMANN, W. — See "Bechstein, C."

HOWARD — See "Baldwin"

HSINGHAI — See "Beijing Hsinghai"

IBACH

Rud. Ibach Sohn GmbH & Co. KG
In der Graslake 20
58332 Schwelm
Germany

+49-(0)2336-935-88 0
+49-(0)2336-935-8830 (fax)
info@ibach.de
www.ibach.de

Pianos made by: Rud. Ibach Sohn, Schwelm, Germany

Established by Johannes Adolf Ibach in 1794, Ibach had the distinction of being the oldest existing manufacturer of fine pianos in the world and was owned and managed by six generations of the original family until discontinuing production in 2008.

Although not as well known in North America as some other European manufacturers, Ibach quietly built a solid reputation in Europe over two centuries through fine craftsmanship and by supplying pianos to a long list of famous composers and artists, such as Wagner, R. Strauss, Liszt, Bartok, Schoenberg, and others.

Economic conditions in Germany during the last couple of decades have hit all the small piano makers very hard. In an attempt to survive, in 1991 Ibach sold a 33 percent interest in the company to Daewoo, the Korean former manufacturer of Sojin pianos. The plan was that Ibach was to sell Korean-made Ibach pianos worldwide in addition to a small number of German-made Ibachs. This joint venture did not survive very long and the Korean manufacturing operation was eventually abandoned by Daewoo.

Although discontinuing production and moving out of the premises that Ibach occupied since 1895, Rud. Ibach Sohn will continue to exist as an enterprise, fulfilling all obligations. The firm cited foreign competition, changes in buying behavior, an excess of second-hand instruments, increased taxes in Germany, and an increasingly weak dollar as primary reasons for ceasing production, but were careful to keep the door open for "a new orientation" in the future.

IRMLER — See "Blüthner"

KAWAI

including Shigeru Kawai

Kawai America Corporation
2055 East University Drive
P.O. Box 9045
Compton, California 90224

310-631-1771
800-421-2177
310-223-0900 (Shigeru Kawai)
acoustic@kawaius.com
www.kawaius.com
www.shigerukawai.com

Pianos made by: Kawai Musical Instrument Mfg. Co., Ltd., Hamamatsu, Japan and Karawan, Indonesia

Kawai was founded in 1927 by Koichi Kawai, an inventor and former Yamaha employee who was the first person in Japan to design and build a piano action. While Kawai is second in size to Yamaha among Japanese piano manufacturers, it has a well-deserved reputation all its own for quality and innovation. Nearly all Kawai grands and taller uprights are made in Japan; most consoles and studios are made in Indonesia. The company closed its North Carolina factory in 2005.

One of Kawai's most important innovations is the use of ABS Styran plastic in the manufacture of action parts. Nearly forty years of use and scientific testing have shown this material to be superior to wood for this purpose. ABS does not swell and shrink with humidity changes, so actions made with it are likely to maintain proper regulation better than wood actions. The parts are stronger and without glue joints, so breakage is rare. These parts are present in every Kawai piano. In the current "Millennium III" version found in some models, the ABS is reinforced with carbon fiber so it can be stronger with less mass. With less mass to "push around" (less inertia), the action can be more responsive to the player's intentions, including faster repetition. Certain contact surfaces on the action parts are also micro-engineered for ideal shape and texture, resulting in a more consistent touch. Although it took a number of years to overcome the idea that plastic parts must be inferior, there is essentially no dispute anymore among piano technicians on this subject.

Kawai's vertical piano offerings change frequently and are sometimes confusing. At present there are three basic series of Kawai vertical pianos. The console series begins with the 44½" model 506, a basic entry-level console in an institutional-style cabinet (legs with toe blocks). Model K-15 is a 44" version of this in a continental-style cabinet (no legs), and model 508 is a 44½" version in a simple furniture-style cabinet (free-standing legs). Model 607 is the same piano in a fancier furniture-style cabinet. All have the same internal workings. The action in this series is slightly smaller than a full-size action, so it will be slightly less responsive. However, it is more than sufficient for beginner or casual use.

The studio series used to consist primarily of the 46" school models UST-7 and UST-8. The UST-7 was a workhorse, with a very strong back, and would stay in tune well even when moved. The UST-8 was a less expensive piano with a thinner back and simpler cabinet, developed to be more competitive in school bidding situations. It didn't have the same tuning stability as the UST-7, especially when moved, but was otherwise adequate. Kawai has replaced both of these models with the 46" model UST-9. This model has the stronger back of the UST-7, but the simpler cabinet of the UST-8. It also contains the Millennium III action; an angled, leather-lined music desk to better hold music; and a stylish, reinforced bench. Because it is made in Indonesia, the price is only a little higher than the UST-8. It is probably one of the better "deals" in the Kawai vertical piano line. Rounding out the studio series is the 46½" model 907, which is essentially the model UST-9 in a fancy, furniture-style cabinet.

Kawai's upright series is known as the "K" series. It consists of the K-2 (45"), K-3 (48"), K-5 (49"), K-6 (52"), and K-8 (52"). All have the Millennium III action, a soft-close fallboard; a wide, leather-lined music desk; a somewhat stylish cabinet; and come with an adjustable bench. The 52" models also features agraffes, duplex scaling, Kawai's NEOTEX synthetic ivory keytops, and various kinds of tone escape mechanisms. The K-8 has a true sostenuto pedal.

Kawai has invented a variable-touch action for vertical pianos in which the player can vary the touchweight by sliding a lever. The lever operates a set of sliding weights behind the fallboard. The touchweight varies depending on the point at which the keys contact the sliding weights. The touchweight can be adjusted from about 48 to 70 grams (normal for Kawai is 56 grams). The "Vari-Touch" feature is currently available only on the 46" VT-118, which is based on the UST-8 studio upright.

Kawai has three series of grand pianos: RX, GE, and GM. The RX series is the most expensive and has the best features. It is designed for the best performance, whereas the GE and GM series are designed more for efficiency in manufacturing, with fewer refinements. The RX pianos have a radial beam structure, focused and connected to the plate using a cast-iron bracket at the tenor break. This system makes for a more rigid structure, which translates into better tone projection. The soundboard of the RX models is tapered for better tonal response, and the rim is thicker and stronger than in the GE and GM models. The RX series pianos also use the new Millennium III action, have duplex scaling, lighter hammers (less inertia), and NEOTEX synthetic ivory keytops (though some of these features are being introduced into the GE and GM pianos as well). The RX grands get more precise key weighting, plus more tuning, regulating, and voicing at the factory. The cabinetry is nicer looking and of better quality than that of the GE and GM series pianos. The difference between the GE and GM pianos is primarily that the GM grands have simpler cabinetry and internal design (no agraffes, for example) than the GE. The 5' model GM-10K is Kawai's first grand made in Indonesia; the others are made in Japan.

Kawai's quality control is excellent. Major problems are rare and after-sale service other than normal maintenance is usually limited to fixing the occasional minor buzz or squeak. Kawai's warranty service is also excellent and the warranty is transferable to future owners within the warranty period (a benefit that is not common these days). The tone of most Kawai pianos, in my opinion, is not as ideal for classical music as some more expensive instruments, but when expertly voiced, it is not far off, and in any case is quite versatile musically. In part because the touch is so good, Kawai grands are often sought by classical pianists as a less-expensive alternative to a Steinway or other high-end piano. Kawai dealers tend to be a little more aggressive about discounting than their competition (Yamaha). There is also a thriving market for used Kawais. (If you are considering buying a used Kawai, please read "Should I Buy a Used 'Gray Market' Yamaha or Kawai Piano?" on pages 176–177 of *The Piano Book*.)

Kawai has invented an Acoustic Piano Recording System (PR-1) that allows one to create a CD of a piano performance right from the piano. It contains two specially designed microphones that attach easily to the piano, and a CD read/write player with built-in reverb and EQ that connects to any sound system. The system retails for $1,595.

The Shigeru Kawai line of grands represents Kawai's ultimate effort in producing world-class pianos. Named after Kawai's former chairman (and son of company founder Koichi Kawai), the limited edition Shigeru Kawai grands are made at the separate facility where Kawai's EX concert grands are made.

Although based on the Kawai RX designs, the Shigeru Kawai models are "hand-made" in the extreme. Very high-grade soundboard spruce is air dried for multiple years and then planed by hand by a worker who knocks on the wood and listens for the optimum tonal response. Ribs are also hand planed for correct stiffness. String bearing is set in the traditional manner by planing the bridges by hand instead of having pre-cut bridges pinned by machine. Bass strings are wound by hand instead of machine wound. Cold-pressed hammers have felt fibers that are sorted bass to treble by the length and texture of the wool fibers for better voicing. Hammer shanks are thinned along the bottom so that their stiffness is matched to the hammer mass. These procedures represent a level of detail relatively few manufacturers indulge in.

Each buyer of a Shigeru Kawai piano receives a visit within the first year by a Kawai master technician from the factory in Japan. These are the same factory technicians who do the final assembly of actions into pianos, as well as the final voicing and regulation. According to those who have watched them work, these Japanese master technicians are amazingly skilled. Although not many U.S. technicians are familiar with Shigeru Kawai pianos, those who are tend to rank them among the world's finest instruments. In addition, Shigeru Kawai pianos have been chosen by top prize winners at a number of prestigious piano competitions.

Warranty: Kawai and Shigeru Kawai—Ten years, parts and labor, transferable to future owners within the warranty period.

KEMBLE

Kemble & Company Ltd.
Mount Avenue
Bletchley, Milton Keynes MK1 1JE
United Kingdom

+44-1908-371771
+44-1908-270448 (fax)
brian.kemble@gmx.yamaha.com
www.kemble-pianos.co.uk

The Kemble family has been manufacturing pianos since 1911. In 1985 Kemble started making pianos for Yamaha for the European market, and in 1988 Yamaha bought a majority interest in the company and expanded and modernized the factory. Kemble is England's only, and Western Europe's largest, piano manufacturer.

Kemble makes verticals from 43" to 52" and a 5' 8" grand. The quality of the materials used in the Kemble is comparable to that in the Yamaha pianos Kemble makes. The soundboard of the Kemble is of German spruce, which the company says gives it more of a European tone. The cabinets tend to be much fancier than Yamaha's, with some very interesting and beautiful designer models and finishes. For example, the 48" Shaker-inspired designer upright, Vermont, was designed by the famous British designers Conran and Partners. The Empire and Prestige models have beautiful inlaid panels of mahogany curl and burr yew, respectively. There is also a 45" model, the Classic-T, available in black and chrome or in a delicious chocolate color called Mocha Oak; a 49" Conservatoire upright with softline design (rounded edges and profile) and brass inlay; and a limited edition (250) Mozart model celebrating the 250th anniversary of the composer's birth. A new 52" model K132SN with sostenuto pedal was introduced in 2007. The 48" K121CL is also available with the new SG silent system from Yamaha that has nineteen different voices and can record and playback through the built-in digital piano.

The 5' 8" model KC173 grand is essentially like the Yamaha model C2 grand, with design differences such as plate color and music desk shape. It is also voiced to

Kemble's specs, sounding to me more "European," i.e., a bass with less-pronounced high overtones.

Warranty: Ten years, parts and labor, to the original purchaser.

KIMBALL

Kimball Piano USA, Inc.
1819 North Major Avenue
Chicago, Illinois 60639

312-212-3635
www.kimballpianousa.com

Kimball, a name with a long history in the piano world (see *The Piano Book* for details), is now being produced by Kimball Piano USA, Inc., which acquired the rights to the Kimball name in 2005. Kimball International, the previous owner of the Kimball brand, which produced Kimball pianos from 1959 to 1996, was primarily a furniture maker that mass-produced a very average piano.

In contrast, Kimball is now controlled by an American piano technician who has returned Kimball to its historical roots in Chicago and says he is placing the company's focus on the musical instrument and on technical details of American piano design and construction. The result of this focus is a new line of Kimball grands that includes the 5' 1" model K1, the 5' 9" model K2, and the 6' 2" model K3. In 2008 Kimball is introducing its new line of verticals. The K-44 is a 49" American furniture console with hand-rubbed lacquer finishes in cherry and oak. The K-49 is a 49" upright utilizing full agraffes and a German Strunz premium solid spruce soundboard.

Parts and components for the new Kimball grands are being sourced from many parts of the world, primarily China and Europe. In the U.S., Kimball is doing final assembly and detailing of the instruments. High-end components include a rim made of maple and oak; full length back posts in verticals; bridges planed and notched by hand in the traditional manner; a wet-sand cast plate; Langer keys, action, and hammers; Röslau strings; Delignit pinblock; and a solid spruce soundboard.

Warranty: Twelve years, parts and labor, to the original purchaser.

KNABE, WM.
See also "Samick"

SMC (formerly Samick Music Corp.)
1329 Gateway Drive
Gallatin, Tennessee 37066

800-592-9393
615-206-0077
info@smcmusic.com
www.smcmusic.com

Pianos made by: Samick Musical Instrument Mfg. Co. Ltd., Incheon, South Korea and Bogor, West Java, Indonesia

Wm. Knabe is an old, distinguished American piano brand dating back to 1854 and eventually becoming part of the Aeolian family of brands. Following Aeolian's demise in 1985, the Knabe name became part of Mason & Hamlin, which was purchased out of bankruptcy in 1996 by the owners of PianoDisc. For a time, a line of Knabe pianos was made for PianoDisc by Young Chang in Korea and China. That line has been discontinued, and Samick has acquired the Wm. Knabe name. (Note: "Knabe" is pronounced using the hard "K" sound followed by "nobby.")

Samick began by using the Wm. Knabe name on some of the pianos formerly sold as the "World Piano" premium line of Samick pianos. The 5' 8" and 6' 4" grand models have been redesigned, however, and the new models are based on the original nineteenth and early twentieth Knabe scale designs and cabinet styles in use when the company was based in Baltimore. Features include sand-cast plates, lacquer semi-gloss wood finishes, Renner actions and hammers, and maple and oak rims. The verticals include unique cabinet designs with bird's-eye maple and mahogany inlays, rosewood key inserts, and tone escapement. As with the other upper-level Samick lines, the pianos are serviced in the company's U.S. facility before being shipped to dealers.

See "Samick" for more information.

Warranty: Twelve years, parts and labor, to the original purchaser; lifetime on "surface tension soundboard" where applicable.

KOHLER & CAMPBELL — See "Samick"

LIVE PERFORMANCE

Live Performance, Inc.
316 California Ave, Suite 825
Reno, Nevada 89509

775-331-5533
sales@live-performance.com
http://www.live-performance.com

Please read "Electronic Player Piano Systems and Hybrid Acoustic/Digital Pianos" on pages 160–161 of *The Piano Book*.

Live Performance was founded in 1992 by Wayne Stahnke, one of the world's foremost authorities in the field of electronic reproducing pianos, perhaps best known for designing the SE reproducing system installed into Bösendorfer pianos during the 1990s.

In 2006 Live Performance introduced its own player piano system, the Model LX, providing playback performance the company says approaches that of the legendary SE system at a price competitive with contemporary retrofitable player systems.

Compatible with any grand piano, the LX shares many of the technical specifications of the SE system, including the use of a high keyboard sample rate (accurate to 1/800 of a second), high-resolution note expression (1020 levels), proportional pedaling (256 positions), and unlimited polyphony. Among the LX's unique features is the immunity of its expression system to variations in line voltage, eliminating a source of playback inconsistency the company says affects competing player piano systems. The LX also features a closed-loop pedal servo mechanism, enabling it to reproduce a pianist's use of the sustain pedal—even subtle half-pedaling effects—with accuracy.

In the interest of being future-proof, the LX does not include an embedded control unit, but rather is driven using specially encoded audio streams delivered by a CD player, MP3 player, wireless link, home music distribution system, or similar audio source. This provides maximum flexibility and reliability.

The Live Performance Model LX plays non-encrypted player piano CDs from all major vendors, as well as Marantz Pianocorder material and its own proprietary high-resolution format. Ten high-resolution albums from a growing catalog of over twenty-five are included with the purchase of each LX system. Third-party software is available to encode MIDI and ESEQ files into audio streams compatible with the LX system.

MASON & HAMLIN

Mason & Hamlin Piano Company
4111 North Freeway Blvd.
Sacramento, California 95834

800-566-3472
916-567-9999
www.masonhamlin.com

Pianos made by: Mason & Hamlin Piano Co., Haverhill, Massachusetts and Sacramento, California

Mason & Hamlin was founded in 1854 by Henry Mason and Emmons Hamlin. Mason was a musician and businessman and Hamlin was an inventor working with reed organs. Within a few years, Mason & Hamlin was one of the largest reed organ manufacturers in the country. The company began making pianos in 1881 in Boston, and soon became, along with Chickering, among the most prestigious of the Boston piano makers. By 1910, Mason & Hamlin was considered Steinway's chief competitor. Over the next eighty-five years, Mason & Hamlin changed hands many times. (You can read the somewhat lengthy and interesting history in *The Piano Book*.) In 1996 the Burgett brothers, owners of PianoDisc, purchased Mason & Hamlin out of bankruptcy and set about reestablishing manufacturing at the factory in Haverhill, Massachusetts. At present, the company manufactures about 350 pianos per year at this factory.

Since acquiring the company, the Burgetts have brought back most of the piano models from the company's Boston era (1881–1932) that originally made the company famous. Some have been refinements of original designs, others have been completely new. First came the 5' 8" model A and 7' model BB, both of which had been manufactured by the previous owner and so needed less work to resurrect. Then, in fairly rapid succession, came the 6' 4" model AA, the 9' 4" model CC concert grand, and the 5' 4" model B. The development of the model AA was an especially interesting project because in the process the engineering staff standardized certain features, refined manufacturing processes, and modernized jigs and machinery, improvements that afterward were applied to the company's other models. The 50" model 50 vertical piano has also been reintroduced and redesigned, with longer keys for a more grand-like touch, and improved pedal leverage. Internal parts for the verticals are made in Haverhill, then installed into an imported cabinet in the company's Sacramento factory, where it also installs PianoDisc systems.

All Mason & Hamlin grands have certain features in common, including a wide-tail design, a full-perimeter plate, an extremely thick and heavy maple rim, solid spruce soundboard; five-ply, quartersawn maple pinblock; and the patented "tension resonator" crown retention system. The tension resonator (illustrated in *The Piano Book*), invented by Richard Gertz in 1900, consists of a series of turnbuckles that connect various parts of the inner rim. In theory this web of turnbuckles, nicknamed "the spider," locks the rim in place so that it cannot expand with stress and age, thereby preserving the soundboard crown (curvature). (The soundboard is glued to the inner rim and would collapse if the rim expanded.) There is no modern-day experimental evidence to confirm or deny this theory, but many technicians believe in its validity nevertheless because unlike most older pianos, the soundboards of old Mason & Hamlins almost always have plenty of crown.

In the early part of the twentieth century, Wessell, Nickel & Gross was a major supplier of actions to American piano manufacturers, including Mason & Hamlin.

Over the years, the name fell into disuse. In 2004 Mason & Hamlin revived the name by registering the trademark, which now refers to the design and specifications of Mason & Hamlin actions.

The grands are available in ebony and several standard and exotic wood finishes, in both satin and high polish. Satin finishes are lacquer, the high polish finishes are polyester. Most sizes are also available in a stylized case design called "Monticello," which has fluted, conical legs, similar to Hepplewhite, with matching lyre and bench.

The tone of Mason & Hamlin pianos is typically American—lush, singing, and powerful, not unlike the Steinway in basic character, but with an even more powerful bass and a clearer treble. The designers have done a good job of making a recognizable Mason & Hamlin sound that is consistent throughout the model line. The 5' 8" model A has a particularly powerful bass for a piano of its size. The treble, notably weak in prior versions, has been beefed up, but the bass is still the showpiece of the piano. The new 5' 4" model B also has a large-sounding bass for its size. The "growling" power of the Mason & Hamlin bass is most apparent in the 7' model BB. The 6' 4" model AA is a little better balanced between bass and treble, one reason why it is a personal favorite.

The basic musical design of Mason & Hamlin pianos is very good, as is most of the workmanship. As with other American-made pianos, musical and cabinet detailing, such as factory voicing and regulation and plate and cabinet cosmetics, are reasonable but lag somewhat behind the company's European competitors in finesse. The company says it is standard procedure for final voicing and regulation to be finished off by thorough and competent dealer prep. Dealers report that like its competitor, Steinway, the Mason & Hamlin piano requires a substantial, but not unreasonable, amount of preparation by the dealer.

In recent years, many companies have turned to China for parts and materials, both to save money and to increase the security of supply. Among makers of high-end pianos, Mason & Hamlin has been pioneering in this regard, though not the only company to do so. As the company explains:

"Mason & Hamlins have always been the costliest pianos to produce, and the demand for them has always outpaced our limited production. Therefore, in an effort to control our pricing and maintain steady production, we have sourced some of our materials and components from the four corners of the earth. We accept only those materials and components whose quality allows us to maintain our reputation for excellence. Using the highest-grade materials, wherever they might come from, ensures longevity in a piano and produces the famous Mason & Hamlin sound. The focus at Mason & Hamlin is, as it always has been, on making a great piano. Mason & Hamlin pianos are still being built the old-fashioned way, by hand, in New England, using the best parts and materials the world has to offer."

Although the company's position on its use of imported materials has raised some eyebrows, and theoretically could entail some risk, it's also likely that for some of the sourced items the quality is actually better than from more traditional sources. Most (though not all) of my contacts felt that the quality of the piano had not diminished during this time and may, in fact, have improved. The worldwide sourcing of materials does seem to have kept the price of the pianos at a reasonable level. After the usual dealer discounts, Mason & Hamlin pianos are a good value among high-end instruments.

Warranty: Twelve years, parts and labor, transferable to future owners within the warranty period; except lifetime, non-transferable warranty on case and action parts.

MAY BERLIN — See "Schimmel"

MEISTER, OTTO

The Piano Group, Inc.
P.O. Box 14128
Bradenton, Florida 34280

941-794-5157
thepianogroup@yahoo.com
www.ottomeisterpianosusa.com

Otto Meister pianos are made by the Beijing Hsinghai Piano Group, Ltd. in Beijing, China. Models include a full range of verticals, and grands from 4' 8" to 5' 7", in traditional and furniture styles. All grands and studios feature slow-fall fallboards. See "Beijing Hsinghai."

MILLER, HENRY F.

Henry F. Miller
236 West Portal Avenue #568
San Francisco, California 94127

800-511-0083
info@henryfmiller.com

Henry F. Miller is the name of an old American piano maker dating back to 1863. The name eventually became owned by Aeolian Pianos, which went out of business in 1985. The name is now owned by the Sherman Clay chain of piano stores and used on a mid-priced line of pianos carried by these and other major piano retailers around the country. Current Henry F. Miller pianos are made by Pearl River in China. Some models are similar to pianos sold under the Pearl River name. The 4' 10" and 5' 3" grands feature solid spruce soundboards.

NORDISKA

Geneva International Corporation
29 East Hintz Road
Wheeling, Illinois 60090

800-533-2388
847-520-9970
pianos@geneva-intl.com
www.geneva-intl.com

Pianos made by: Dongbei Piano Company, Ltd., Yingkou, Liaoning Province, China

Nordiska was a hundred-year-old Swedish piano manufacturer that sold its designs, equipment, and technology to the Chinese company Dongbei when it went out of business in 1988. See "Dongbei" for more information.

Dongbei pianos are sold in the United States under a number of different brand names, among them Nordiska. The importer says the Nordiska brand differs from the others in several ways: The Nordiska brand has Abel hammers (except the 43" model). The grands use a higher grade of felt, cloth, and buckskin throughout the action, keys, and key frame, resulting in an action that is quieter and more durable than that of its competitors. The Nordiska pianos utilize the best quality soundboard wood and are worked on by the most experienced technicians. Finally, only the Nordiska pianos use the Petrof leg attachment system. The importer says that other exclusive upgrades are planned for the future.

Nordiska grands now utilize the focused beam structure described under "Dongbei," plus a maple rim, heavier plate, and better plate cosmetics. The 7' and 9' models also feature Renner actions assembled by Renner, Kluge keys and key frame, and a Bolduc (Canadian) white spruce soundboard. Imported American veneers are being used on all grands. The 7' grand has an especially good sound and touch, one of the best on a Chinese-made piano.

Warranty: Ten years, parts and labor, to the original purchaser.

OPUS II — See "Cristofori"

PALATINO

The Music Link
P.O. Box 162
Brisbane, California 94005

888-552-5465
piano@palatinousa.com
www.palatinausa.com

Pianos made by: AXL Musical Instrument Co., Ltd. Corp., Shanghai, China

Although this company is new to the piano world, it is not new to music. For some time, AXL has been manufacturing a full range of musical instruments under its own name and under OEM agreements with other companies. The company says that its factory is very automated, employing CNC routers from Japan and Germany, and that it sources materials for the pianos from around the world. Palatino makes about 7,000 pianos annually.

At present the company makes three sizes of vertical piano and four sizes of grand. Specifications include solid spruce soundboard in both verticals and grands, hard rock maple pinblock and bridges, maple rims and wet-sand cast plates in the grands, and an adjustable artist bench and slow-close fallboard on all models. New models 123TU-A and 123TU-AR also feature Abel hammers from Germany and agraffes throughout the scale.

Based on personal observation and dealer reports, Palatino pianos appear to have good quality control and are prepared well at the factory before being shipped to dealers.

Warranty: Ten years, parts and labor, transferable to future owners within the warranty period.

PEARL RIVER

including Ritmüller

Pearl River Piano Group America, Ltd.
2260 South Haven Avenue, Suite F
Ontario, California 91761

909-673-9155
800-435-5086
sales@pearlriverusa.com
www.pearlriverusa.com

Pianos made by: Guangzhou Pearl River Piano Group Ltd., Guangzhou, Guangdong Province, China

Originally established in 1954 through the consolidation of several piano making facilities, the Guangzhou Pearl River piano factory is now China's largest piano manufacturer and one of the largest in the world, with production of over 100,000 pianos annually by move than 4,000 workers. The company says the average length of service of its workers is seventeen years. Pianos are made under the Pearl River and Ritmüller names, and under a few other names under OEM contract with distributors, such as Henry F. Miller (with Sherman Clay) and Essex (with Steinway) (see separate listings under those names).

Pearl River verticals begin with 42½" console model 108 in continental style (no legs) and in a style with curved leg and toe block, and with 43½" model 110 in a variety of American furniture styles. It continues with a series of studio models, including 45" model 115 in a traditional institutional style (legs with toe blocks), a school-friendly institutional style, and a furniture style; and 47" model 118 in institutional style. Finally, there are upright models 120 (48"), 125 (49"), and 130 (51½") in institutional style. The 49" model is a joint venture with Yamaha. The 51½" model has a decorative upper panel.

Pearl River grands come in ten sizes, from 4' 7" to 9'. In addition to a number of models with decorative legs and music desk, there are two unusual pianos: a 6' 1" model 186 in "European" style with angled case sides and a cast-iron plate in silver; and a 6' 6" model 198 "Butterfly" style with U-shaped body, clear acrylic lid that hinges in the middle, and other modern design features.

Pearl River's Ritmüller line uses the same strung back (structural and acoustical components) as the Pearl River line, but has upgraded cabinets and finishes. It also has more furniture options in the larger sizes of vertical. The 7' and 9' grand models in both lines come with Renner actions; all other models use Pearl River–manufactured actions. Most Pearl River and Ritmüller pianos have a veneer-laminated soundboard, but now that the company has invested in climate control in its tropically situated factory, it is in the process of switching over to solid spruce soundboards in some of its models.

Warranty: Ten years, parts and labor, to the original purchaser.

PERZINA, GEBR.
including Carl Ebel and Gerh. Steinberg

Piano Empire, Inc.
13370 East Firestone Blvd., Suite A
Santa Fe Springs, California 90670

800-576-3463
562-926-1906
info@pianoempire.com
www.perzinapianos.com

Pianos made by: Yantai-Perzina Piano Manufacturing Co., Ltd., Yantai, Shandong Province, China

The Gebr. Perzina (Brothers Perzina) piano company was established in the German town of Schwerin in 1871, and was a prominent piano maker until World War I, after which its fortunes declined. In more recent times, the factory was moved to the nearby city of Lenzen and the company became known as Pianofabrik Lenzen GmbH. In the early 1990s, the company was purchased by Music Brokers International B.V. in the Netherlands. Eventually it was decided that making pianos in Germany was not economically viable, so manufacturing was moved to Yantai, China, where a range of verticals and grands were made for a number of years by the Yantai Longfeng Piano Co. under the Perzina name. In 2003, Music Brokers International established its own factory in Yantai, called Yantai-Perzina, where it now builds the Perzina, Carl Ebel, and Gerh. Steinberg pianos. (Note: Do not confuse Gerh. Steinberg with Wilh. Steinberg, a German piano brand.)

The Carl Ebel and Gerh. Steinberg pianos are based on the same scale design, but the Perzina scale design is different. Further technical differences revolve primarily around the choice of action, hammers, and soundboard design, among other things. In particular, the Perzina brand is distinguished by use of a solid, tapered, Austrian white spruce soundboard in both verticals and grands, whereas the Carl Ebel and Gerh. Steinberg soundboards are of veneer-laminated Austrian white spruce. The Perzina pianos also receive greater attention to detail than the other two brands. In addition, the Perzina verticals have several interesting features rarely found in other pianos, including a "floating" soundboard that is unattached to the back at certain points for freer vibration, and a reverse, or concave, soundboard crown. (There may be something to this, as the Perzina verticals are the best sounding verticals from China, the bass being particularly notable.) Later in 2008 the company plans to introduce a premium vertical piano series featuring the German Renner action.

Perzina grands are available with either Detoa ("G" models) or Renner ("E" models) action. Also available are three new deluxe grand models featuring new scale designs and other upgrades and modifications, with three different actions available. The "GX" has a factory action (with European materials and design); the "DX" action is made by Detoa (Czech Republic); and "EX" has a Renner action. All three have Renner "AA" hammers.

The company's European headquarters says it ships many European materials to Yantai, including Degen copper wound strings, Röslau strings, Delignit pinblocks,

71

Renner hammers, English felts, European veneers, and Austrian white spruce soundboards. New machinery is from Germany, Japan, and Italy. According to the company, all the piano designs are the original German scales. The Renner actions used by Perzina are ordered complete from Germany, not assembled from parts.

Warranty: Ten years, parts and labor, to the original purchaser

PETROF
See also Weinbach

Petrof USA, LLC
5400 Lawrenceville Hwy., Suites B1&2
Lilburn, Georgia 30047

877-9-PETROF
770-564-4974
sales@petrofpianosusa.com
www.petrof.com

Geneva International Corp.
29 East Hintz Road
Wheeling, Illinois 60090

800-533-2388
847-520-9970
pianos@geneva-intl.com
www.geneva-intl.com

Pianos made by: Petrof, spol. s.r.o., Hradec Králové, Czech Republic

[Note: In 2007 Petrof cancelled its distribution agreement with Geneva International Corporation, which had been distributing Petrof pianos in the United States since 1985, and set up its own distribution network under the name Petrof USA, LLC. Geneva International sued, and as this *Supplement* goes to press, the case is in arbitration, with a final decision expected very soon. Since late 2007, all Petrof pianos entering North America have been via Petrof USA. Contact information for both distributors is included here. The Petrof product line and specifications remain substantially the same, though some furniture styles and model numbers may have changed. Prices are from Petrof USA.]

The Petrof piano factory was founded in 1864 by Antonin Petrof in Hradec Králové, an industrial town located 100 kilometers east of Prague in the Czech Republic. Three generations of the Petrof family owned and managed the business, during which time the company kept pace with technical developments and earned prizes for its pianos at international exhibitions. The Czech Republic has long been known for its vibrant musical instrument industry, which also includes makers of brass, woodwind, and stringed instruments.

In 1947 all businesses in the Czech Republic were nationalized by the state and the Petrof family was forced out of the business. In 1965 Petrof, along with other piano manufacturers, was forced to join Musicexport, the state-controlled import-export company for musical instruments. Since the fall of the Soviet Union and the liberation of Eastern Europe, the various factories that were part of Musicexport have been spun off as private businesses, including Petrof, which is once again owned and controlled by the Petrof family. Currently Petrof manufactures 5,000 vertical pianos and 900 grands annually.

Petrof makes seven sizes of grand and three sizes of vertical. The majority of components are produced in Petrof or other Czech factories, including hardware, plates, and cabinetry. Soundboards are of solid Bohemian spruce, grand rims are largely of beech, and plates are of the wet sand-cast type. The grands and largest verticals use compressed beech plywood pinblocks. All grands produced for the United States now use Abel or Renner hammers. Keys are individually weighted. The grands all have a sostenuto pedal, the verticals a practice pedal (except 53" model P135, which has a sostenuto).

For many years Petrof used a combination of Czech Detoa actions and German Renner actions or action parts, depending on the model. The company has recently designed new grand and vertical actions, called "Petrof Original," which are being manufactured in a separate section of the Detoa factory under the supervision of Petrof engineers. The larger grands and larger verticals use Renner actions. The smaller grands and mid-sized verticals use either Renner parts on a Petrof action frame or the new Petrof Original action. Most of the smaller verticals use a standard Detoa action.

Petrof has also invented and patented a version of its new grand action that uses tiny opposing magnets on the wippens and wippen rail. These magnets allow for the removal of the usual lead counterweights in the keys and, according to the company, significantly alter the dynamic properties of the action. "The hammer receives an inertial boost from the magnets as the key begins to move from the rest position. When the key is fully depressed, the effect of the magnets is minimal, allowing gravity to work in giving the hammer another inertial boost on the way down. The effect is faster repetition, less fatigue, and less physical work needed to reach higher dynamic levels." The new action also furthers the European Union's stated environmental goal of phasing out the use of lead in pianos. The action is adjusted in the factory for a standard touchweight and is serviced in exactly the same way as a standard action. The "Magnetic Accelerated Action" action, as it is known, is a special-order option on the grands. Petrof also offers as an option the "Magnetic Balanced Action," which allows the player to quickly and easily change the touchweight in the range of ± 4–5 grams simply by turning a knob.

Petrof's research and development department, one of the largest in the piano industry, has been busy of late. In addition to the innovations mentioned above, Petrof recently introduced the 6' 10½" "Pasat B" grand, which contains a myriad of novel and interesting technical features. The inner rim is built up by hand of alternating layers of solid pieces of red beech and spruce instead of laminations bent around a mold. The company says this is the way several piano makers formed their grand rims in the nineteenth century before modern technology made the bent-lamination rim possible, and that this method results in a more stable, stress-free rim. The bridges are of solid maple, but the treble bridge is capped with solid ebony wood to increase sound projection of the higher frequencies. The piano is single-strung with front and rear tuned duplexes (duplex scale) throughout the treble. The solid spruce soundboard is asymmetrically crowned, and each soundboard is custom-tapered based on tests of its vibrating characteristics. The piano utilizes a focused beam structure to increase rigidity of the structure for better tonal projection. A densified beam of red beech further stiffens the treble area to enhance projection of the treble tone. The result is a very impressive sounding and playing instrument. The Pasat is the first of a series of new Petrof grands based on similar design principles, the others to be released in 2008 and 2009. The company says the new grands can be recognized by the polished bright gold cast-iron plate with "diamond effect" and by the dark macassar ebony veneer on the inner face of the rim.

Petrofs are known for their warm, rich, singing tone, full of color. The pianos are solidly built and workmanship is good, but can vary a little as they come from the factory. After careful preparation, though, the pianos can sound and feel quite beautiful and hold their own against some of the better-known European pianos. Due to lower labor costs, however, the prices are significantly lower than many other European instruments and sometimes even less expensive than pianos from Japan. As a result, they are a very good value.

Note: For years, Weinbach pianos were made by the Petrof company and were virtually identical to Petrof brand pianos. The Weinbach name is now being used differently. See under "Weinbach" for more information.

Warranty (Petrof USA): Ten years, parts and labor, to the original purchaser. The first five years are from Petrof, the second five from Petrof USA, the importer.

Warranty (Geneva International): Ten years, parts and labor, to the original purchaser. The first five years are from Petrof, the second five from Geneva International.

PIANODISC

PianoDisc
4111 North Freeway Blvd.
Sacramento, California 95834

800-566-3472
916-567-9999
www.pianodisc.com

Please read "Electronic Player Piano Systems and Hybrid Acoustic/Digital Pianos" on pages 160–161 of *The Piano Book*.

PianoDisc is an electronic player piano system that can be installed into virtually any piano, grand or vertical, new or used. Most piano manufacturers offer factory-installed PianoDisc products, and piano dealers can also have the installation done at their own locations by certified PianoDisc technicians.

Like other such systems, the basic components of a PianoDisc system consist of a solenoid rail installed in a slot cut into the piano keybed, a processor unit mounted under the piano, and a control box mounted under the keybed at the front of the piano, hidden inside, or placed on or near the piano, depending on the model. There is one solenoid for each note and a solenoid for the damper pedal. When playing PianoDisc's music, one channel contains the MIDI signal that drives the piano solenoids, the other is an instrumental or vocal accompaniment that plays through a stereo system or through optional amplified speakers. Models vary by control box and by storage and playback capabilities. Consumers can choose between models that use floppy disks, CD/DVDs, and internal and/or external hard drives to store and play back music.

PianoDisc's newest system is iQ. Hidden within the piano body, iQ can play back PianoDisc music using almost any media player (iPod, iTunes, CD/DVD, and multi-media players) as a source. The most popular configuration is bundled with an Apple iPod. Unique within the industry, iQ features a patent-pending method of detecting changes to the volume of the music player and automatically adjusts the piano volume to match. Customers can operate all functions of the piano from one familiar device.

PianoDisc's basic system is the model 228CFX. It has both a floppy drive and a CD drive as standard equipment. Its slimline controller can be mounted on the piano or located up to 100 feet away and operated with the included infrared wireless remote control. The 228CFX has several options: SymphonyPro, a 128-voice General MIDI sound module set to provide sampled-sound orchestration as an accompaniment to the piano; TFT ("Touch Film Technology") MIDI Record, a sensor strip installed beneath the keys that allows the user to record his performance or turn the piano into a MIDI controller; and MX (Music Expansion), a flash memory in which to store music and play it back without having to change a disc.

PianoDisc's entry-level system is called Piano CD, an easy to use system that plays only CDs—both PianoDisc CDs and regular audio CDs—and has fewer features than the 228CFX.

The flagship of the PianoDisc line is the Opus7 system (released in 2004), the first player system to connect to the Internet. Its playback system, hidden within the piano, can be operated from a wireless, Internet-ready Web Tablet with touchscreen and full color. It has the ability to download music and system upgrades directly from PianoDisc's Web site, and surf the Web and receive email (broadband connection required), among other features. Opus7 comes in two versions, Opulence and Luxury. Opulence is the full system. Luxury is designed to integrate with home automation systems, and so does not come with the Web Tablet or router, as it is assumed that the home automation system will already include these or similar interfaces.

The Opus7's MX3 hard drive comes with forty hours of pre-loaded music and will accept standard MIDI files type 0 and 1 available from a wide variety of standard MIDI file publishers, PianoDisc CDs, and standard audio CDs. Music saved to the MX3 can be organized into separate "libraries" and played back from a single source for convenience. A "Schedule" feature allows one to program a start time and end time for selected music to play.

Using PianoDisc's PianoCast technology and broadband Internet, Opus7 can connect to one of PianoDisc's Internet radio streams and listen to special events, interviews, and performances, combining a traditional audio broadcast with a piano performance that will play the Opus7. The "Classical and More" stream features 24/7 classical music—of interest to hotels or restaurants that need royalty-free background music.

PianoDisc maintains a growing library of music available as digital downloads, floppy disks, CDs, DVDs, and high definition Blu-ray discs for use on its systems. The library includes solo piano performances from famous artists, piano with orchestrated accompaniment (some "live"), and vocals. PianoDisc systems also play any standard MIDI file (type 0 format), and some disks of other producers.

MusiConnect is a free PianoDisc application for Windows or Macintosh computers that allows consumers to download music purchased from PianoDisc's online music store. With MusiConnect, consumers can import PianoDisc album files or download purchases directly to their computer. All of their PianoDisc albums and songs are displayed within the MusiConnect main interface. Consumers can even mix and match songs from different albums to create unique playlists. Once all the music is downloaded, MusiConnect gives the option of syncing an album or playlist with iTunes. This process creates a matching playlist in iTunes, imports each PianoDisc song, and includes album, artist, and genre information (when available).

PianoSync is a MIDI-controlled piano performance that synchronizes with a commercially available audio CD of a major recording artist. PianoSyncs are purchased as downloads or on CD from PianoDisc's Web site and stored using MusiConnect. The consumer also purchases the original artist's CD and loads it into iTunes where the two are merged. The consumer plays the merged file on their piano and hears the original CD with its new live piano accompaniment.

PianoVideo HD is the first high definition video (combining MIDI, audio, and video) created specifically for the modern player piano system. PianoVideo HD technology gives PianoDisc owners the ultimate entertainment experience: as they watch a high definition video, their piano will play along with it live, in sync with the pianist on the screen. PianoVideo HD performances come in standard definition DVD or in high definition Blu-ray discs.

PianoDisc also offers a stable of complementary products such as Sync-A-Vision, which brings the element of HD video to the PianoDisc experience. Sync-A-Vision consists of a 19" high definition monitor that's built into a piano music rack, is powered by Apple's Mac mini computer, and comes with educational and entertainment programs pre-loaded. Included are seventy-two piano lessons, sing-and-play-along karaoke, cartoon and silent film entertainment, PianoDisc music, and PianoVideo HD performances.

Another product is QuietTime MagicStar. Once installed, MagicStar can mute the acoustic piano and let the user hear their performance via sampled sound through headphones. MagicStar has a control unit with 128 sampled instruments—a full General MIDI (GM) sound set. It also includes a built-in adjustable metronome. A MIDI key sensor strip is installed under the keys, and a padded mute rail prevents the hammers from hitting the strings while still allowing the motion and feel of the piano action. The mute rail is activated by moving a small lever under the keyboard, which also turns on the sampled sound. MagicStar comes with a control unit, power supply, MIDI cable, MIDI strip, pedal switches, headphones, and a mute rail. An entry-level version of MagicStar, QuietTime model GT-2, comes with just piano and organ sound instead of the full sound set. *Note*: If you purchase the PianoDisc playback system with the SymphonyPro sound module, the TFT MIDI Record system, and the PianoMute rail, you have already purchased virtually all the components of the MagicStar system. The separate listings for MagicStar and GT-2 QuietTime in the price list are for those who wish to purchase it without the PianoDisc playback.

PIANOFORCE

Pianoforce LLC
1251 East Fowler Avenue
Tampa, Florida 33612

813-631-8888
sales@pianoforce.com
www.pianoforce.com

Please read "Electronic Player Piano Systems and Hybrid Acoustic/Digital Pianos" on pages 160–161 of *The Piano Book*.

Pianoforce is a new entrant into the player piano market under its own name, but the company that makes the Pianoforce product—Ncode Ltd. of Bratislava, Slovakia—has been developing and manufacturing front-end controllers for the player piano systems of other companies, such as Baldwin and QRS, since 1995. In 2005, Pianoforce was first offered as a complete system in the pianos of selected piano makers. In 2006, it was introduced as a retrofit kit that can be installed into any piano, new or old. The kit is designed and built by Ncode in Europe. It is ordered through a piano dealer and is typically installed in a new piano either at a distribution point or at the dealer location.

Like other such systems, Pianoforce consists of a solenoid rail installed into a slot cut in the keybed of the piano, with one solenoid for each note and one for the damper pedal, and a CD drive/controller mounted under the keybed at the front of the piano. Traditionally, one CD channel contains the MIDI information that drives the piano solenoids, while the other channel contains instrumental or vocal accompaniment that plays through a stereo system or optional amplified speakers. In addition, the new Pianoforce CD format uses both channels for full stereo audio, with embedded MIDI information for the player mechanism. An infrared remote control device is included.

The company says that its system differs from that of its competitors in that the main rail component also contains all the controlling electronics, eliminating the need for a lot of complicated wiring and making for a neater and simpler installation. Also, a technician can plug a laptop computer into a USB port on the rail and, using software supplied by the company, can customize the system to the piano and to the customer's preferences through the software control of many playing parameters, such as solenoid force, note release, and pedal release. These customized parameters can then be archived on the laptop. The system automatically calibrates itself with the help of a small sensor mounted on the soundboard. The combination of automatic calibration with manual setup ensures the best playback performance for each individual piano after installation.

In 2007 Pianoforce introduced its latest controller, called "Performance." Expanding on its experience supplying control components for other companies in the past, the new controller contains some of the newest and most advanced features in the player piano arena, such as the ability to read the software of other systems, including Yamaha Disklavier, QRS (except SyncAlong), and Web Only software, plus standard MIDI files; onboard connections to the Internet via an ethernet or wireless hookup through which the user can download music from Pianoforce, or even have system problems diagnosed and fixed from Europe; and three USB ports for greater versatility, such as plugging in flash memory. There is a digital optical stereo output and a dedicated sub-woofer output line.

The system comes with 256 MB of internal memory, pre-loaded with approximately 25 hours of piano music, and is expandable to 8 GB. The units are also shipped with approximately 400 "Star Tracks" piano recordings. A "Star Track" is a piano file in MIDI format synchronized to an original audio CD. When the audio CD is inserted, the corresponding Star Track is activated and plays a 30-second sampler piano accompaniment on the piano. The customer can then order a key via email or phone to unlock the entire song or album from Pianoforce.

The company says that a record strip, a General MIDI sound card, and other optional accessories are coming in the near future. In addition to the system's ability to play other makers' software, Pianoforce is also building its own library of CDs. To start the customer's collection, five Pianoforce CDs are supplied with the system.

The MSRP for the installed system, including pedal solenoid, two amplified speakers, and remote control, is $5,695. As with other such systems, discounts may be available, especially as an incentive to purchase a piano.

Warranty: Five years parts, one year labor, to the original purchaser.

PLEYEL

Ignace Pleyel, an accomplished musician and composer, patron of music, and publisher, began manufacturing pianos in 1807 with the aim of adapting instruments to the new requirements of the composers and musicians of his day. By the time of his death in 1831, Pleyel pianos were known and exported throughout the world. His son, Camille, an accomplished pianist, continued the family business and brought it to new heights of success. As part of his work, Camille established the legendary music salons that served as a focus for the Parisian music scene of his time and where many famous musicians and composers were heard for the first time. It was at one of these concerts, in 1832, that Frederic Chopin made his Paris debut, and he played his final concert there in 1848. In addition to Chopin, who is closely associated with Pleyel pianos, other notable users included Claude Debussy, Cesar Frank, Edward Grieg, and Maurice Ravel. In 1927 the company established the Salle Pleyel, an important Paris concert venue.

Pleyel was also responsible for some of the technical innovations of his day. The company first introduced iron bracing into a piano in 1826, was the first to bring the upright piano to France, and is credited with inventing the sostenuto in 1860.

Over the years, Pleyel acquired the piano names of former French piano makers Rameau, Gaveau, and Erard. From 1971, these names were made under contract by Schimmel in Germany, returning to France in 1994. In 2000, a private investor associated with the Salle Pleyel acquired the trademarks under the name Manufacture Française de Pianos and moved the factory to the south of France, where for several years it produced high-quality instruments using a combination of high-tech machinery and hand craftsmanship. As this edition of the *Supplement* goes to press, the company has just moved to a new location in the outskirts of Paris, not far from its original factory and the Salle Pleyel. The company says that due to competition from China and other economic factors, it cannot survive in its present form. It plans to drastically reduce the size of production and concentrate only on building a very small number of instruments to the highest standards. There are no plans to continue distribution in the United States. Pleyel is France's only piano manufacturer.

PRAMBERGER

See also "Samick"

SMC (formerly Samick Music Corp.)
1329 Gateway Drive
Gallatin, Tennessee 37066

800-592-9393
615-206-0077
info@smcmusic.com
www.smcmusic.com

Pianos made by: Samick Musical Instrument Mfg. Co. Ltd., Incheon, South Korea and Bogor, West Java, Indonesia

Pramberger is a name that was used by Young Chang for its premium-level pianos under license from the late piano engineer Joseph Pramberger, who at one time was head of manufacturing at Steinway & Sons. When Mr. Pramberger died in 2003, his estate terminated its relationship with Young Chang and signed up with Samick. However, since Young Chang still holds the rights to its piano designs, Samick has designed new pianos to go with the name.

The "J.P. Pramberger Platinum Series" piano is a higher-end instrument made in Korea, then shipped to the U.S. for inspection, voicing, and regulation. Several American technicians who had known and worked with Joe Pramberger went to Korea at Samick's request to design this piano. Benefiting by work previously done by Bechstein engineers at the Samick factory, they began with a modified Bechstein scale, then added several features found on current or older Steinways, such as an all-maple rim, an asymmetrically tapered white spruce soundboard, vertically laminated maple and mahogany bridges with maple cap, duplex scaling, and Renner action and hammers. One of the technicians told me the group feels that its design is an advancement of Mr. Pramberger's work that he would have approved of.

The "Pramberger Signature Series" (formerly known as "J. Pramberger") is a more modestly priced instrument from Indonesia. Its design is based on the former Korean-built Young Chang version. The grands start at the 5' model PS150, with a duplex scale starting at the 5' 2" model PS157 and continuing through the rest of the line to the 6' 1" model PS185. This line uses Samick's Pratt-Reed Premium action, Renner hammers, and a Bolduc (Canadian) solid spruce soundboard. The institutional verticals in this line have all-wood cabinet construction and agraffes in the bass section, and the decorator versions include Renner hammers and a slow-close fallboard.

The Pramberger Legacy Series is the newest edition to the Pramberger line and provides a reasonably priced option for the budget-minded consumer. (The Remington brand is no longer a regular part of the Pramberger lineup, but is available to dealers on special order.)

[Note: Samick's Pratt-Reed Premium action should not be confused with the Pratt-*Read* action used in many American-made pianos in the mid to late twentieth century and eventually acquired by Baldwin. Samick says its Pratt-Reed action is made in Korea and designed by their research and development team after the German Renner action.]

See "Samick" for more information.

Warranty: Twelve years, parts and labor, to the original purchaser; lifetime on "surface tension soundboard" where applicable.

QRS / PIANOMATION

QRS Music Technologies, Inc.
2011 Seward Avenue
Naples, Florida 34109

800-247-6557
www.qrsmusic.com

Please read "Electronic Player Piano Systems and Hybrid Acoustic/Digital Pianos" on pages 160–161 of *The Piano Book*.

Pianomation is an electronic player piano system that can be installed into virtually any piano, grand or vertical, new or used. Most manufacturers endorse Pianomation and install it at dealer request at one of their manufacturing or distribution points, and QRS also does factory installations on all major brands of pianos at its U.S. facilities. It can also be installed at a dealer location by a technician who has been specially trained by QRS.

As with all such systems, Pianomation consists of a solenoid rail installed in a slot cut in the piano keybed, a processor unit mounted under the piano, and a control box that usually plays CDs, either mounted under the keybed at the front of the piano or that sits on or near the piano. There is one solenoid for each note and a solenoid for the damper pedal. (If this solenoid is for any reason disabled, software-based commands called "Magic Pedal" will simulate it.)

"Pianomation" refers to the engine that makes the keys move up and down. The source of the music can either be a MIDI signal or a QRS analog MIDI signal. This feature provides customers with a migration path to new controller technology without requiring them to purchase an entirely new system

QRS offers several different Pianomation systems and options. The simplest and least expensive controller is the model 2000C. The control box is hidden under the piano. It has no built-in disk drives, but instead uses the owner's stereo components (a CD player, DVD player, or MP3 player) to drive the Pianomation engine and play QRS content. The background music comes from the user's stereo system, while a wireless transmitter sends the piano data to the Pianomation system, even through walls.

The Petine is just over one-and-a-half inches tall, and includes both a DVD ROM drive and a compact flash reader. The drive will play both audio CDs and data CDs (CD ROMs), the latter potentially containing thousands of MIDI files on a single CD. This controller will also play Standard MIDI files type 1 and 0. The unit features a 3-digit LED display and can be controlled by either a data wheel or infrared remote control. The Petine has a headphone output, microphone input for karaoke, and internal memory storage capacity. The operating system is flash upgradeable. Petine comes standard with a CompactFlash card containing a large sampling of free music from the QRS music library.

The Ancho controller has all the functionality of the Petine, but with the more user-friendly, 20-character alpha-numeric display plus dedicated transport controls, unique among Pianomation controllers. It comes standard with a sound card (optional on the Petine) as well as a CompactFlash card with free content.

Both systems come standard with a speaker. Both the Ancho and Petine have mixed and unmixed audio outputs so that the background music track and the piano track can be mixed for piping around the house, but the piano track can be omitted from the speakers located in the room containing the piano. Individual sources of audio sound can be finely adjusted so they will sound properly balanced at any volume level. On board but not yet implemented on both controllers are dual USB ports and an S-video output.

The MIDI information on Pianomation CDs is in analog format, which is compressed by QRS' patented AMI (Analog MIDI interface) technology, then uncompressed and translated back into digital format as it is sent to the piano for playback. The analog signal can also be transmitted to the piano by radio waves using the optional wireless transmitter and receiver, which could be handy for use in commercial establishments or when one doesn't want to run wires from the CD player to the piano.

SyncAlong is a MIDI-controlled piano performance that synchronizes with a commercially available audio CD of a major recording artist. SyncAlong CDs play on the Ancho and Petine. QRS has prepared a piano track in MIDI format, stored on a CompactFlash card, to go along with each of a number of popular audio CDs available on the general market. When the owner plays the CD, SyncAlong links it with the stored piano track, enabling Pianomation to accurately play along with the CD. A Transcription series, similar to SyncAlong but without the background music, is also available. In this series, a solo performance audio CD is transcribed and offered as a Pianomation CD so the customer can hear the performance on his or her own piano.

Qsync™ is a DVD interface designed to implement QRS' patent-pending DVD SyncAlong technology. With the addition of Qsync, a Pianomation player piano will play along with any of a number of popular concert DVDs available to the general market. The owner plays the DVD on his or her own DVD player, which is hooked up to the Pianomation system. Qsync links it with the stored piano track, enabling Pianomation to accurately play along with the DVD.

QRS offers an optical recording strip called PNOscan™ that now comes standard on all Story & Clark pianos (see "Story & Clark"). Placed under the keys, PNOscan translates each key stroke into MIDI information on note, speed, and duration without affecting the piano's touch. This MIDI information can be output to Pianomation for storage and later playback, or stored as a standard MIDI file on CompactFlash for computer editing if desired. Coupled with Ancho or Petine (with optional sound card), the pianist can play General MIDI sounds. SilentPNO™ consists of the PNOscan record strip, a piano sound module, and a stop rail for muting the acoustic piano. By muting the piano and turning on the sound card, the pianist can play in privacy with headphones.

Playola is a portable Pianomation system that sits atop the keys and plays them with little rubber fingers, either alone or with accompaniment. It comes configured with one of the controllers described earlier, and does not require professional installation by a technician.

Pianomation systems and controllers, excluding the Ancho, can be ordered or installed through any dealer doing business with QRS. The Ancho can be purchased through Story & Clark dealers only.

QRS has developed an extensive library of CDs, with over 3,000 selections in every imaginable genre, for use with its systems. The library is made up almost entirely of live performance recordings rather than synthesized music, including solo piano, piano with orchestral accompaniment, and piano with background music and vocals.

CDs can be purchased one at a time or obtained through NetPiano™, a service through which customers can download any of the thousands of songs from the QRS library to their Pianomation-equipped piano through their personal computer. A wireless transmitter plugged into the computer's audio jack transmits the music to the piano. The service is subscription-based, and allows the customer to have access to songs anytime, day or night, without having to build their own CD library. Subscriptions are available only through QRS dealers or through the QRS Web site.

Apart from its player piano systems, QRS is constantly inventing new gadgets and gizmos for pianos that can be installed independently of Pianomation. Recent inventions include a mute rail for quieting the sound of a grand piano (these have existed for verticals before, but not for grands); a Grand Fallboard Closer that allows a grand fallboard to close gently and avoid hurting the player's fingers (available on many new pianos for some time, but not previously as an add-on accessory); the PNObar™, a bar attachment designed to fit any Story & Clark grand piano, creating a natural setting for socializing (it comes with four bar stools); and GloKeys™, a customized keyboard option where the black keys have been replaced by clear keys that are illuminated using state-of-the-art Superflux RGB LED (red, green, blue light emitting diode) technology to produce a wide array of dazzling colors and effects.

RAVENSCROFT

Spreeman Piano Innovations, LLC
7898 East Acoma Drive, Suite 105
Scottsdale, Arizona 85260

480-664-3702
info@spreemanpianoinnovations.com
www.spreemanpianoinnovations.com

Crafted in Scottsdale, Arizona by piano rebuilder Michael Spreeman, the Ravenscroft piano entered the market for high-end performance pianos in 2006. There are two models available: a 7' 3" model 220 and a 9' model 275. The model 220 made its debut at the Piano Technicians Guild Annual Convention in 2007, where it received a very favorable reception.

While the general trend in the industry seems to be toward outsourcing to less expensive suppliers, Spreeman says his concept is the exact opposite. Appealing to the niche market of high-end consumers, Spreeman's approach is more along the lines of the early European small shop builders, with an emphasis on quality and exclusivity.

The case and iron frame of the Ravenscroft piano are constructed in Germany by Sauter to Ravenscroft specifications and shipped to the Arizona facility. The Renner action and Kluge keys of each individual piano are computer designed to optimize performance. The scale design, Italian Fiemme spruce soundboard panels, and vertically laminated bridge bodies (maple, mahogany, and ebony) with solid caps are meticulously designed and built by Mr. Spreeman.

Initially, only four to six pianos will be produced yearly, with pricing beginning at $250,000 for a handcrafted model 220, and up to $350,000 for a model 275 with "all the extras," including exotic veneers, titanium bridge pins and hitch pins, and titanium front and rear treble duplex terminations. Most instruments are custom ordered and can take up to one year to complete.

REMINGTON — See "Samick"

RITMÜLLER — See "Pearl River"

SAMICK

including Kohler & Campbell and Conover Cable.

See separate listings for Wm. Knabe, Pramberger, and Sohmer & Co.

SMC (formerly Samick Music Corp.)
1329 Gateway Drive
Gallatin, Tennessee 37066

800-592-9393
615-206-0077
info@smcmusic.com
www.smcmusic.com

Pianos made by: Samick Musical Instrument Mfg. Co. Ltd., Incheon, South Korea
and Bogor, West Java, Indonesia

Samick was founded by Hyo Ick Lee in 1958 as a Baldwin distributor in South Korea. Facing an immense challenge in an impoverished and war-torn country, in the early 1960s Lee began to build and sell a very limited quantity of vertical pianos using largely imported parts. As the economy improved, Lee expanded his operation, and in 1964 began exporting to other parts of the world, eventually becoming one of the world's largest piano manufacturers, making most of the parts in-house. Over the next several decades, Samick expanded into manufacturing guitars and other instruments and opened factories in China and Indonesia, where it shifted much of its production as Korean wages rose. The Asian economic crisis of the late 1990s forced Samick into bankruptcy, but it emerged from bankruptcy in 2002 and is now on a sound financial footing.

In 2002 Samick and C. Bechstein, a major European piano maker, each acquired a financial interest in the other and agreed to cooperate on technical issues and marketing. Samick has used that collaboration to upgrade its manufacturing capabilities. The two companies also own a joint-venture factory in Shanghai, China. For a few years, Samick distributed Bechstein pianos in North America, but that arrangement has ended (see "Bechstein, C.").

In 2004, Samick acquired a controlling interest in its competitor Young Chang and briefly took over distribution of Young Chang and Bergmann pianos in the United States. However, anti-trust rulings in Korea and the United States ended this arrangement a year later. Young Chang is once again an independent company and distributes those brands itself (see "Young Chang").

The company says that "Samick" means "Three Benefits" in Korean, symbolizing the wish that the activities of the company benefit not only the company itself, but also the customers and the Korean economy.

Samick Music Corporation, the North American marketing arm of the Korean company, is now known as SMC, and distributes Samick, Kohler & Campbell, Conover Cable, Pramberger, Remington, Wm. Knabe, and Sohmer & Co. pianos in North America. (See separate listings for Knabe, Pramberger, and Sohmer.) Samick no longer makes pianos under the Bernhard Steiner and Hazelton Bros. names. SMC is in the process of building a new manufacturing, warehousing, and office facility in Tennessee, and intends one day to assemble its upper-level instruments there instead of in Korea. Some parts and assemblies will continue to be made elsewhere, especially in Indonesia, and Samick will continue to make pianos in Korea.

Until just a few years ago, Samick primarily made pianos under the Samick and Kohler & Campbell brand names. (For historical information about the original Kohler & Campbell piano company, see *The Piano Book*.) In the 1980s Klaus Fenner, a German piano designer, was hired to revise the Samick scale designs and make them more "European." Most of the present Samick and Kohler & Campbell pianos are based on these designs. The Conover Cable name (another old American name), identical to the Samick piano, was introduced to markets that needed an additional line. It is now available to dealers by special order only, as is the Remington brand that Samick makes. (For Conover Cable models and prices, see under "Samick" in the Model and Pricing Guide section.)

Although in most respects the Samick and Kohler & Campbell pianos are similar in quality, so as not to compete with one another the grands are available in different sizes and have some different features. The two lines are primarily differentiated by the fact that Kohler & Campbell grands (except the 4' 7" model) have solid spruce soundboards and individually hitched stringing (also known as single-stringing), whereas the Samick grands have veneer-laminated soundboards and conventional loop stringing. A veneer-laminated soundboard (which Samick calls a "surface tension soundboard") is essentially a solid spruce soundboard surrounded by two very thin veneers. Samick pioneered the use of this soundboard with Mr. Fenner's technical advice in early 1980, and it is now used by others as well. Tonally, it behaves much more like a solid spruce soundboard than the old kind of laminated soundboard that was essentially plywood. Like the old kind, however, it won't crack or lose its crown. The solid spruce soundboard may have a slight advantage tonally, but the laminated one will last longer, so take your pick. Likewise, single stringing is more elegant to those who know pianos, but otherwise offers little or no advantage over loop stringing. The two brands' vertical pianos are more alike: They have the same difference in soundboard as the grands, but are all loop-strung and come more or less in the same sizes.

Kohler & Campbell has an upper-level group of models called the "Millennium" series with higher-quality features. The grands have a maple rim, premium Canadian Bolduc tapered solid spruce soundboard, Renner action and hammers, and satin wood finishes available in lacquer semi-gloss. The verticals have Renner parts on a Samick-made "Pratt-Reed" hornbeam action rail, Bolduc solid spruce soundboard, Renner hammers, lacquer semi-gloss wood finishes, and a sostenuto pedal on the 52" model. All Samick pianos and regular series Kohler & Campbell pianos are made in Indonesia for the U.S. market. Smaller Millennium series verticals and grands are made in Indonesia, larger ones in Korea. However, all Millennium series pianos are shipped to the U.S. for inspection and tone and action regulation before being shipped to dealers.

[Note: Samick's Pratt-Reed Premium action should not be confused with the Pratt-*Read* action used in many American-made pianos in the mid to late twentieth century and eventually acquired by Baldwin. Samick says its Pratt-Reed action is made in Korea and designed after the German Renner action.]

In the Kohler & Campbell price list, KC models are Indonesian-made, regular series verticals; KM are Indonesian-made Millennium series verticals; KMV are Korean-made Millennium series verticals; KCG are Indonesian-made regular series grands; KCM are Indonesian-made Millennium series grands; KFM are Korean-made Millennium series grands.

Quality control in Samick's Korean and Indonesian factories has steadily improved, especially in the last few years, and the Indonesian product is said to be almost as good as the Korean. Many large-scale issues have been addressed and engineers are now working on smaller refinements. The company says that new CNC machinery installed in 2007 has revolutionized the consistency and accuracy of its manufacturing. Climate control in the tropically situated Indonesian factory and action geometry issues are also among the areas that have recently seen improvement. Samick's upper-level pianos—Kohler & Campbell Millennium series, J.P. Pramberger, and Wm. Knabe—have met with a very positive response from technicians as to their musical design and performance, exceeding comparably priced pianos from Japan in that regard. Workmanship is good, although still not quite as consistent as in the Japanese pianos. Many of Samick's Indonesian pianos are priced similarly to low-cost pianos from China, and some technicians find the Samicks to be more consistent than those. Although many of the Samick-made pianos are inspected and prepared in the U.S. prior to being shipped to dealers, the quality of the preparation can vary, so preparation by the dealer is very important. With good dealer prep, I recommend Samick-made pianos for average use. In difficult climates humidity control is recommended.

[Samick-made pianos have an odd serial numbering system consisting of a series of letters and numbers. The system appears to vary from one factory to another. Please contact SMC for information on the date of manufacture of a Samick-made piano.]

Warranty: Samick, Kohler & Campbell, Conover Cable—Twelve years, parts and labor, to the original purchaser; lifetime on "surface tension soundboard" where applicable.

SAUTER

Sauter USA
P.O. Box 1130
Richland, Washington 99354

509-946-8078 (U.S.)
877-946-8078 (toll-free)
+49-7424-94820 (factory)
info@sauteramerica.com (U.S.)
info@sauter-pianos.de (factory)
www.sauter-pianos.de
www.sauterforum.com

Pianos made by: Carl Sauter Pianofortemanufaktur GmbH&Co.KG, Max-Planck-Strasse 20, 78549 Spaichingen, Germany

The Sauter piano firm was founded in 1819 by Johann Grimm, stepfather to Carl Sauter I, and has been owned and managed by members of the Sauter family for six generations, currently by Ulrich Sauter. The factory produces about 800 vertical pianos and 120 grand pianos a year in its factory in the extreme south of Germany at the foot of the Alps. Structural and acoustical parts are made of high-quality woods, including solid Bavarian spruce soundboards and beech pinblocks. Actions are made by Renner and Sauter makes its own keys. The keybed is reinforced with steel to prevent warping and all pianos are fully tropicalized for humid climates. The larger verticals use an action, designed and patented by Sauter, that contains an auxiliary jack spring to aid in faster repetition. Sauter calls this the "R2 Double Escapement" action. (Although the term "double escapement" does not apply here as it has historically been used, the mechanism has some of the same effect.)

Sauter pianos are especially known for the variety of finishes and styles in which they are available, many with intricate detail and inlay work. It is common to find such rare woods as Yew, Burl Walnut, Pyramid Mahogany, and genuine Ebony in the cabinets of Sauter pianos, as well as special engravings, which can be customized to any customer's desires. Sauter has a line of vertical pianos designated the "M line" which feature exclusive cabinet detailing and built-in features such as a hygrometer to measure relative humidity. "Amadeus" is a special-edition 6' 1" grand in celebration of the 250th anniversary of Mozart's birth. The styling of this model is reminiscent of that in Mozart's time. The natural keytops are of polished bone, the sharps of rosewood with ebony caps. Only thirty-six are to be made, one for each year of Mozart's life.

The company also has introduced versions of its 48" upright and 6' 11" and 7' 6" grands with cabinets designed by the famous European designer Peter Maly. Some recent Peter Maly designs include the 48" upright "Vitrea," after the Latin word for "glass," with a veneer of greenish glass covering the front of the cabinet; and "Ambiente," a 7' 6" grand that is curved asymmetrically on both the bass and treble sides. In the recent past, Sauter has won several prestigious design awards for its Peter Maly–designed pianos.

A couple of extremely unusual models bear mentioning. The 7' 3" model 220 contains colored lines painted on the soundboard and white inlays on the tops of the dampers as guides for musicians performing music for "prepared piano," ultra-modern music requiring the insertion of foreign objects between the strings or the plucking or striking of strings directly by the performer. The 1/16 tone microtonal piano is an upright with ninety-seven keys that has a total pitch range from the lowest to the highest note of only one octave, with the pitch difference from key to key being only 1/16 of a tone (1/8 of a semitone). You can read more about these strange instruments in *The Piano Book*.

Sauter's 190-year anniversary will be celebrated by a limited edition grand piano to be presented at a musical instrument trade show in 2009. Only three instruments will be built, one each for the Asian, European, and U.S. markets.

Sauter pianos are high quality instruments with a lush, full, singing tone, closer to an "American" sound than most other European pianos.

Warranty: Ten years, parts and labor, to the original purchaser.

SCHIMMEL

including Vogel and May Berlin

Schimmel Piano Corporation
577B Hackman Road
Lititz, Pennsylvania 17543

800-426-3205
schimmel@ptd.net
www.schimmel-piano.de

Pianos made by: Wilhelm Schimmel Pianofortefabrik GmbH, Braunschweig, Germany (Schimmel pianos); Schimmel Holzwerkstätten Leipzig GmbH (all cabinets), Leipzig, Germany; PianoEurope, Kalisz, Poland (Vogel pianos); various factories in China (May Berlin)

Wilhelm Schimmel began making pianos in Leipzig in 1885, and his company enjoyed steady growth through the late nineteenth and early twentieth centuries. The two world wars and the Depression disrupted production several times, but the company has gradually rebuilt itself over the past sixty years with a strong reputation for quality. Today, Schimmel is managed by Hannes Schimmel-Vogel, the husband of Viola Schimmel. Schimmel makes about 3,700 verticals and 800 grands per year and is one of Europe's most important piano makers. Yamaha owns a 24.9 percent non-voting interest in the Braunschweig company.

Among European piano manufacturers, Schimmel has been a pioneer in the use of computer-aided design and manufacturing. The company has used its CAPE software (Computer Assisted Piano Engineering) to research, design, and implement virtually every aspect of making a piano, from keyboard layout and action geometry to soundboard acoustics and scale design. According to Schimmel the combination of CNC machinery and hand craftsmanship leads to better results than hand work alone. Schimmel also believes that precision is aided by controlling as much of the production process as possible. To that end, it says it is the only German piano manufacturer making its own keyboards. For the same reason, Schimmel established its current Leipzig factory to produce piano cabinet components, which it also supplies to other German piano makers.

Over the last few years, Schimmel has reorganized its model lineup into two categories: "Konzert" (models beginning with "K") and "Classic" (models beginning with "C"). The Konzert series consists of some of the newer and larger vertical models and the six most recently designed and advanced grand models. The company says that the purpose of the Konzert series was to expand the Schimmel line upward to a higher level of quality than it had previously attained. The Classic series consists of the rest of the verticals, the 6' grand model 182, and the 6' 10" grand model 208. This series represents models that have been tested over time and are solid, traditional, high-quality instruments, but without the latest refinements. Certain Schimmel Classic models are getting their finish and some action work done at the Schimmel factory in Kalisz, Poland before returning to Braunschweig for further preparation and voicing.

The Konzert series uprights—48" model K122, 49" model K125, and 52" model K132—are based on a more sophisticated philosophy of construction than the Classic series. These models also incorporate triplex scaling and other advanced design features. Schimmel's philosophy for these uprights was to design them to be as much like the grands as possible. The treble scales, in fact, are exactly the same as in the Konzert series grands.

The Konzert series grands consist of two model groups. In the first, Schimmel has created a "trilogy" of redesigned grands by marrying the front end (keyboard) of its 7' grand to two new models: 5' 7" and 6' 3". The company says the new models all have the same treble scale, keyboard, and action as the 7' grand, and so all three have a similar sound and touch. The case sides are angled slightly to obtain a larger soundboard, a technique now applied to all the grand models. The pianos also have triplex scaling for greater tonal color. The second group, also a "trilogy," consists of the 7' 5", 8' 4", and 9' 2" semi-concert and concert grand models. In this group, all three models have the same keyboard and action as the concert grand. These models also have tunable front and rear duplex scales, reinforced keys for optimal energy transmission, and mineral keytops to mimic the feel of ivory, among other advanced features.

The 6' 3" model K189 and 7' model K213 are currently available in a "Nikolaus W. Schimmel" (NWS) model. Built to commemorate the retirement of the elder Mr. Nikolaus Schimmel, this model has many small technical and cosmetic refinements, uses top quality soundboard material, and receives greater final preparation at the factory to create a really superior instrument.

Schimmel grand pianos have historically had a tone that was very bright and clear, but a bit thin and lacking in color in the treble. The grands were redesigned, in part, to add additional color to the tone. The result is definitely more interesting than before. Sustain is also very good. The pianos are being delivered to U.S. dealers voiced less bright than previously, as this is what the American ear tends to prefer. As for the verticals, the smaller ones tend to have a very big bass for their size, with a tone that emphasizes the fundamental, giving the bass a warmer character. The 51" model K132, which features a grand-shaped soundboard, has a very big sound, and listening to it, one might think one was in the presence of a grand.

In 2002, Schimmel acquired the PianoEurope factory in Kalisz, Poland, a piano restoration and manufacturing facility. Schimmel is using this factory to manufacture its Vogel brand, a moderately priced line named after the company's president. Schimmel says that although the skill level of the employees is high, lower wages and other lower costs result in a piano approximately 30 percent less costly than the Schimmel. Vogel grand pianos feature full Renner actions, with other parts mainly made by Schimmel in Braunschweig or by the Kalisz factory. The pianos are designed by Schimmel, but don't have all the refinements and advanced features of the latest Schimmel models. Nevertheless, the pianos have received praise from many quarters for their high-quality workmanship and sound. The company also uses the Kalisz factory to perform some work on selected Schimmel Classic pianos (as mentioned earlier).

Schimmel now imports an entry-level series of pianos from China under the name "May Berlin," a name long owned by Schimmel but not used for a number of years. The pianos are made by several selected suppliers. The company says it sends soundboard wood and hammer felt for grand pianos to the factory in China for use in its pianos. When completed, the pianos are first shipped to the Schimmel factory in Germany for inspection. Those that do not conform to Schimmel's standards are returned to China. The rest are prepared further before being sent on to dealers around the world.

Warranty: Schimmel, Vogel, May Berlin—Ten years, parts and labor, to the original purchaser.

SCHULZE POLLMANN

North American Music Inc.
11 Kay Fries Drive
Stony Point, New York 10980

800-782-2694
www.schulzepollmann.com
www.namusic.com

Pianos made by: Schulze Pollmann s.r.l., Fermingnano, Italy

Schulze Pollmann was formed in 1928 by the merger of two German piano builders who had moved to Italy, where the company still resides today. Since 1973 the firm has been owned by Generalmusic, best known for its digital pianos and organs and other musical electronics. Schulze Pollmann utilizes both sophisticated technology and hand work in its manufacturing. The pianos contain Delignit pinblocks, solid European spruce soundboards, and Renner actions and hammers. Interesting features include a one-piece solid lock (laminated) back and agraffes on the larger verticals, and finger-jointed construction on all soundboards to discourage future cracking. Many of the cabinets have beautiful designs and inlays. A new entry-level 45" vertical has a traditional back, Czech Detoa action, Renner hammers, and a lesser-quality solid spruce soundboard.

The two larger uprights are well built and have a sound that is warm and colorful with a good amount of sustain. The treble is not nearly as brittle sounding as in some of the other European uprights. The smallest vertical is quite different and clearly made to lower quality standards, though with nicely finished furniture. Schulze

Pollmann grands are likewise very nicely crafted and arrive at the dealer in good condition. However, they need solid preparation by the dealer to sound their best.

Italian auto manufacturer Ferrari Motor Car has selected Schulze Pollmann as a partner in the launch of its new Ferrari 612 Scaglietti series of automobiles. For the occasion, Schulze Pollmann has crafted a limited edition grand piano whose case sports the Ferrari racing red while the cast-iron plate is in the Ferrari gray carbon, the same as the engine of the Scaglietti. The car and the piano are being exhibited together in cities around the world.

Warranty: Ten years, parts and labor, transferable to future owners within the warranty period.

SEILER

Ed. Seiler Pianofortefabrik
GmbH & Co. KG
Schwarzacher Strasse 40
97318 Kitzingen, Germany

+49 9321 933 0
+49 9321 933 50 (fax)
america@seiler-pianos.de
www.seiler-pianos.com

Pianos made by: Ed. Seiler Pianofortefabrik, Kitzingen, Germany

Eduard Seiler, the company's founder, began making pianos in Liegnitz, Silesia, Germany in 1849. The company grew to over 435 employees, producing up to 3,000 pianos per year in 1923. Seiler was the largest piano manufacturer in Eastern Europe at that time. In 1945 and after World War II, the plant was occupied by Poland and the Seiler family left their native homeland with millions of other refugees. In 1951 Steffan Seiler reestablished the company in Copenhagen under the fourth generation of family ownership, and in 1962 moved it to Kitzingen, Germany, where it resides today. The company produces approximately 2,000 pianos annually.

Seiler makes high quality pianos using a combination of traditional methods and modern technology. The scale designs are of relatively high tension, producing a brilliant, balanced tone that is quite consistent from one Seiler to the next. The grands have wide tails for greater soundboard area and string length. Although brilliant, the tone also sings well due to, the company says, a unique soundboard feature called a Membrator—a tapered groove running around the perimeter of the board—that gives the soundboard flexibility without losing necessary stiffness. The pianos feature Bavarian spruce soundboards, multi-laminated beech pinblocks, quarter-sawn beech bridges, Renner actions, and slow-close fallboards. A few years ago, the grands were redesigned with a duplex scale for greater treble tonal color, and with longer keys and a lighter touch. Musically, these redesigns were very successful. They retained the typical Seiler clarity, but with longer sustain and a marvelously even-feeling touch. Both the verticals and the 6' 1" grands are available in dozens of models with beautiful wood inlays and brass ornamentation.

Seiler's 48" and 52" uprights are now available with the optional "Super Magnet Repetition" (SMR) action, a patented feature that uses magnets to increase repetition speed. Tiny magnets are attached to certain action parts of each note. During playing, the magnets repel each other, forcing the parts to return to their rest position faster, ready for a new key stroke.

Warranty: Five years, parts and labor, to original purchaser.

SEJUNG

including Falcone, Hobart M. Cable, Geo. Steck

America Sejung Corporation
5300 East Ontario Mills Parkway
Suite 100
Ontario, California 91764

909-484-7498
866-473-5864
sales@sejungusa.com
www.sejungusa.com

Pianos made by: Sejung Corporation, Qingdao, Shandong Province, China

Sejung is a Korean-based company established in 1974. The musical instrument division of the business began production in 2001 with the creation of a partnership with Qingdao Sejung Musical Instruments in China. They began by building a 700,000 square foot factory in Qingdao, a port city on the eastern coast with a temperate climate; hired dozens of managers who had once worked for Young Chang and Samick; and staffed the factory with some 2,000 workers. In order to attract skilled labor and reduce turnover, the company built dormitories to house and feed this labor force. The company has invested substantially in automated production equipment to achieve high quality standards and produces just about every piano component in its own factories.

Sejung currently manufactures the Falcone, George Steck, and Hobart M. Cable brand names. These lines are similar technically and are differentiated by cabinetry. Most of the models have a solid spruce soundboard, slow-close fallboard, cast pedals, and maple trapwork. In addition, an upscale Falcone Georgian (FG) series includes such features as Abel hammers on grands 5' 4" and larger, upgraded soundboard material, bubinga veneer on the inside of the grand rim, real ebony sharps, and gold-plated hardware.

The first pianos from Sejung were sold in the U.S. in fall of 2002, less than one year after production began. A number of their first offerings were examined by technicians, and although still a little rough, they were definitely satisfactory, and remarkably good for such a new company. Since then, the factory has grown to become one of the largest musical instrument exporters from China, production has been refined, and quality has improved. After proper regulation and tuning, the pianos offer good value in an entry-level instrument. The 4' 8" grand and the continental console in particular are most appropriate for those buyers whose primary considerations are price or furniture.

For model and price information, see under "Sejung" in the Model and Pricing Guide section of this *Supplement*.

Warranty: Twelve years on parts and ten years on labor, to the original purchaser.

SOHMER (& CO.)

Founded by German immigrant Hugo Sohmer in 1872, Sohmer & Co. was owned and managed by the Sohmer family in New York City for 110 years. Having no descendants to take over the business, the founder's grandsons sold the company in 1982. As the company changed hands several times over the following decade, limited production of Sohmer pianos took place in Connecticut and Pennsylvania, finally ceasing in 1994 (see the Sohmer entry in *The Piano Book* for a more detailed recent history).

Pianos are again being made under this venerable name, once considered among the finest of American-built instruments. However, there appears to be a dispute over the ownership of the Sohmer trademark, with pianos bearing this name being manufactured and distributed by two different companies.

SMC, North American distributor of Samick pianos, says it holds a license from the Burgett brothers, owners of PianoDisc, to use the Sohmer name. The Burgetts acquired the Sohmer trademark registrations when they purchased the assets of Mason & Hamlin out of bankruptcy in 1996. A distributor doing business under the name Persis International, Inc., who applied for the Sohmer trademark in 2001, claims that the registrations acquired by the Burgetts are expired and have been legally abandoned, not having been used since the 1994 closing of the Sohmer factory in Pennsylvania. The U.S. Patent and Trademark Office confirms that the government considers all past registrations of the Sohmer trademark to be expired or canceled and that the Burgetts' new application was refused. Further action on Persis' application has been temporarily suspended pending the Burgetts' appeal. At press time, the application process was still ongoing and it may be some time before the issue is settled for good. In the meantime, piano shoppers may find two "Sohmer" pianos in the marketplace. (Note: Persis' pianos are labeled "Sohmer" and SMC's are labeled "Sohmer & Co.") Both companies submitted product information, including model and price data, for this *Supplement*.

Persis International, Inc.
3540 North Southport #116
Chicago, Illinois 60657

773-342-4212
www.sohmer-piano.com

Sohmer pianos from this distributor are manufactured by Royale, a Korean firm that is descended from the former joint venture between Ibach and Daewoo (see "Ibach"). During the German-Korean joint venture, the string scales, bridges, soundboards, rib dimensions, actions, keys, and hammers were redesigned by Ibach to German standards. Models include a 50" vertical and 5' 3", 5' 10", and 7' 2" grands. The pianos have high quality European components, such as Renner actions, Abel hammers, Delignit pinblocks, Röslau strings, and Ciresa solid spruce soundboards.

Warranty: Ten years, parts and labor, to the original purchaser

SMC (formerly Samick Music Corp.)
1329 Gateway Drive
Gallatin, Tennessee 37066

615-206-0077
800-592-9393
www.smcmusic.com

The Sohmer & Co. model 34, a 42" vertical, features full-length backposts, a sand-cast plate, solid spruce soundboard, exposed 16-ply pinblock, and a slow-close fallboard—virtually identical (except for the slow-close fallboard) to the original, highly regarded Sohmer & Co. console. A new Sohmer & Co. studio piano has a design based on the Bechstein 116 centimeter scale. At present, the consoles are made in Indonesia, the studio pianos in Korea. [Note: This description from Samick of the Sohmer verticals is not consistent with the Sohmer models listed in the Pricing Guide section of the *Supplement*. It appears that some models may be identical to the verticals sold under the Wm. Knabe name. At press time, the Samick contact could not be reached for an explanation.]

Sohmer & Co. grands are similar to the pianos Samick made for Baldwin under the Chickering label. They have maple outer rims, sand-cast plates, German solid spruce soundboards, Renner hammers, spruce beams, solid brass hardware, agraffes, lacquer semi-gloss wood finishes, and other higher quality features, and are available in a variety of furniture styles. Sohmer & Co. grands are made in Korea, except the 5' model and selected others, which are from Indonesia. All Sohmer & Co. pianos are inspected, voiced, and regulated in the U.S. before being shipped to dealers.

Warranty: Twelve years, parts and labor, to original purchaser.

STECK, GEO. — See "Sejung"

STEIGERMAN

Steigerman Music Corporation
4902 — 217B Street
Langley, British Columbia
Canada V3A 9K1

888-651-8119
pianos@steigerman.com
www.steigerman.com

Pianos made by: Ningbo Hailun Musical Instruments Co. Ltd., Ningbo, Zhejiang
    Province, China and Beijing Hsinghai Piano Group, Ltd., Beijing, China

Steigerman is a name, owned by Canadian piano distributor Steigerman Music Corporation, which has appeared over the years on pianos from a number of Asian manufacturers, including Yamaha, Samick, Beijing Hsinghai and, more recently, Hailun.

At present, Steigerman's "Classic" line of pianos is made by the Beijing Hsinghai Piano Group in Beijing, China (see "Beijing Hsinghai"). These models have a three-ply laminated spruce soundboard, except for the 6' grand, which has a solid spruce board.

Steigerman now has a "Premium" line of pianos made by Hailun in Ningbo, China (see "Hailun"). Features of both grands and verticals include a tapered, solid spruce soundboard; sand-cast plate, agraffes, Renner hammers, and optional Renner action. Additionally, the verticals have a maple back and an easy-to-remove practice rail; grands have a maple rim and front and rear duplex scale.

Warranty: Ten years, parts and labor, to the original purchaser.

STEINBERG, GERH. — See "Perzina, Gebr."

STEINBERG, WILH.

Thüringer Pianoforte GmbH
Mozartstrasse 3
07607 Eisenberg, Germany
+49-36691-5950
+49-36691-59540 (fax)
WSTPianos@aol.com
www.Wilh-Steinberg.com

Pianos made by: Thüringer Pianoforte GmbH, Eisenberg, Germany

This company, formerly known as Wilhelm Steinberg Pianofortefabrik, was formed from the merger of several East German piano companies following the unification of Germany. These companies collectively trace their origin back to 1877. Steinberg also makes cabinets for other German piano makers, and makes several European piano brands under OEM agreement. The company also specializes in custom cabinets and finishes. Piano production is about 900 verticals and 50 grands per year.

Steinberg makes four models of vertical piano (46", 48", 48½", and 51") and two sizes of grand (5' 8" and 6' 4"). These high quality pianos have beech rims with spruce bracing (grands), solid Bavarian spruce soundboards, maple bridges with maple cap, Renner actions and hammers, and Kluge keys.

Warranty: Five years, parts and labor, to the original purchaser.

STEINGRAEBER & SÖHNE

Unique Pianos
Brian Gatchell
25 South Wickham Rd.
Melbourne, Florida 32904

888-725-6633
321-725-5690
www.steingraeber.de
www.steingraeberpianos.com

Pianos made by: Steingraeber & Söhne, Bayreuth, Germany

Bayreuth is famous the world over for its annual summer Wagner festival. But tucked away in the old part of town is a second center of Bayreuth musical excellence and one of the piano world's best-kept secrets: Steingraeber & Söhne. Founded in Bayreuth in 1852, and in its present factory since 1872, Steingraeber is one of the smaller piano manufacturers in the world, producing fewer than 250 pianos per year for the top end of the market. It is owned and operated by sixth-generation family member Udo Steingraeber, who still makes pianos using the traditional methods of his forebearers.

Steingraeber makes three sizes of vertical piano—48", 51", and 54". One interesting option on the vertical pianos is "twist and change" panels. These are two-sided top and bottom panels, one side finished in polished ebony and the other in a two-toned combination of a wood veneer and ebony. The panels can be reversed as desired by the piano owner to match room décor or just for a change of scenery.

The company also makes four sizes of grand piano—5' 7", 6' 9", 7' 7", and 8' 11". The 5' 7" grand model has an unusually wide tail, allowing for a larger soundboard area and longer bass strings than is customary for an instrument of its size. The 6' 9" model 205, known as the "Chamber Concert Grand," was designed to embody the same tone quality of the Steingraeber Liszt grand piano of circa 1873. The 8' 11" model E-272 concert grand was introduced in 2002 for Steingraeber's 150th anniversary. Unique features include: a drilled capo bar for more sustain in the treble, unusually shaped rim bracing, and smaller soundboard resonating area in the treble to better match string length. In 2007, Steingraeber introduced a new 7' 7" concert grand to provide an additional smaller, concert-size instrument. Its design features many of the innovations of the E-272. (I had an opportunity recently to experience the new 7' 7" grand, and it is phenomenal!)

Steingraeber is known for its many innovative technical improvements to the piano. One new one is a cylindrical knuckle (grand piano action part) that revolves. It acts like a normal knuckle until the hammer reaches the let-off position. After that point, in soft playing, the knuckle revolves, reducing friction and making pianissimo playing easier, smoother, and more accurate. Another innovation is a new action for upright pianos. The "SFM" action, as it is called, contains no jack spring, instead using magnets to return the jack more quickly under the hammer butt for faster repetition. It is available in all three models of vertical piano. Steingraeber also specializes in so-called ecological or biological finishes, available as an option on most models. This involves the use of only organic materials in the piano, such as natural paints and glues in the case, and white keytops made from cattle bone.

Steingraeber pianos have a unique sound, with an extensive tonal palette derived from a mixture of clarity and warmth.

In addition to its regular line of pianos, Steingraeber makes a piano that can be used by physically handicapped players who don't have the use of their legs for pedaling. A switch in a backrest cushion operates the sustain pedal and a switch under the keybed operates the soft pedal. This mechanism can be installed in pianos of other makers if certain technical requirements are met.

The Steingraeber engineering department has designed and manufactured prototypes of new piano models for a number of other European piano manufacturers. These designs are not the same as Steingraeber's own current models.

Warranty: Ten years, parts and labor, to original purchaser.

STEINWAY & SONS

Steinway & Sons, Inc.
Steinway Place
Long Island City, New York 11105

718-721-2600
800-366-1853
www.steinway.com

Heinrich Englehard Steinweg, a cabinetmaker and piano maker from Seesen, Germany, emigrated with his family to the United States in 1850 and established Steinway & Sons in 1853. Within a relatively short time, the Steinways were granted patents that revolutionized the piano, and which were eventually adopted or imitated by other makers. Many of these patents concerned the quest for a stronger frame, a richer, more powerful sound, and a more sensitive action. By the 1880s, the Steinway piano was in most ways the modern piano we have today, and in the next generation the standards set by the founder were strictly adhered to. (The early history of Steinway & Sons is fascinating, and is intimately connected to the history of New York City and the piano industry in general. You can read a summary of it in *The Piano Book*, and there are several excellent books devoted to the subject as well.)

Jumping ahead to the 1960s, the fourth generation of Steinways found themselves without any heirs willing or able to take over the business and with a lack of capital with which to finance much needed equipment modernization, so in 1972 the Steinways sold their company to CBS. CBS exited the musical instrument business in 1985, selling Steinway to an investment group. In 1995 the company was sold again, this time to a major manufacturer of brass and woodwind instruments. The combined company, now known as Steinway Musical Instruments, Inc., is listed on the New York Stock Exchange under the symbol LVB. Steinway also owns a branch factory in Hamburg, Germany, which serves the world market outside of the Americas, and two major suppliers, the Herman Kluge company, Europe's largest maker of piano keys, and the O.S. Kelly company, the only remaining piano plate foundry in the U.S.

Steinway makes two types of vertical piano in three sizes: a 45" model 4510 studio, a 46½" model 1098 studio, and a 52" model K-52 upright. Models 4510 and 1098 are technically identical—only the cabinet is different—the former being in a period style for home use, the latter in an institutional cabinet for school use or less furniture-conscious home use. In all three models, the middle pedal operates a sostenuto mechanism. All Steinway verticals use a solid spruce soundboard, have no particleboard, and in many other ways are similar in design, materials, and quality of workmanship to Steinway grands. Actions are made by Renner. Model K-52 in ebony and model 1098 in ebony, mahogany, and walnut come with an adjustable artist bench, the others with a regular bench.

Technicians have always liked the performance of Steinway verticals, but used to complain that the studio models in particular were among the most difficult pianos to tune and would jump out of tune unexpectedly. Over the last few years, Steinway has made small design changes to alleviate this problem. The feedback I'm receiving is that the pianos are now mechanically more normal to tune and are stable, but an excess of false beats (tonal irregularities) still make the pianos difficult to tune at times.

Steinway makes six sizes of grand piano, two of which are new within the last few years. All ebony, mahogany, and walnut grand models come with an adjustable artist bench, the others with a regular bench.

The 5' 1" model S is very good for a small grand, but has the usual limitations of any small piano and so is only recommended where space considerations are paramount. The 5' 7" model M is a full six inches longer, but costs little more than the S. Historically, it has been one of Steinway's more popular models and is found in living rooms across the country. Its medium size makes the tone in certain areas slightly less than perfect, but it's an excellent home instrument.

The 5' 10½" model L has been replaced with the model O of the same size. Model O was first produced in 1902, but discontinued in 1924 in favor of the model L. Changes over time in both engineering and musical taste, as well as a desire to better synchronize the offerings of the New York factory with Hamburg, where the model O was never abandoned, seemed to dictate a return to the O. The main difference between the two models is in the shape of the tail—the L has a squared-off tail and the O has a round tail—but this can also affect the soundboard and bridges and therefore the tone.

Reintroduction of the model O followed by one year the reintroduction of the legendary 6' 2" model A. First offered in 1878 and discontinued in New York in 1945, model A revolutionized piano making by featuring for the first time radial rim bracing and one-piece bent rim construction, now used in all Steinway grands. Over the years, the model A has gone through several makeovers, each of slightly different size and scaling. The version being reintroduced was made in New York from 1896 to 1914 and is the same size as the model A that has been made at the Hamburg factory for more than a century. Models O and A are suitable for the larger living room or for many school and teaching situations.

The 6' 10½" model B is the favorite of many piano technicians. It is the best choice for the serious pianist, recording or teaching studio, or small recital hall. Small design changes and other refinements to this model in recent years have brought a steady stream of accolades. The 8' 11¾" model D, the concert grand, is the flagship of the Steinway line and the piano of choice for the overwhelming majority of concert pianists. It's too large for most places other than the concert stage.

Steinway uses excellent materials and construction techniques in the manufacture of its grands. The rims, both inner and outer, are made in one continuous bend from layers of maple, and the beams are of solid spruce. The keybed is of quartersawn spruce planks freely mortised together, and the keys are of Bavarian spruce. The pinblock consists of seven laminations of maple with successive grain orientations of 45 and 90 degrees. The soundboard is of solid Sitka spruce, the bridges are vertically laminated of maple with a solid maple cap, and all models have duplex scaling.

It is well known that Steinway's principal competition comes from used and rebuilt Steinways, many of which come in exotic veneers or have elaborately carved or customized "art cases." The company has responded by expanding its product line to include modern-day versions of these collector's items. The Crown Jewel Collection consists of the regular models in natural wood (non-ebonized) veneers, many of them exotic. They are finished in a semi-gloss finish Steinway calls Satin Lustre. Limited Edition models, issued at irregular intervals, are reproductions of turn-of-the-century designs, available only in models O and B. The newest Limited Edition model is one honoring Henry Z. Steinway, the oldest living member of the Steinway family, now in his nineties. This model has Victorian-style legs and lyre, an intricately carved music desk and period cabinet detailing, and is available in Ebony with chrome-plated hardware, or East Indian Rosewood. Each instrument is personally signed by Henry Steinway.

During the early 1900s, ownership of art case Steinways became a symbol of wealth and culture. Steinway has resumed this tradition by regularly commissioning noted furniture designers to create new ones. Most are created around a theme. For example, in 1999 Frank Pollaro designed an art case called "Rhapsody" to commemorate the 100th anniversary of the birth of George Gershwin. The piano featured a blue-dyed maple veneer adorned with more than 400 hand-cut mother-of-pearl stars and a gilded silver plate. Each year sees new art case pianos from Steinway and they are truly stunning. Steinway's Legendary Collection consists of occasional one-of-a-kind reproductions of historical art case pianos.

As another way of capitalizing on the popularity of older Steinways, the company also operates the world's largest Steinway piano rebuilding facility at the factory for the restoration of older Steinways. *The Piano Book* contains a great deal of additional information on the purchase of an older or restored Steinway.

The underlying excellence of the Steinway musical designs and the integrity of the construction process are the hallmarks of the Steinway piano. Steinway pianos at their best have the quintessential American piano sound: a powerful bass, a resonant mid-range, a singing treble with plenty of tonal color. Although other brands have some of these characteristics, it is perhaps the particular combination of harmonics that comprise the Steinway's tonal coloration that distinguishes it from other brands more than anything else and gives it its richness, depth, and power. The construction process creates a very durable and rigid framework, which also contributes to the power of its sound. As with other American-made pianos, musical and cabinet detailing such as factory voicing and regulation and plate and cabinet cosmetics, are reasonable but lag somewhat behind the company's European competitors in finesse. Some of this can be finished off by thorough and competent dealer make-ready.

Steinway pianos require more preparation by the dealer than most pianos in their class, but over the last several years the factory preparation has greatly improved, so the work required by the dealer is no longer excessive. Still, some dealers are more conscientious than others, and I occasionally hear of piano buyers who "can't find a good Steinway." How much of this is due to inherent weaknesses in some pianos, how much to lack of dealer preparation, and how much to customer bias or groundless complaining is hard to tell. I suspect it is a little of each. Piano technicians who work on these pianos do sometimes remark that some seem to have more potential than others. Many dealers do just enough regulating and voicing to be acceptable to the average customer, but reserve the highest level of work for those situations where a fussy customer for one of the larger models is trying to decide between a few particular instruments. Most customers for a Steinway will probably find one they like on the sales floor. However, if you are a discriminating buyer who has had trouble finding a Steinway that suits your preferences, I recommend letting the salesperson know as precisely as you can what you are looking for. Give the salesperson some time to have a few instruments prepared for you before making a decision. It may also help to tactfully let the salesperson know that you are aware there are other options available to you in the market for high-end pianos. By the way, customers seeking to purchase a model B or D Steinway who have not found the piano they are looking for at their local dealer can make arrangements with that dealer to visit the Steinway factory in New York, where a selection of the larger models is kept on hand for this purpose.

As mentioned earlier, Steinway owns a branch factory in Hamburg, Germany, established in 1880. The "fit and finish" (detailing) of the pianos at this factory is reputed to be better than at the one in New York, although pianists sometimes prefer the sound of the New York Steinway. Traditionally, the Hamburg factory has operated somewhat autonomously, but more recently, the company has been synchronizing the two plants through technical exchanges, model changes, jointly built models, and materials that are shipped from New York to Hamburg. It's possible to special-order a Hamburg Steinway through an American Steinway dealer, or an enterprising American customer could travel to Europe, buy one there, and have it shipped back home.

In 2008 Steinway underwent a change in management, the first in twenty-three years. For the first time, the company's top executives have been recruited from its European operations rather than from America. It is speculated that this may signal a subtle change of direction with regard to quality issues and that we soon may see European quality standards more strictly applied to the American-made instruments.

Warranty: Five years, parts and labor, to the original purchaser.

STORY & CLARK

Story & Clark Piano Co.
269 Quaker Drive
Seneca, Pennsylvania 16346

800-247-6557
www.qrsmusic.com

Owned by: QRS Music Technologies, Inc., Naples, Florida

Pianos made by: Samick Musical Instrument Mfg. Co. Ltd., Bogor, West Java, Indonesia

Hampton Story began making pianos in 1857 and was joined by Melville Clark in 1884. The business settled in Grand Rapids, Michigan in 1901, where it remained, under various owners, until about 1986. Around 1990, a new owner moved the company to its present location in Seneca, Pennsylvania. Over the years, pianos were manufactured under a number of different names, including in recent years, Story & Clark, Hobart M. Cable, Hampton, and Classic. In 1993 QRS Piano Rolls, Inc., now QRS Music Technologies, Inc., purchased Story & Clark. (Ironically, QRS itself was founded in 1901 by Melville Clark of the Story & Clark Piano Co. of old.) QRS, historically the nation's major source of music rolls for traditional player pianos, now manufactures electronic player piano systems that can be retrofitted into any piano (see "QRS/Pianomation").

In an effort to offer unique and exclusive scales and styles, Story & Clark recently moved its source of manufacturing from China, where the pianos had for some time been made by Dongbei, to Indonesia, where they are now made by Samick.

The company now offers two series of vertical and grand pianos. The "Heritage Series" is a popularly priced line of vertical pianos with a "Storytone II" soundboard—Story & Clark's name for the veneer-laminated soundboard developed by Samick (see "Samick").

The "Signature Series" comes in both vertical and grand models. These pianos feature premium Renner hammers, Röslau strings, maple and mahogany rims, solid brass hardware, Bolduc tapered soundboards of solid spruce, sand-cast plates and advanced low-tension scales. The pianos have cabinet designs that offer lots of detail for the money and coordinate with major furniture trends. In spite of their beauty, the company says, these pianos are also appropriate for school and commercial applications.

In keeping with the tradition started by Hampton Story of integrating technology into pianos, all Story & Clark pianos are now equipped with an exclusive feature called PNOscan™. PNOscan is an optical sensor strip attached to the key frame directly under the keys. This optical device senses the velocity and up/down movement of each key so it can precisely recreate every detail of an original performance including the force, speed, and duration of each note played without affecting the touch or response of the keyboard. The data captured by PNOscan is then transmitted through either a USB connection or MIDI output to a computer, general MIDI sound module, or other digital device. The addition of PNOscan to every Story & Clark acoustic piano gives customers the potential to have all the features of a digital piano; when combined with various accessories, PNOscan gives users the ability to learn, record, compose, practice in silence, and more.

Many Story & Clark grands are outfitted with QRS Pianomation systems, which necessitates pre-slotting and modifying the pianos to accept the player systems without cutting into the keys and key frame. By combining PNOscan with a Petine or Ancho Pianomation system, a player can record, playback, and save digital performances. See "QRS/Pianomation" for more details.

Warranty: Fifteen years, parts and labor, to the original purchaser. Lifetime limited warranty to the original purchaser and 25-year transferable warranty to subsequent purchasers on the Storytone II soundboard.

SUZUKI

Suzuki Corporation
P.O. Box 261030
San Diego, California 92196

800-854-1594
858-566-9710
www.suzukipianos.com

Pianos made by: Artfield Piano Co., Qingpu, Shanghai, China; possibly others

Suzuki Corporation, the world's largest producer of musical instruments for education, has entered the acoustic piano business with a line of vertical and grand pianos made in China. The pianos are sold online at www.suzukipianos.com and through Costco, as well as through regular piano dealers. The company prefers not to be specific as to the source of its pianos, but it appears to me that most are now manufactured by Artfield Piano Co.

Warranty: Ten years, parts and labor, to the original purchaser.

VIVACE — See "Cristofori"

VOGEL — See "Schimmel"

VOSE & SONS

Wrightwood Enterprises, Inc.
717 St. Joseph Drive
St. Joseph, Michigan 49085

616-828-0618

Pianos made by: Dongbei Piano Company, Ltd., Yingkou, Liaoning Province, China

Vose & Sons was established in 1851 in Boston by James Whiting Vose. Ownership eventually transferred to the American Piano Company, and later to Aeolian Pianos, which went out of business in 1985. Since 2004, the brand has been used by a different distributor on pianos from the Dongbei Piano Company in China (see "Dongbei").

WALTER, CHARLES R.

Walter Piano Company, Inc.
25416 CR 6
Elkhart, Indiana 46514

574-266-0615
www.walterpiano.com

Charles Walter, an engineer, was head of Piano Design and Developmental Engineering at C.G. Conn in the 1960s, when Conn was doing important research in musical acoustics. In 1969 Walter bought the Janssen piano name from Conn, and continued to make Janssen pianos until 1981. In 1975 he brought out the Charles R.

Walter line of consoles and studios, based on his continuing research in piano design. Walter began making grands in 1997.

The Walter Piano Company is fairly unique among U.S. piano manufacturers in that it is a family business, staffed by Charles and his wife, several of their grownup children and various in-laws, in addition to unrelated production employees. The Walters say that each piano is inspected and signed by a member of their family before being shipped. Dealers and technicians report that doing business with the Walters is a pleasure in itself.

The Charles R. Walter line consists of 43" and 45" studio pianos in various decorator and institutional styles, and 5' 9" and 6' 4" grands. The 43" pianos are called "consoles" for marketing purposes because of their styling, but both the 43" and 45" pianos are really studios (as I define the term) by virtue of their full-size actions, and are actually identical pianos in different sized cabinets. Because of the larger action, the "console" will outperform many real consoles on the market.

Although Mr. Walter is not oblivious to marketing concerns, his vertical piano bears the mark of being designed by an engineer who understands pianos and strives for quality. The pianos are built in a traditional manner, with heavy-duty, full-length, spruce backposts; a solid spruce soundboard; and Delignit pinblock. Exceptionally long, thick keys that are individually lead-weighted provide a very even feel across the keyboard. The scale design is well thought out and the bass sounds good most of the way to the bottom. The cabinetry is substantial, contains no particle board, and is beautifully finished. Some of the fancy consoles in particular, such as the Queen Anne models, are strikingly beautiful. The pianos are well prepared at the factory and so need minimal preparation by the dealer.

The vertical pianos now use Renner actions, but a Chinese-made action is available as a lower-cost option, reducing the price of the piano by about $1,200 (list). The Chinese parts are virtually indistinguishable from the Renner parts, but they make the action feel just slightly lighter due to differing spring tensions.

The Walter 5' 9" and 6' 4" grands were designed by Del Fandrich, one of the nation's most respected piano design engineers. Both models have high-quality features such as a maple rim, Renner action, Kluge keys, Delignit pinblock, tapered solid spruce soundboard, and Abel hammers (Ronsen hammers in the 5' 9" model). The 5' 9" grand also has a number of innovative features: A portion of the inner rim and soundboard at the bass end of the piano are separated from the rest of the rim and allowed to "float." Less restricted in its movement, the soundboard can reproduce the fundamental frequencies of the lower bass notes more like a larger piano can. A special extension of the tenor bridge creates a smoother transition from bass to treble. Eight plate nosebolts increase plate stability, helping to reduce energy loss to the plate and thus increase sustain. Inverted half-agraffes embedded in the capo bar maintain string alignment and reduce unwanted string noise. The Walter grands are competently built and play very well.

Warranty: Twelve years, parts and labor, transferable to future owners within the warranty period.

WEBER — See "Young Chang"

WEINBACH

Geneva International Corporation
29 East Hintz Road
Wheeling, Illinois 60090

800-533-2388
847-520-9970
pianos@geneva-intl.com
www.geneva-intl.com

Pianos made by: Dongbei Piano Company, Ltd., Yingkou, Liaoning Province, China

Formerly made by Petrof and for years virually identical to Petrof pianos, the Weinbach piano line was given a complete makeover in 2006. The pianos are now assembled in the section of the Dongbei Piano Co. in China in which Nordiska pianos are manufactured (see "Nordiska" and "Dongbei").

The Weinbach grand rim structure is the same as for the Nordiska, but the scale designs are modified, and the plate designs are completely new. The pianos are strung with a combination of loop and single stringing (one loop and one single-tied string per unison), with bass strings made in the U.S. by Mapes. Like the Nordiska, the Weinbach grands have maple rims, solid spruce soundboards, Abel hammers, and an advanced leg plate design, among other features. The action is Petrof's new "Petrof Original" action made by Detoa (see "Petrof" for details). Fully assembled actions, keys, and key frames are shipped from Petrof to Dongbei and added to the Chinese-made strung back and cabinet. At present only grand models exist, but vertical models will follow soon.

Warranty: Ten years, parts and labor, to original purchaser.

WEINBERGER

Cathy Harl
Harl Pianos
318 Montgomery Street
Alexandria, Virginia 22314

703-739-2220
800-440-HARL (4275)

Pianos made by: Klavierhaus Weinberger, Enns, Austria

Bruno Weinberger is an Austrian piano technician who markets his own line of pianos. Distribution in the U.S. is very limited. For the most part, the pianos are manufactured in Germany by Thüringer Pianoforte GmbH, maker of Wilh. Steinberg pianos, with Mr. Weinberger providing the musical and technical finishing work. Mr. Weinberger says the verticals are similar to the Wilh. Steinberg line, but that the grands are built to his own design. The grands have a couple of unique cabinet design features. The closed lid is supported on short posts so that even in the closed position there is a small space for sound to escape. The music desk folds down into the front part of the lid. For model and price information, contact the distributor.

WURLITZER — See "Baldwin"

WYMAN

Wyman Piano Company
P.O. Box 218802
Nashville, Tennessee 37221

615-356-9143
206-350-7912 (fax)
info@wymanpiano.com
www.wymanpiano.com

Pianos made by: Beijing Hsinghai Piano Group, Ltd., Beijing, China

Wyman Piano Company was created by experienced former Baldwin (Cincinnati) executives with more than sixty years combined piano industry experience. Although a relatively new company, Wyman distribution has grown to include the UK, Germany, and Japan, as well as the U.S.

The regular Wyman line consists of six vertical piano sizes and four grand models in a variety of cabinet sizes and finishes. All are based on German scale designs and are manufactured in China by the Beijing Hsinghai Piano Group (see "Beijing

Hsinghai") at that company's new 1.2 million square foot factory. A new limited production premium line of Wyman "Pianoforte" models, made in a small production facility in the Beijing area, features deluxe cabinets and some upgraded technical features.

Wyman offers the model CD2 player piano system by Pianoforce, a new entrant into the field of player piano systems (see "Pianoforce"). The optional CD system features a unique stamped rail designed specifically for these pianos that, according to the company, allows a much lower profile than other player systems that use universal rails to fit any piano. They are installed at the Beijing factory.

Wyman says that its executives make frequent trips to the factory in Beijing to monitor manufacturing and inspect finished instruments.

Warranty: Ten years, parts and labor, transferable to future owners within the warranty period. Lifetime warranty on the soundboard.

XINGHAI — See "Beijing Xinghai"

YAMAHA

including Cable-Nelson. See separate listing for Disklavier.

Yamaha Corporation of America
P.O. Box 6600
Buena Park, California 90622

714-522-9011
800-854-1569
infostation@yamaha.com
www.yamaha.com

Pianos made by: Yamaha Corporation, Hamamatsu, Japan and other locations (see text)

Torakusu Yamaha, a watchmaker, developed Japan's first reed organ, founding Yamaha Reed Organ Manufacturing in 1887. In 1899 Yamaha visited the United States to learn to build pianos. Within a couple of years, he began making grand and vertical pianos under the name Nippon Gakki, Ltd. Beginning in the 1930s, Yamaha expanded its operations, first into other musical instruments, then into other goods and services, such as sporting goods and furniture, and finally internationally.

Export of pianos to the United States began about 1960. In 1973 Yamaha acquired the Everett Piano Co. in South Haven, Michigan, and made both Yamaha and Everett pianos there until 1986. In that year, the company moved its piano manufacturing to a plant in Thomaston, Georgia, where it has made Yamaha consoles, studios, and some grands until last year. Citing a depressed piano market and increasing competition from China and Indonesia, Yamaha closed its Thomaston facility in 2007. Since then, the company has introduced new models, made in other Yamaha factories, to replace those formerly made in Thomaston.

Yamaha is probably the most international of the piano manufacturers. In addition to its factories in Japan, Yamaha has plants and partnerships with other companies all over the world, including Germany (with Schimmel), England (with Kemble), Mexico, China, Indonesia, and Taiwan. Currently, Yamaha pianos sold in the U.S. are made in Japan, China, Indonesia, and Taiwan.

Yamaha's console line consists of 44" models M460 and M560 in furniture style (free-standing legs) with increasing levels of cabinet sophistication and price. All are the same internally and have a compressed action typical of a console, so the action will not be quite as responsive as with larger models.

The studio line consists of the popular 45" model P22 in institutional style (legs with toe blocks) with school-friendly cabinet; the furniture-style version P660, and 47" model T118 in a less-expensive, traditional institutional-style cabinet. All are more or less the same internally, with a full-size action. The institutional-style studios are made in China, the furniture-style consoles and studios in Taiwan.

The uprights are the very popular 48" model U1, the 48" model T121 in a less-expensive cabinet (otherwise the same), and the 52" model U3. Models U1 and U3 now sport a longer music desk—a very welcome addition. Model U3 joins model U5 (discontinued in this form) in the use of a "floating" soundboard—the soundboard is not completely attached to the back at the top, allowing it to vibrate a little more freely to enhance tonal performance. A new "Super U" series of uprights (YUS1, YUS3, YUS5) have different hammers and get additional tuning and voicing at the factory, including voicing by machine to create a more consistent, more mellow tone. Model YUS5 uses German Röslau music wire instead of Yamaha wire, also for a more mellow tone. This top-of-the-line 52" upright also has agraffes, duplex scaling, and a sostenuto pedal. (All other Yamaha verticals have a practice/mute pedal.) The uprights are made in Japan.

Yamaha vertical pianos are very well made for a mass-produced piano. The taller uprights in particular are considered a "dream" to service by technicians and are very much enjoyed by musicians. Sometimes the pianos can sound quite bright, though much less so than in previous years. The current version of the model P22 school studio is said to have been redesigned to sound less bright and have an improved spectrum of tonal color. Double-striking of the hammer in the low tenor on a soft or incomplete stroke of the key is a problem occasionally mentioned in regard to Yamaha verticals by those who play with an especially soft touch. This tendency is a characteristic of the action design, the trade-off being better-than-normal repetition for a vertical piano. It's possible that a technician can lessen this problem if necessary with careful adjustment, but at the risk of sacrificing some speed of repetition.

Yamaha grands come in four levels of sophistication and size. The "Classic Collection" consists of the 4' 11" model GB1 and the 5' 3" model GC1. The GB1 has simplified case construction and cabinetry, no duplex scale, and the middle pedal operates a bass sustain mechanism. It is currently the only Yamaha grand sold in the U.S. that is made in Indonesia. The GC1 has regular case construction and duplex scale, but simplified cabinetry and a bass sustain.

The "Conservatory Collection" consists of the 5' 3" model C1, 5' 8" model C2, 6' 1" model C3, and 6' 7" model C5. The "Conservatory Concert Collection" is the 6' 11" model C6 and the 7' 6" model C7. Both collections have the advanced construction, scaling, and cabinetry mentioned above, plus a true sostenuto pedal and a soft-close fallboard. Both now have vertically laminated bridges with maple or boxwood cap. The vertically laminated design is similar to that found in Steinways and other fine pianos, and is considered to give the bridges greater strength and resistance to cracking and better transmission of vibrational energy. The larger grands also use Yamaha's ivory-alternative Ivorite™ keytops.

Finally, the "Handcrafted Concert Collection" consists of the 9' model CFIIIS concert grand and the two "S" series Yamahas: 6' 3" model S4B and 6' 11" model S6B. The pianos in this collection are "hand-built" in a separate factory to much higher standards and with some different materials. For example, they use maple and mahogany in the rim, which has recently been made more rigid for greater tonal power; higher-grade soundboard material; a treble "bell" (as in the larger Steinways) to enhance the treble tone; German strings and recent hammer and scaling changes for a more mellow tone; as well as the more advanced features of the other collections. The result is an instrument capable of greater dynamic range, tonal color, and sustain than the regular Yamahas. The CFIIIS concert grand made in this factory is endorsed and used by a number of notable musicians, including Michael Tilson Thomas, Chick Corea, and Elton John, among others.

Other than the special grands just described, historically Yamaha grands have been a little on the percussive side and have been said not to "sing" as well as some more expensive pianos. The tone has been very clear and often bright, especially in the smaller grands, although the excessive brightness that once characterized Yamahas seems to be a thing of the past. The clarity and percussiveness are very attractive, but are sometimes said to be less well-suited for classical music, which tends to require a singing tone and lush harmonic color. On the other hand, Yamaha is the piano of choice for jazz and popular music, which may value the clarity and brightness more than the other qualities mentioned. More recently, however, Yamaha has been trying to move away from this image as a "bright" piano that is limited to jazz. First with the larger grands and more recently with the smaller ones, Yamaha has changed bridge construction and hammer density, and provided more custom voicing at the factory, to bring out a broader spectrum of tonal color in the pianos.

Both Yamaha's quality control and its warranty and technical service are legendary in the piano business. They are the standard against which every other company is measured. For general home and school use, piano technicians probably recommend Yamaha pianos more often than any other brand. Their precision, reliability, and performance make them a very good value for a consumer product.

The Yamaha Servicebond program encourages Yamaha dealers to provide customers with follow-up service during the first six months of ownership by reimbursing the dealers for part of the cost of providing the service. Services for which a dealer can be reimbursed include a tuning and a general maintenance check (tightening screws, among other things). The program is voluntary, however, on the part of the dealer. When negotiating the sale, the customer might wish to inquire as to whether the dealer participates in the program, and if so, to make sure the service is actually provided.

Yamaha now makes a piano under the name Cable-Nelson. It is made in Yamaha's factory in Hangzhou, Zhejiang Province, China, southwest of Shanghai, where the company also makes guitars. The Cable-Nelson 45" model CN116 is identical in quality and musical specifications to Yamaha's former model T116 (no longer available), except that the Cable-Nelson has a laminated soundboard, whereas all Yamaha pianos sold in the U.S. have a solid spruce soundboard. The Cable-Nelson model CN216 is a furniture-style version of the 116.

Cable-Nelson is the name of an old American piano maker that traces its roots back to 1903. Yamaha acquired the name when it bought the Everett Piano Company in 1973, and used the name in conjunction with Everett pianos until 1981.

There is a thriving market for used Yamahas. If you are considering buying a used Yamaha, please read "Should I Buy a Used, 'Gray Market' Yamaha or Kawai Piano?" on pages 176–177 of *The Piano Book*.

To help its dealers overcome competition from "gray market" pianos, Yamaha has begun an "Heirloom Assurance" program that provides a five-year warranty on a used Yamaha piano less than twenty-five years old purchased from an authorized Yamaha dealer. See a Yamaha dealer for details.

Yamaha also makes electronic player pianos called Disklaviers, as well as a hybrid acoustic/digital instrument called Silent Piano (formerly called MIDIPiano), that account for a substantial percentage of the company's sales. These products are reviewed separately under "Disklavier."

Warranty: Yamaha and Cable-Nelson—Ten years, parts and labor, to the original purchaser. Cable-Nelson pianos do not come with the Yamaha Servicebond.

YOUNG CHANG

including Bergmann, Weber, Albert Weber

Young Chang North America, Inc.
19060 South Dominguez Hills Drive
Rancho Dominguez, California 90220

310-637-2000
800-874-2880
www.youngchang.com

Pianos made by: Young Chang Akki, Ltd., Inchon, South Korea and Tianjin, China

In 1956 three brothers, Young-Sup, Chang-Sup, and Jai-Sup Kim founded Young Chang and began selling Yamaha pianos in Korea under an agreement with that Japanese firm. Korea was recovering from a devastating war, and only the wealthy could afford pianos. But the prospects were bright for economic development, and as a symbol of cultural refinement the piano was much coveted. In 1962 the brothers incorporated as Young Chang Akki Co., Ltd.

In 1964 Yamaha and Young Chang entered into an agreement in which Yamaha helped Young Chang set up a full-fledged manufacturing operation. Yamaha shipped partially completed Yamaha pianos from Japan to the Young Chang factory in Inchon, South Korea, where Young Chang would perform the final assembly work such as cabinet assembly, stringing, and action installation. This arrangement reduced high import duties. As time went by, Young Chang built more of the components to the point where they were making virtually the entire piano. In 1975 the arrangement between the two companies ended when Young Chang decided to expand domestically and internationally under its own brand name, thus becoming a competitor. Young Chang began exporting to the United States in the late 1970s. In addition to making pianos under its own name, it also made pianos for a time for Baldwin under the Wurlitzer name, for Samsung under the Weber name, and private-label names for large dealer chains and distributors worldwide.

In 1995, in response to rising Korean wages and to supply a growing Chinese domestic market, Young Chang built a 750,000 square foot factory in Tianjin, China and gradually began to move manufacturing operations there for some of its models.

In 2004, Young Chang's Korean rival Samick acquired a controlling interest in the company and began to consolidate the two companies' administrative and distribution functions in North America. A few months later, however, the Korean Fair Trade Commission ruled that the purchase violated Korean anti-monopoly laws and ordered Samick to sell its interest. Naturally, Samick stopped making payments to creditors on Young Chang's behalf, forcing Young Chang into bankruptcy. For a couple of years, while these issues wound their way through the courts, there was a question of which of the two companies was entitled to distribute Young Chang pianos in North America, but the courts finally ruled that Young Chang was a separate entity entitled to distribute its own pianos.

In 2006, Hyundai Development Company purchased Young Chang and is in the process of re-establishing Young Chang's presence in North America. Hyundai Development is a Korean civil engineering and construction company that helped create Hyundai Motor Company. The company says that Hyundai Development has brought the necessary capital for factory renovations and has instituted new quality control systems on a par with automobile manufacturing. Young Chang also owns Kurzweil Music Systems, a manufacturer of professional keyboards and digital pianos.

In 1995 Young Chang employed the services of Joseph Pramberger, a highly respected piano design engineer who had spent much of his professional career as an engineer and manufacturing executive at Steinway & Sons, to evaluate its piano designs and make improvements. The pianos that resulted from this process were known as the "Pramberger Signature Series." The company also produced a completely new line of premium pianos designed by Mr. Pramberger with maple inner rim (grands), upgraded hammers and soundboard material, Renner action parts (grands), and exotic veneers that was called the "Pramberger Platinum Series" and said "Pramberger" on the fallboard instead of "Young Chang."

After Mr. Pramberger died in 2003, his estate terminated its relationship with Young Chang and signed up with Samick. Samick now uses the Pramberger name on a completely different piano design (see "Samick"). Young Chang owns and continues to use the original Pramberger designs. The Pramberger Signature Series is now called the Young Chang Professional Artist Series (PG). The Pramberger Platinum Series is now called the Young Chang Platinum Edition (YP). The PG and YP lines are made in Korea. Pianos made in Young Chang's factory in Tianjin, China are made to Young Chang's original specifications (known as the "Gold" series) and are priced lower than the Korean-made pianos. For many years they bore the name "Bergmann," a name Young Chang is now phasing out.

Following the demise of the Samsung-owned Weber Piano Company, Young Chang reacquired the Weber name and brought out a line of Weber pianos patterned after existing Young Chang pianos and the former Pramberger line. The Weber "Legend" series is made in the Tianjin factory and is like the Young Chang pianos manufactured there. The "Sovereign" series is similar to the Young Chang Professional Artist series, and the "Albert Weber" series is comparable to the Young Chang Platinum Edition.

Quality control in Young Chang's Korean factory has improved little by little over the years, always with the promise that it would one day be as good as Yamaha, but never quite making it. Still, most of the problems are minor ones that can be cured by a good dealer make-ready and a little follow-up service, and the pianos seem to hold up pretty well in the field, even in institutions. The tone of Young Chang pianos used to be bright and sterile, but the work of Joseph Pramberger changed that. He introduced some tonal color and sustain into the pianos he designed. The medium-level pianos are still not exactly what I would call "warm," but with some voicing, they can definitely be made reasonably musical. The Platinum Edition and Albert Weber pianos have greater musical potential and respond well to expert voicing. Pianos from the factory in China, like other pianos from that country, have been uneven in quality, but greatly improving. Young Chang says that Hyundai Development has upgraded the factories in both countries and that the pianos made at the Tianjin factory are now on a par with those made in Korea.

Young Chang also makes "Essex" pianos under contract with Steinway for sale by Steinway dealers. See "Essex" for more information.

Warranty: Young Chang Platinum Edition—Fifteen years, parts and labor, transferable to future owners. Young Chang Professional Artist series—Fifteen years, parts and labor, to original owner. Young Chang Gold series—Ten years, parts and labor, to original owner. Parts are further warranted for the lifetime of the original owner.

MODEL and PRICING GUIDE

This guide contains the "list price" for nearly every brand, model, style, and finish of new piano that has regular distribution in the United States and, for the most part, Canada. Some marginal, local, or "stencil" brands are omitted. Except where indicated, prices are in U.S. dollars and the pianos are assumed to be for sale in the U.S. (Canadians will find the information useful after translation into Canadian dollars, but there may be differences in import duties and sales practices that will affect retail prices.) Prices and specifications are, of course, subject to change. Most manufacturers revise their prices at least once a year; two or three times a year is not uncommon when currency exchange rates are unstable. The prices in this edition were compiled in the spring of 2008.

Note that prices of European pianos vary with the value of the dollar against the Euro. For this Supplement, the exchange rate used by most manufacturers was in the range of Euro = $1.40-1.60. All prices are "landed" prices, i.e., including import duties and estimated costs of freight to the U.S. warehouse or port of entry. However, such costs will vary depending on the shipping method employed, the port of entry, and other variables.

Some terms used in this guide require special explanation and disclaimers:

Style and Finish

Unless otherwise indicated, the cabinet style is assumed to be "traditional" and is not stated. Exactly what "traditional" means varies from brand to brand. In general, it is a "classic" styling with minimal embellishment and straight legs. The vertical pianos have front legs, which are free-standing on smaller verticals and attached to the cabinet with toe blocks on larger verticals, the latter often called "institutional-style." "Continental" or European styling refers to vertical pianos without decorative trim and usually without front legs. Other furniture styles (Chippendale, French Provincial, Queen Anne, etc.) are as noted. The manufacturer's own trademarked style name is used when an appropriate generic name could not be determined.

"Satin" finishes reflect light but not images. "Polished" finishes, also known as "high-gloss" or "high-polish," are mirror-like. "Oiled" finishes are usually matte (not shiny). "Open-pore" finishes, common on some European pianos, are slightly grainier satin finishes due to the wood pores not being filled in prior to finishing. In fact, many finishes labeled "satin" on European pianos are actually open-pore. "Ebony" is a black finish.

Special-order-only styles and finishes are in italics.

Some descriptions of style and finish may be slightly different from the manufacturer's own for the purpose of clarity, consistency, saving space, or other reason.

Size

The height of a vertical piano is measured from the floor to the top of the piano. The length of a grand piano is measured from the very front (keyboard end) to the very back (tail end), usually with the lid closed.

List Price

The list price is usually a starting point for negotiation, not a final sales price. The term "list price," as used in this *Supplement*, is a "standard" or "normalized" list price computed from the published wholesale price according to a formula commonly used in the industry. Some manufacturers use a different formula, however, for their own "manufacturer's suggested retail price" (MSRP), usually one that raises the price above "standard" list by ten to fifty percent so that their dealers can advertise a larger "discount" without losing profit. Because the formula for MSRP varies from one company to another, price-shopping by comparing discounts from the MSRP may result in a faulty price comparison. To provide a level playing field for comparing prices, most prices in this guide are computed according to a uniform "standard" formula, *even though it may differ from the manufacturers' own suggested retail prices*. Where my list prices and those of a manufacturer differ, then, no dishonesty should be inferred; we simply employ different formulas.

To see how this might affect your shopping experience, consider the following scenario: Manufacturer A sells brand A through its dealer A. The wholesale price to the dealer is $1,000, but the manufacturer sets the MSRP at $2,000, doubling the wholesale price. Dealer A offers a 25 percent discount off the MSRP, for a "street price" of $1,500. Manufacturer B sells brand B through its dealer B. The wholesale price to the dealer is also $1,000, but manufacturer B sets the MSRP at $3,000, tripling the wholesale price. Dealer B offers a generous 50 percent discount, for a street price of $1,500. Although the street price is the same for both pianos, a customer shopping at both stores, not knowing anything about the wholesale price or how the MSRP is figured, is likely to come away with the idea that brand B is a more "valuable" piano and that dealer B is offering a more "generous" discount. Other factors aside, which dealer do you think will get the sale?

It's important to note that there is nothing about brand B that makes it deserving of a higher MSRP than brand A—how to compute the MSRP is essentially a marketing decision on the part of the manufacturer. If both these brands had been listed in this *Supplement*, their "list prices" would have been identical—derived from the wholesale price using a formula uniformly applied among brands. This would have enabled the customer to discover that although the MSRPs differed, the underlying value of the pianos, based on the wholesale price, was the same. The formula I use is based on a traditional formula that endeavors to stay close enough to what the customer is likely to actually pay so that the information will be useful (since most customers are, after all, on a budget), while still giving the dealer a little wiggle room to entice the customer with a discount. By agreement with the manufacturers, the formula is confidential so as not to disclose the wholesale prices to the public. However, the actual formula used is not as important as the fact that it is applied uniformly among brands. (In most cases, the formula also includes an allowance for freight, dealer prep, and where applicable, duty to more accurately reflect the dealer's actual costs.)

Turning wholesale prices into standardized list prices is essentially an exercise in arithmetic. Unfortunately, the job is made more difficult by another obstacle. A growing number of companies now issue phony, inflated *wholesale* price lists, specially computed so that when I employ my formula, my "list price" will equal their MSRP. These manufacturers are more than happy to give me their wholesale price lists! Although given enough time and resources I could probably find out what dealers are really paying for each and every model, the size of the piano market and the price of this book will not support such an enterprise and, reluctantly, I must sometimes publish "list prices" that are based on wholesale prices I know or suspect are substantially inflated. Where possible, I make up for it by taking the price inflation into account when I suggest typical "street price" discounts (see below).

Actual Selling or "Street" Price

Buying a piano is something like buying a car—as mentioned above, the list price is deliberately set high in anticipation of negotiating.[*] But sometimes this is carried to extremes, as when the salesperson reduces the price three times in the first fifteen minutes to barely half the sticker price. In situations like this, the customer, understandably confused, is bound to ask in exasperation, "What is the real price of this piano?"

Unfortunately, there is no "real" price. In theory, the dealer pays a wholesale price and then marks it up by an amount sufficient to cover the overhead and produce a profit. In practice, however, the markup can vary considerably from sale to sale depending on such factors as:

- how long the inventory has been sitting around, racking up finance charges for the dealer

- how much of a discount the dealer received at the wholesale level for buying in quantity or for paying cash, or because the wholesale price list itself was artificially inflated

---

[*] A relatively small number of dealers have non-negotiable prices.

- the dealer's cash flow situation

- the ease of comparison shopping in that geographic area

- the competition in that geographic area for a particular brand or type of piano

- special piano sales events taking place in the area

- how the salesperson sizes up your situation and your willingness to pay

- the level of pre- and post-sale service the dealer seeks to provide

- the dealer's other overhead expenses

Keeping in mind that there can be a large variation from one situation to another, here are some discounts from "list price" I typically see for selected brands:

Discounts for Yamaha pianos are usually limited to about twenty percent in most cases. Kawai dealers tend to discount a little more than Yamaha; twenty-five percent off is not uncommon in a competitive environment. Inexpensive Chinese pianos tend to be service intensive and it's not cost-effective to sell them at a steep discount. Some dealers use the least expensive pianos from China as "loss leaders," that is, just to get people into the store, whereupon the customer is sold on a more expensive piano. On the other hand, the wholesale (and therefore retail) prices are sometimes vastly inflated. Therefore, discounts can vary a lot—from ten to thirty percent or more. For example, a dealer of Brodmann pianos—one of the better brands from China—would make a typical piano-dealer profit margin when discounting thirty to forty percent from list. Discounts on other Asian pianos vary a lot, too, from twenty to perhaps thirty percent.

The Boston piano, although manufactured in Asia, is generally viewed as being a little more "exclusive" due to its association with Steinway, so deep discounting is much less likely. Discounts in the range of ten to fifteen percent or so are common. Selling-price information is scarce on Baldwin products because of the company's re-establishment, the sharp trimming of its dealerships, and the move of much of its manufacturing to China. Discounts of twenty-five percent or so are probable on its American-made products.

Western European instruments tend to be extremely expensive here due to their high quality, the high European cost of doing business, additional middlemen/importers and, recently, unfavorable exchange rates. Discounts generally range from twenty-five to thirty percent, but can go as high as forty percent if the piano has gone unsold for an extended period of time. Eastern European brands like Petrof, Bohemia, and Estonia are already seen as being a good deal for the money, so expect moderate discounts of perhaps fifteen to twenty-five percent.

Steinway pianos have always been in a class by themselves, historically the only expensive piano to continually command high profit margins. Except for older

Steinways and the occasional Mason & Hamlin, Steinway has little competition and only about seventy dealers in the United States. Service requirements can be quite high, at least in part because of the higher standards often required to satisfy a fussier clientele. Historically, Steinway pianos have sold at or near full list price. (Some dealers even sell above list!) This is still true in some places, but in recent years I have seen a little more discounting than in the past. Five percent is most common in the largest metropolitan areas (except New York, where there is no discounting). Ten to fifteen percent is not unusual in some less populated areas. As much as twenty percent would be rare, and is usually limited to institutional purchases of larger instruments. Mason & Hamlin pianos are typically sold at discounts of twenty-five percent or more.

For brands not mentioned or implied in the above discussion, it's usually a safe bet to figure a discount of fifteen to twenty-five percent, with greater discounts possible in selected situations. (Note: Remember that the suggested "street price" discounts should be subtracted from the "list prices" in this *Supplement*, not from the manufacturer's suggested retail price.)

For most brands, but not all, the price includes a bench and the standard manufacturer's warranty for that brand. Prices listed here for some European brands do not include a bench, though the dealer will almost always provide a bench and quote a price that includes it. Most dealers will also include moving and one or two tunings in the home, but these are optional and a matter of agreement between you and the dealer.

There is no "fair" price for a piano except the one the buyer and seller agree on. The dealer is no more obligated to sell you a piano at a deep discount than you are obligated to pay the list price. Many dealers are simply not able to sell at the low end of the range consistently and still stay in business. It's understandable that you would like to pay the lowest price possible, and there's no harm in asking, but remember that piano shopping is not just about chasing the lowest price. Be sure you are getting the instrument that best suits your needs and preferences and that the dealer is committed to providing the proper pre- and post-sale service.

For more information on shopping for a new piano and on how to save money, please see pages 60–75 in *The Piano Book* (fourth edition).

Model	Size	Style and Finish	List Price*

Altenburg

Verticals

Model	Size	Style and Finish	List Price
AV108	42½"	Continental Polished Ebony	3,690.
AV108	42½"	Continental Polished Cherry/Mahogany	3,750.
AV110	43"	Classic Polished Ebony	4,090.
AV110	43"	Classic Polished Cherry/Mahogany	4,150.
AV110	43"	Am. Country Oak/Brown Mahogany	4,690.
AV110	43"	French Prov. Cherry/Country French Oak	4,790.
AV115	45"	Polished Ebony	4,290.
AV115	45"	Polished Cherry/Mahogany	4,350.
AV118	46"	Institutional Polished Ebony	4,890.
AV118	46"	Institutional Satin Walnut	4,950.
AV120	48"	Polished Ebony	4,690.
AV120	48"	Polished Mahogany	4,750.
AV132	52"	Classic Polished Ebony	5,790.

Grands

Model	Size	Style and Finish	List Price
AG145	4' 9"	Polished Ebony	8,590.
AG145	4' 9"	Polished Mahogany/White	8,990.
AG160	5' 3"	Polished Ebony	10,580.
AG160	5' 3"	Polished Mahogany/White	10,980.
AG170	5' 7"	Polished Ebony	11,790.
AG170	5' 7"	Polished Mahogany/White	12,190.
AG185	6' 1"	Polished Ebony	13,590.
AG185	6' 1"	Polished Mahogany/White	13,990.
All models		With Round or Curved Legs, add'l	1,000.
All models		Satin Ebony/Mahogany/Cherry, add'l	800.

Astin-Weight

Verticals

Model	Size	Style and Finish	List Price
U-500	50"	Oiled Oak	16,180.
U-500	50"	Santa Fe Oiled Oak	17,580.
U-500	50"	Lacquer Oak	16,580.
U-500	50"	Oiled Walnut	16,780.
U-500	50"	Lacquer Walnut	17,180.

Grands

Model	Size	Style and Finish	List Price
———	5' 9"	Satin Ebony	38,500.

Baldwin

Please see text for special information about Baldwin vertical pianos.

Verticals

Model	Size	Style and Finish	List Price
DHB242	42"	Polished Ebony	6,190.

Model	Size	Style and Finish	List Price*
H110	43"	Polished Ebony	4,140.
H110	43"	Satin Mahogany/Cherry	4,140.
H110	43"	Polished Mahogany	4,140.
H112	44"	Satin Mahogany/Cherry	4,340.
H115	45"	Polished Ebony	4,540.
H115	45"	Satin Mahogany/Walnut	4,540.
H115	45"	Polished Mahogany	4,540.
DHB247	47"	Polished Ebony	6,690.
H121	48"	Polished Ebony	4,740.
H121	48"	Polished Mahogany	4,740.
DHB252	52"	Satin Ebony	7,890.
6000E	52"	Satin Ebony	9,800.

Grands

Model	Size	Style and Finish	List Price*
M1	5' 2"	Satin Ebony	31,806.
M1	5' 2"	Polished Ebony	33,872.
M1	5' 2"	Satin Mahogany/Walnut	34,832.
M1	5' 2"	Polished Mahogany/Walnut/Cherry	36,912.
225E	5' 2"	French Provincial Satin Cherry	41,552.
225E	5' 2"	French Provincial Polished Cherry	43,632.
R1	5' 8"	Satin Ebony	35,706.
R1	5' 8"	Polished Ebony	38,032.
R1	5' 8"	Satin Mahogany/Walnut/Cherry	39,372.
R1	5' 8"	Polished Mahogany/Walnut	41,624.
226E	5' 8"	French Provincial Satin Cherry	46,272.
226E	5' 8"	French Provincial Polished Cherry	48,524.
227E	5' 8"	Louis XVI Satin Mahogany	46,272.
L1	6' 3"	Satin Ebony	40,146.
L1	6' 3"	Polished Ebony	42,588.
L1	6' 3"	Satin Mahogany/Walnut	44,336.
L1	6' 3"	Polished Mahogany/Walnut/Cherry	46,784.
SF10E	7'	Satin Ebony	55,986.
SF10E	7'	Polished Ebony	60,608.
SD10	9'	Satin Ebony	87,636.
SD10	9'	Polished Ebony	99,920.

ConcertMaster (approximate, including installation by factory or dealer)

Grands		ConcertMaster CD	4,000.
		ConcertMaster with Playback only	5,000.
		ConcertMaster with Performance Option	6,000.
		With stop rail, add $1,000	

Note: Discounts may apply, especially as an incentive to purchase the piano.

*For explanation of terms and prices, please see pages 117–121.

Model	Size	Style and Finish	List Price*

Bechstein, (C.)

Models beginning with "A" say only "Bechstein" on the fallboard. Others say "C. Bechstein."

Bechstein Verticals

Model	Size	Style and Finish	List Price
A-3	45½"	Polished Ebony	19,200.
A-3	45½"	Satin Mahogany/Walnut/Cherry	19,200.
A-3	45½"	Polished Mahogany/Walnut/Cherry/White	20,600.
A-3	45½"	Satin Alder/Beech	19,200.
A-2	47½"	Polished Ebony	20,600.
A-2	47½"	Satin Mahogany/Walnut/Cherry/Alder	20,600.
A-2	47½"	Polished Mahogany	24,800.
A-2	47½"	Polished Walnut/Cherry	22,000.
A-2	47½"	Polished White	22,000.
A-2	47½"	Polished Blue	23,600.
A-1	49½"	Polished Ebony	22,000.
A-1	49½"	Satin Mahogany/Walnut/Cherry/Beech	22,000.
A-1	49½"	Polished Mahogany/White	24,000.
A-1	49½"	Polished Walnut/Cherry	24,000.

C. Bechstein Verticals

Model	Size	Style and Finish	List Price
M-116	45½"	Polished Ebony	22,000.
M-116K	45½"	Polished Ebony	25,200.
Balance	45½"	"ProBechstein" Polished Ebony	29,600.
Classic 124	49"	Polished Ebony	33,600.
Classic 124	49"	Satin Walnut/Mahogany/Cherry	33,600.
Classic 124	49"	Polished Walnut/Mahogany/Cherry	35,400.
Elegance 124	49"	Polished Ebony	36,200.
Elegance 124	49"	Satin Walnut/Cherry	36,200.
Elegance 124	49"	Polished Walnut/Mahogany/Cherry	40,000.
Ars Nova	49"	"ProBechstein" Polished Ebony	41,400.
Concert 8	51½"	Polished Ebony	50,800.
Concert 8	51½"	Satin Walnut/Mahogany/Cherry	50,800.
Concert 8	51½"	Polished Walnut/Mahogany	53,200.
Concert 8	51½"	Special Woods	62,600.

Bechstein Grands

Model	Size	Style and Finish	List Price
A-160	5' 3"	Polished Ebony	51,400.
A-160	5' 3"	Polished Mahogany	54,800.
A-160	5' 3"	Polished White	58,200.
A-160	5' 3"	Special Woods	69,600.
A-190	6' 3"	Polished Ebony	61,400.
A-190	6' 3"	Polished Mahogany	64,800.
A-190	6' 3"	Polished White	68,000.
A-190	6' 3"	Special Woods	79,600.
A-208	6' 8"	Polished Ebony	71,400.

Model	Size	Style and Finish	List Price*
A-208	6' 8"	Polished Mahogany	74,600.
A-208	6' 8"	Polished White	78,000.
A-228	7' 5"	Polished Ebony	81,800.

C. Bechstein Grands

Model	Size	Style and Finish	List Price*
L-167	5' 6"	Ebony and Polished Ebony	91,800.
L-167	5' 6"	Satin Mahogany/Walnut/Cherry	91,800.
L-167	5' 6"	Polished Mahogany/Walnut/Cherry/White	97,000.
L-167	5' 6"	Special Woods	109,000.
M/P 192	6' 4"	Satin and Polished Ebony	106,600.
M/P 192	6' 4"	Satin Mahogany/Walnut/Cherry	106,600.
M/P 192	6' 4"	Polished Mahogany/Walnut/Cherry/White	112,200.
M/P 192	6' 4"	Special Woods	125,600.
L, M/P		Classic Finish, add'l	16,200.
L, M/P		Chippendale, add'l	14,900.
B-210	6' 11"	Satin and Polished Ebony	127,200.
C-234	7' 8"	Polished Ebony	159,600.
B, C		Classic Finish, add'l	18,200.
D-280	9' 2"	Polished Ebony	207,600.

Blüthner

Prices do not include bench.

Verticals

Model	Size	Style and Finish	List Price*
I	45"	Satin and Polished Ebony	25,666.
I	45"	Satin and Polished Walnut	27,026.
I	45"	Satin and Polished Mahogany	26,888.
I	45"	Satin and Polished Cherry	26,888.
I	45"	Satin and Polished White	27,026.
C	46"	Satin and Polished Ebony	27,140.
C	46"	Satin and Polished Walnut	28,704.
C	46"	Satin and Polished Mahogany	28,440.
C	46"	Satin and Polished Cherry	28,576.
C	46"	Satin and Polished White	28,704.
C	46"	Satin/Polished Bubinga/Yew/Rosewd/Macassar	30,302.
C	46"	Saxony Polished Pyramid Mahogany	35,798.
C	46"	Polished Burl Walnut/Camphor Polish	36,154.
A	49"	Satin and Polished Ebony	34,570.
A	49"	Satin and Polished Walnut	36,560.
A	49"	Satin and Polished Mahogany	36,214.
A	49"	Satin and Polished Cherry	36,386.
A	49"	Satin and Polished White	36,560.
A	49"	Satin/Polished Bubinga/Yew/RosewdMacassar	38,582.
A	49"	Saxony Polished Pyramid Mahogany	45,598.
A	49"	Polished Burl Walnut/Camphor Polish	46,046.

*For explanation of terms and prices, please see pages 117–121.

Model	Size	Style and Finish	List Price*

Blüthner (continued)

Model	Size	Style and Finish	List Price*
B	52"	Satin and Polished Ebony	39,468.
B	52"	Satin and Polished Walnut	41,744.
B	52"	Satin and Polished Mahogany	41,354.
B	52"	Satin and Polished Cherry	41,550.
B	52"	Satin and Polished White	41,744.
B	52"	Satin/Polished Bubinga/Yew/RosewdMacassar	44,058.
B	52"	Saxony Polished Pyramid Mahogany	52,070.
B	52"	Polished Burl Walnut/Camphor Polish	52,566.
—	—	*Sostenuto pedal on vertical piano, add'l*	2,680.

Grands

Model	Size	Style and Finish	List Price*
11	5' 1"	Satin and Polished Ebony	69,988.
11	5' 1"	Satin and Polished Walnut	74,038.
11	5' 1"	Satin and Polished Mahogany	73,324.
11	5' 1"	Satin and Polished Cherry	73,680.
11	5' 1"	Satin and Polished White	74,038.
11	5' 1"	Satin/Polished Bubinga/Yew/Rosewd/Macassar	78,132.
11	5' 1"	Saxony Polished Pyramid Mahogany	92,334.
11	5' 1"	Polished Burl Walnut /Camphor Polish	93,232.
11	5' 1"	"President" Polished Ebony	78,132.
11	5' 1"	"President" Polished Mahogany	81,258.
11	5' 1"	"President" Polished Walnut	82,042.
11	5' 1"	"President" Polished Bubinga	85,946.
11	5' 1"	Louis XVI Satin and Polished Ebony	81,684.
11	5' 1"	Louis XVI Satin and Polished Mahogany	85,768.
11	5' 1"	Louis XVI Satin and Polished Walnut	84,950.
11	5' 1"	"Kaiser Wilhelm II" Polished Ebony	82,396.
11	5' 1"	"Kaiser Wilhelm II" Polished Mahogany	85,686.
11	5' 1"	"Kaiser Wilhelm II" Polished Walnut	86,514.
11	5' 1"	"Kaiser Wilhelm II" Polished Cherry	86,100.
11	5' 1"	"Ambassador" Satin East Indian Rosewood	95,886.
11	5' 1"	"Ambassador" Satin Walnut	88,790.
11	5' 1"	"Nicolas II" Satin Walnut with Burl Inlay	95,886.
11	5' 1"	Louis XIV Rococo Satin White with Gold	102,994.
11	5' 1"	"Alexandra" Polished Ebony	79,556.
11	5' 1"	"Alexandra" Polished Mahogany	83,526.
11	5' 1"	"Alexandra" Polished Walnut	82,732.
11	5' 1"	Julius Blüthner Edition	95,886.
10	5' 5"	Satin and Polished Ebony	80,672.
10	5' 5"	Satin and Polished Walnut	85,342.
10	5' 5"	Satin and Polished Mahogany	84,526.
10	5' 5"	Satin and Polished Cherry	84,940.
10	5' 5"	Satin and Polished White	85,342.
10	5' 5"	Satin/Polished Bubinga/Yew/Rosewd Macassar	90,068.

Model	Size	Style and Finish	List Price*
10	5' 5"	Saxony Polished Pyramid Mahogany	106,444.
10	5' 5"	Polished Burl Walnut/Camphor Polish	107,468.
10	5' 5"	"President" Polished Ebony	90,068.
10	5' 5"	"President" Polished Mahogany	93,666.
10	5' 5"	"President" Polished Walnut	94,576.
10	5' 5"	"President" Polished Bubinga	99,072.
10	5' 5"	"Senator" French Satin Walnut with Leather	98,256.
10	5' 5"	"Senator" Jacaranda Satin Rosewood w/Leather	104,810.
10	5' 5"	Louis XVI Satin and Polished Ebony	94,164.
10	5' 5"	Louis XVI Satin and Polished Mahogany	98,878.
10	5' 5"	Louis XVI Satin and Polished Walnut	97,934.
10	5' 5"	"Kaiser Wilhelm II" Polished Ebony	94,980.
10	5' 5"	"Kaiser Wilhelm II" Polished Mahogany	98,784.
10	5' 5"	"Kaiser Wilhelm II" Polished Walnut	99,728.
10	5' 5"	"Kaiser Wilhelm II" Polished Cherry	99,256.
10	5' 5"	"Ambassador" Satin East Indian Rosewood	110,538.
10	5' 5"	"Ambassador" Satin Walnut	102,350.
10	5' 5"	"Nicolas II" Satin Walnut with Burl Inlay	110,538.
10	5' 5"	Louis XIV Rococo Satin White with Gold	118,738.
10	5' 5"	"Alexandra" Polished Ebony	91,702.
10	5' 5"	"Alexandra" Polished Mahogany	96,290.
10	5' 5"	"Alexandra" Polished Walnut	95,370.
10	5' 5"	Julius Blüthner Edition	95,886.
6	6' 3"	Satin and Polished Ebony	87,998.
6	6' 3"	Satin and Polished Walnut	93,082.
6	6' 3"	Satin and Polished Mahogany	92,196.
6	6' 3"	Satin and Polished Cherry	92,644.
6	6' 3"	Satin and Polished White	93,082.
6	6' 3"	Satin/Polished Bubinga/Yew/RosewdMacassar	98,244.
6	6' 3"	Saxony Polished Pyramid Mahogany	116,104.
6	6' 3"	Polished Burl Walnut/Camphor Polish	117,218.
6	6' 3"	"President" Polished Ebony	98,244.
6	6' 3"	"President" Polished Mahogany	102,166.
6	6' 3"	"President" Polished Walnut	103,144.
6	6' 3"	"President" Polished Bubinga	108,054.
6	6' 3"	"Senator" French Satin Walnut with Leather	107,168.
6	6' 3"	"Senator" Jacaranda Satin Rosewood w/Leather	114,310.
6	6' 3"	Louis XVI Satin and Polished Ebony	102,706.
6	6' 3"	Louis XVI Satin and Polished Mahogany	107,836.
6	6' 3"	Louis XVI Satin and Polished Walnut	106,812.
6	6' 3"	"Kaiser Wilhelm II" Polished Ebony	103,592.
6	6' 3"	"Kaiser Wilhelm II" Polished Mahogany	107,734.
6	6' 3"	"Kaiser Wilhelm II" Polished Walnut	108,778.
6	6' 3"	"Kaiser Wilhelm II" Polished Cherry	108,260.
6	6' 3"	"Ambassador" Satin East Indian Rosewood	120,566.

*For explanation of terms and prices, please see pages 117–121.

Model	Size	Style and Finish	List Price*

Blüthner (continued)

Model	Size	Style and Finish	List Price*
6	6' 3"	"Ambassador" Satin Walnut	111,630.
6	6' 3"	"Nicolas II" Satin Walnut with Burl Inlay	120,566.
6	6' 3"	Louis XIV Rococo Satin White with Gold	129,490.
6	6' 3"	"Alexandra" Polished Ebony	100,016.
6	6' 3"	"Alexandra" Polished Mahogany	105,030.
6	6' 3"	"Alexandra" Polished Walnut	104,030.
6	6' 3"	Julius Blüthner Edition	120,566.
6	6' 3"	*Jubilee Edition Plate, add'l*	5,980.
4	6' 10"	Satin and Polished Ebony	104,362.
4	6' 10"	Satin and Polished Walnut	110,400.
4	6' 10"	Satin and Polished Mahogany	109,354.
4	6' 10"	Satin and Polished Cherry	109,872.
4	6' 10"	Satin and Polished White	110,400.
4	6' 10"	Satin/Polished Bubinga/Yew/Rosewd/Macassar	116,518.
4	6' 10"	Saxony Polished Pyramid Mahogany	137,690.
4	6' 10"	Polished Burl Walnut/Camphor Polish	139,024.
4	6' 10"	"President" Polished Ebony	116,518.
4	6' 10"	"President" Polished Mahogany	121,176.
4	6' 10"	"President" Polished Walnut	122,336.
4	6' 10"	"President" Polished Bubinga	128,166.
4	6' 10"	"Kaiser Wilhelm II" Polished Ebony	122,866.
4	6' 10"	"Kaiser Wilhelm II" Polished Mahogany	127,788.
4	6' 10"	"Kaiser Wilhelm II" Polished Wainut	129,018.
4	6' 10"	"Kaiser Wilhelm II" Polished Cherry	128,398.
4	6' 10"	"Ambassador" Satin East Indian Rosewood	142,992.
4	6' 10"	"Ambassador" Satin Walnut	132,412.
4	6' 10"	"Alexandra" Polished Ebony	118,634.
4	6' 10"	"Alexandra" Polished Mahogany	124,568.
4	6' 10"	"Alexandra" Polished Walnut	123,372.
4	6' 10"	Julius Blüthner Edition	142,992.
2	7' 8"	Satin and Polished Ebony	116,644.
2	7' 8"	Satin and Polished Walnut	123,394.
2	7' 8"	Satin and Polished Mahogany	122,210.
2	7' 8"	Satin and Polished Cherry	122,808.
2	7' 8"	Satin and Polished White	123,396.
2	7' 8"	Satin/Polished Bubinga/Yew/Rosewd/Macassar	130,226.
2	7' 8"	Saxony Polished Pyramid Mahogany	153,904.
2	7' 8"	Polished Burl Walnut/Camphor Polish	155,388.
2	7' 8"	"President" Polished Ebony	130,226.
2	7' 8"	"President" Polished Mahogany	135,422.
2	7' 8"	"President" Polished Walnut	136,734.
2	7' 8"	"President" Polished Bubinga	143,244.
2	7' 8"	"Kaiser Wilhelm II" Polished Ebony	137,332.

Model	Size	Style and Finish	List Price*
2	7' 8"	"Kaiser Wilhelm II" Polished Mahogany	142,820.
2	7' 8"	"Kaiser Wilhelm II" Polished Walnut	144,186.
2	7' 8"	"Kaiser Wilhelm II" Polished Cherry	143,508.
2	7' 8"	"Ambassador" Satin East Indian Rosewood	159,816.
2	7' 8"	"Ambassador" Satin Walnut	147,982.
2	7' 8"	Julius Blüthner Edition	159,816.
2	7' 8"	"Queen Victoria" JB Edition Polished Rosewood	184,552.
1	9' 2"	Satin and Polished Ebony	150,420.
1	9' 2"	Satin and Polished Walnut	159,126.
1	9' 2"	Satin and Polished Mahogany	157,608.
1	9' 2"	Satin and Polished Cherry	158,378.
1	9' 2"	Satin and Polished White	159,126.
1	9' 2"	"President" Polished Ebony	167,924.
1	9' 2"	"President" Polished Mahogany	174,662.
1	9' 2"	"President" Polished Walnut	176,318.
1	9' 2"	"President" Polished Bubinga	184,724.
1	9' 2"	Julius Blüthner Edition	190,658.
1	9' 2"	"Queen Victoria" JB Edition Polished Rosewood	215,832.

Bohemia

Adjustable Artist Bench included with all pianos.

Verticals

122A	48"	Demi-Chippendale Satin and Polished Ebony	11,460.
122A	48"	Demi-Chippendale Satin Walnut/Mahogany	12,500.
122A	48"	Demi-Chippendale Polished Walnut/Mahogany	12,500.
122A	48"	Demi-Chippendale Polished Pomele	13,680.
122A	48"	Chippendale Satin Walnut/Mahogany	13,620.
122A	48"	Chippendale Polished Walnut/Mahogany	13,620.
122A	48"	"Romance" Satin Ebony with Mahogany Oval	12,940.
123A	48"	"Exclusive" Satin and Polished Ebony	10,920.
123A	48"	"Exclusive" Open-pore Wal./Mahogany/Cherry	10,820.
123A	48"	"Exclusive" Satin and Polished Wal./Mahogany	11,940.
123A	48"	"Exclusive" Polished Pomele	13,060.
123A	48"	"Exclusive" Polished White	11,940.
122A-123A	48"	With Bohemia/Renner Action, add'l	1,100.
122A-123A	48"	With Full Renner Action, add'l	2,100.
125A	49"	"Professional" Satin and Polished Ebony	12,240.
125A	49"	"Professional" Satin and Polished Wal./Mahog.	14,480.
125A	49"	"Professional" Polished Pomele	14,640.
125A	49"	"Professional" Polished White	13,380.
125A-BR	49"	125A with Bohemia/Renner Action, add'l	1,200.
132	52"	"Concerto" Satin and Polished Ebony	13,880.
132	52"	"Concerto" Polished Mahogany	15,180.

*For explanation of terms and prices, please see pages 117–121.

Model	Size	Style and Finish	List Price*

Bohemia (continued)

Model	Size	Style and Finish	List Price*
132BR	52"	132 with Bohemia/Renner Action, add'l	1,400.

Grands

Model	Size	Style and Finish	List Price*
156A-B	5' 2"	"Martinu" Satin and Polished Ebony	33,380.
156A-B	5' 2"	"Martinu" Satin and Polished Wal./Mahogany	36,640.
156A-B	5' 2"	"Martinu" Hand-Rub. Satin Ebony/Wal./Mahog.	38,640.
156A-B	5' 2"	"Martinu" Polished Pomele	38,600.
156A-B	5' 2"	"Martinu" Polished White	36,640.
156A-B	5' 2"	Demi-Chip. Satin and Pol. Walnut/Mahogany	40,220.
156A-B	5' 2"	Chippendale Satin and Pol. Walnut/Mahogany	42,020.
156A-BR	5' 2"	156A-B with Bohemia/Renner Action, add'l	2,000.
173-B	5' 8"	"Mahler" Satin and Polished Ebony	36,560.
173-B	5' 8"	"Mahler" Satin and Polished Wal./Mahog.	40,140.
173-B	5' 8"	"Mahler" Hand-Rub. Satin Ebony/Wal./Mahog.	42,140.
173-B	5' 8"	Demi-Chip. Satin and Pol. Walnut/Mahogany	44,080.
173-B	5' 8"	Chippendale Satin and Pol. Walnut/Mahogany	46,040.
185A-B	6' 1"	"Janacek" Satin and Polished Ebony	39,740.
185A-B	6' 1"	"Janacek" Satin and Polished Walnut/Mahogany	43,640.
185A-B	6' 1"	"Janacek" Hand-Rub. Satin Ebony/Wal./Mahog.	47,280.
185A-B	6' 1"	"Janacek" Polished White	43,640.
185A-BR	6' 1"	185A-B with Bohemia/Renner Action, add'l	2,000.
185AE-B	6' 1"	"Empire" Satin and Polished Ebony	43,700.
185AE-B	6' 1"	"Empire" Satin and Polished Walnut/Mahogany	47,980.
185AE-BR	6' 1"	185AE-B w/ Bohemia/Renner Action, add'l	2,000.
225R	7' 4"	"Smetana" Satin and Pol. Ebony (Full Renner)	59,460.
272R	8' 11"	"Dvorak" Satin and Pol. Ebony (Full Renner)	100,600.

Bösendorfer

Verticals

Model	Size	Style and Finish	List Price*
130	52"	Satin and Polished Ebony	53,576.
130	52"	Satin and Polished White, other colors	57,594.
130	52"	Polished, Satin, Open-pore: Walnut, Cherry, Mahogany, Pomele, Bubinga, Wenge	58,934.
130	52"	Polished , Satin, Open-pore: Pyramid Mahogany, Amboyna, Rio Rosewood, Burl Walnut, Birdseye Maple, Yew, Macassar	61,614.

Grands

Model	Size	Style and Finish	List Price*
170	5' 8"	Satin and Polished Ebony	93,530.
170	5' 8"	Satin and Polished White, other colors	100,546.
170	5' 8"	Polished, Satin, Open-pore: Walnut, Cherry, Mahogany, Pomele, Bubinga, Wenge	102,884.
170	5' 8"	Polished, Satin, Open-pore: Pyramid Mahogany, Amboyna, Rio Rosewood, Burl Walnut, Birdseye Maple, Yew, Macassar	107,560.

Model	Size	Style and Finish	List Price*
170	5' 8"	"Johann Strauss" Satin and Polished Ebony	101,106.
170	5' 8"	"Johann Strauss," other finish	119,812.
170	5' 8"	"Franz Schubert" Satin and Polished Ebony	101,106.
170	5' 8"	"Franz Schubert," other finish	119,812.
170	5' 8"	"Vienna"	149,070.
170	5' 8"	"Senator"	112,236.
170	5' 8"	"Chopin"	136,822.
170	5' 8"	"Liszt"	119,812.
170	5' 8"	"Yacht"	123,460.
170	5' 8"	"Artisan," Satin and Polished	173,032.
170	5' 8"	"Edge"	101,014.
170	5' 8"	Baroque	128,138.
170	5' 8"	Louis XVI	128,138.
170	5' 8"	180th Anniversary Special Edition	98,208.
185	6' 1"	Satin and Polished Ebony	95,920.
185	6' 1"	Satin and Polished White, other colors	103,114.
185	6' 1"	Polished, Satin, Open-pore: Walnut, Cherry, Mahogany, Pomele, Bubinga, Wenge	105,512.
185	6' 1"	Polished, Satin, Open-pore: Pyramid Mahogany, Amboyna, Rio Rosewood, Burl Walnut, Birdseye Maple, Yew, Macassar	110,308.
185	6' 1"	"Johann Strauss" Satin and Polished Ebony	103,688.
185	6' 1"	"Johann Strauss," other finish	122,872.
185	6' 1"	"Franz Schubert" Satin and Polished Ebony	103,688.
185	6' 1"	"Franz Schubert," other finish	122,872.
185	6' 1"	"Vienna"	149,084.
185	6' 1"	"Senator"	115,104.
185	6' 1"	"Chopin"	140,098.
185	6' 1"	"Porsche Design," Satin and Polished	141,210.
185	6' 1"	"Porsche Design," Polished Colors	150,976.
185	6' 1"	"Liszt"	122,872.
185	6' 1"	"Yacht"	126,614.
185	6' 1"	"Artisan," Satin and Polished	177,450.
185	6' 1"	"Edge"	103,592.
185	6' 1"	Baroque	131,410.
185	6' 1"	Louis XVI	131,410.
185	6' 1"	180th Anniversary Special Edition	100,716.
200CS	6' 7"	"Conservatory" Satin Ebony	86,456.
200	6' 7"	Satin and Polished Ebony	105,786.
200	6' 7"	Satin and Polished White, other colors	113,720.
200	6' 7"	Polished, Satin, Open-pore: Walnut, Cherry, Mahogany, Pomele, Bubinga, Wenge	116,366.
200	6' 7"	Polished, Satin, Open-pore: Pyramid Mahogany, Amboyna, Rio Rosewood, Burl Walnut, Birdseye Maple, Yew, Macassar	121,654.

*For explanation of terms and prices, please see pages 117–121.

Model	Size	Style and Finish	List Price*

Bösendorfer (continued)

Model	Size	Style and Finish	List Price*
200	6' 7"	"Johann Strauss" Satin and Polished Ebony	114,356.
200	6' 7"	"Johann Strauss," other finish	135,512.
200	6' 7"	"Franz Schubert" Satin and Polished Ebony	114,356.
200	6' 7"	"Franz Schubert," other finish	135,512.
200	6' 7"	"Vienna"	155,032.
200	6' 7"	"Senator"	126,944.
200	6' 7"	"Chopin"	152,026.
200	6' 7"	"Liszt"	135,512.
200	6' 7"	"Yacht"	139,638.
200	6' 7"	"Artisan," Satin and Polished	195,706.
200	6' 7"	"Edge"	114,250.
200	6' 7"	Baroque	144,928.
200	6' 7"	Louis XVI	144,928.
200	6' 7"	180th Anniversary Special Edition	111,076.
214CS	7'	"Conservatory" Satin Ebony	94,274.
214	7'	Satin and Polished Ebony	123,226.
214	7'	Satin and Polished White, other colors	132,468.
214	7'	Polished, Satin, Open-pore: Walnut, Cherry, Mahogany, Pomele, Bubinga, Wenge	135,550.
214	7'	Polished, Satin, Open-pore: Pyramid Mahogany, Amboyna, Rio Rosewood, Burl Walnut, Birdseye Maple, Yew, Macassar	141,710.
214	7'	"Johann Strauss" Satin and Polished Ebony	133,208.
214	7'	"Johann Strauss," other finish	157,854.
214	7'	"Franz Schubert" Satin and Polished Ebony	133,208.
214	7'	"Franz Schubert," other finish	157,854.
214	7'	"Vienna"	173,750.
214	7'	"Senator"	147,872.
214	7'	"Chopin"	169,780.
214	7'	"Porsche Design," Satin and Polished	172,518.
214	7'	"Porsche Design," Polished Colors	181,144.
214	7'	"Liszt"	157,854.
214	7'	"Yacht"	162,660.
214	7'	"Artisan," Satin and Polished	227,970.
214	7'	"Edge"	133,084.
214	7'	Baroque	168,820.
214	7'	Louis XVI	168,820.
214	7'	180th Anniversary Special Edition	129,388.
225	7' 4"	Satin and Polished Ebony	129,192.
225	7' 4"	Satin and Polished White, other colors	138,882.
225	7' 4"	Polished, Satin, Open-pore: Walnut, Cherry, Mahogany, Pomele, Bubinga, Wenge	142,112.
225	7' 4"	Polished, Satin, Open-pore: Pyramid Mahogany, Amboyna, Rio Rosewood, Burl Walnut, Birdseye	148,572.

Model	Size	Style and Finish	List Price*
		Maple, Yew, Macassar	
225	7' 4"	"Johann Strauss" Satin and Polished Ebony	139,658.
225	7' 4"	"Johann Strauss," other finish	165,496.
225	7' 4"	"Franz Schubert" Satin and Polished Ebony	139,658.
225	7' 4"	"Franz Schubert," other finish	165,496.
225	7' 4"	"Vienna"	182,162.
225	7' 4"	"Senator"	155,032.
225	7' 4"	"Chopin"	180,740.
225	7' 4"	"Liszt"	165,496.
225	7' 4"	"Yacht"	170,534.
225	7' 4"	"Artisan," Satin and Polished	239,006.
225	7' 4"	"Edge"	139,528.
225	7' 4"	Baroque	176,994.
225	7' 4"	Louis XVI	176,994.
225	7' 4"	180th Anniversary Special Edition	135,652.
280	9' 2"	Satin and Polished Ebony	167,514.
280	9' 2"	Satin and Polished White, other colors	180,078.
280	9' 2"	Polished, Satin, Open-pore: Walnut, Cherry, Mahogany, Pomele, Bubinga, Wenge	184,266.
280	9' 2"	Polished, Satin, Open-pore: Pyramid Mahogany, Amboyna, Rio Rosewood, Burl Walnut, Birdseye Maple, Yew, Macassar	192,642.
280	9' 2"	"Johann Strauss" Satin and Polished Ebony	181,084.
280	9' 2"	"Johann Strauss," other finish	214,586.
280	9' 2"	"Franz Schubert" Satin and Polished Ebony	181,084.
280	9' 2"	"Franz Schubert," other finish	214,586.
280	9' 2"	"Vienna"	236,196.
280	9' 2"	"Senator"	201,018.
280	9' 2"	"Chopin"	232,680.
280	9' 2"	"Porsche Design," Satin and Polished	234,520.
280	9' 2"	"Porsche Design," Polished Colors	246,246.
280	9' 2"	"Liszt"	214,586.
280	9' 2"	"Yacht"	221,120.
280	9' 2"	"Artisan," Satin and Polished	265,632.
280	9' 2"	Baroque	229,496.
280	9' 2"	Louis XVI	229,496.
280	9' 2"	180th Anniversary Special Edition	175,890.
290	9' 6"	Satin and Polished Ebony	190,462.
290	9' 6"	Satin and Polished White, other colors	204,746.
290	9' 6"	Polished, Satin, Open-pore: Walnut, Cherry, Mahogany, Pomele, Bubinga, Wenge	209,508.
290	9' 6"	Polished, Satin, Open-pore: Pyramid Mahogany, Amboyna, Rio Rosewood, Burl Walnut, Birdseye Maple, Yew, Macassar	219,032.
290	9' 6"	"Johann Strauss" Satin and Polished Ebony	205,890.

*For explanation of terms and prices, please see pages 117–121.

Model	Size	Style and Finish	List Price*

Bösendorfer (continued)

Model	Size	Style and Finish	List Price*
290	9' 6"	"Johann Strauss," other finish	243,982.
290	9' 6"	"Franz Schubert" Satin and Polished Ebony	205,890.
290	9' 6"	"Franz Schubert," other finish	243,982.
290	9' 6"	"Vienna"	268,552.
290	9' 6"	"Senator"	228,554.
290	9' 6"	"Chopin"	262,312.
290	9' 6"	"Liszt"	243,982.
290	9' 6"	"Yacht"	251,410.
290	9' 6"	"Artisan," Satin and Polished	280,512.
290	9' 6"	Baroque	260,932.
290	9' 6"	Louis XVI	260,932.
290	9' 6"	180th Anniversary Special Edition	199,986.
170–280	5' 8"–9' 2"	"CEUS" Computer Grand, add'l	63,858.
290	9' 6"	"CEUS" Computer Grand, add'l	70,388.

Boston

Verticals

Model	Size	Style and Finish	List Price*
UP-118E	46"	Satin and Polished Ebony	10,620.
UP-118E	46"	Satin Walnut	11,790.
UP-118E	46"	Polished Walnut/Mahogany	12,020.
UP-118E	46"	Polished White	11,860.
UP-118A	46"	Art Deco Satin Aniegre	8,790.
UP-118S	46"	Open-Pore Honey Oak/Black Oak/Red Oak	6,940.
UP-118S	46"	Satin Mahogany	8,400.
UP-126E	50"	Satin and Polished Ebony	12,720.
UP-126E	50"	Polished Mahogany	14,560.
UP-132E	52"	Polished Ebony	13,900.

Grands

Model	Size	Style and Finish	List Price*
GP-156	5' 1"	Satin and Polished Ebony	17,990.
GP-163	5' 4"	Satin Ebony	21,340.
GP-163	5' 4"	Polished Ebony	21,900.
GP-163	5' 4"	Satin Mahogany	23,280.
GP-163	5' 4"	Polished Mahogany	23,900.
GP-163	5' 4"	Satin Walnut	23,480.
GP-163	5' 4"	Polished Walnut	24,160.
GP-163	5' 4"	Polished White/Ivory	22,480.
GP-178	5' 10"	Satin Ebony	24,500.
GP-178	5' 10"	Polished Ebony	25,100.
GP-178	5' 10"	Satin Mahogany	26,140.
GP-178	5' 10"	Polished Mahogany	26,840.
GP-178	5' 10"	Satin Walnut	26,440.
GP-178	5' 10"	Polished Walnut	27,320.

Model	Size	Style and Finish	List Price*
GP-178	5' 10"	Polished White/Ivory	25,620.
GP-193	6' 4"	Satin Ebony	30,920.
GP-193	6' 4"	Polished Ebony	31,700.
GP-193	6' 4"	Satin Walnut	34,360.
GP-193	6' 4"	Polished Mahogany	34,600.
GP-193	6' 4"	Polished White	33,320.
GP-215	7' 1"	Satin Ebony	39,720.
GP-215	7' 1"	Polished Ebony	40,700.

Brodmann

Verticals

PE 116	45"	Polished Ebony	6,990.
PE 121	47"	Polished Ebony	7,690.
PE 123C	48"	Italian Provincial Satin Cherry	8,590.
PE 123M	48"	French Provincial Satin Mahogany	8,590.
PE 123W	48"	Satin Walnut	8,590.
PE 125	49"	Polished Ebony	8,390.
PE 128	50"	Polished Ebony	9,490.
PE 132	52"	Polished Ebony	9,990.

Grands

PE 150	4' 11"	Polished Ebony	17,970.
PE 162	5' 4"	Polished Ebony	20,970.
PE 187	6' 2"	Polished Ebony	24,970.
PE 212	7'	Polished Ebony	31,970.
PE 228	7' 5"	Polished Ebony	39,970.
PE 228R	7' 5"	With Renner Action, add'l	10,000.

Cable, Hobart M. — see "Sejung"

Cable-Nelson

Verticals

CN 116	45"	Polished Ebony	3,995.
CN 216	45"	Satin Walnut	4,190.

Grands

CN 151	4' 11"	Polished Ebony	10,190.
CN 161	5' 3"	Polished Ebony	13,790.

Chase, A. B.

Verticals

EV-112	44"	Continental Polished Ebony	4,380.
EV-112	44"	Continental Polished Mahogany	4,500.

*For explanation of terms and prices, please see pages 117–121.

Model	Size	Style and Finish	List Price*

Chase, A. B. (continued)

EV-113	45"	Polished Ebony	4,580.
EV-113	45"	Polished Mahogany	4,700.
EV-121	48"	Polished Ebony	4,980.
EV-121	48"	Polished Mahogany	5,100.

Grands

EV-152	5'	Polished Ebony	11,580.
EV-152	5'	Polished Mahogany	12,080.
EV-165	5' 5"	Polished Ebony	12,380.
EV-165	5' 5"	Polished Mahogany	12,880.
EV-185	6' 1"	Polished Ebony	14,380.

Conover Cable — see "Samick"

Cristofori

Verticals

CRV425	42½"	Continental Satin Ebony	3,698.
CRV425	42½"	Continental Polished Ebony	3,498.
CRV425	42½"	Continental Polished Mahogany	3,698.
CRV430	43"	French Provincial Satin Cherry	4,398.
CRV430	43"	Mediterranean Satin Oak	4,398.
CRV430	43"	Satin Cherry	4,398.
CRV450S	45"	Satin Ebony	4,698.
CRV450S	45"	Satin Walnut	4,598.
CRV450S	45"	Satin Oak	4,698.
CRV465	46½"	Satin Ebony	4,798.
CRV465	46½"	Polished Ebony	4,598.
CRV465	46½"	Satin/Polished Mahogany	4,798.
CRV480	48"	Satin Ebony	5,798.
CRV480	48"	Polished Ebony	5,598.
CRV480	48"	Polished Mahogany	5,798.
CRV480L	48"	Satin Ebony	5,698.
CRV480L	48"	Polished Ebony	5,498.
CRV480L	48"	Polished Mahogany	5,698.

Grands

CRG48	4' 8"	Polished Ebony	7,398.
CRG48	4' 8"	Polished Mahogany	7,798.
CRG410	4' 10"	Satin Ebony	8,498.
CRG410	4' 10"	Polished Ebony	8,198.
CRG410	4' 10"	Polished Mahogany	8,598.
CRG410	4' 10"	French Provincial Satin Cherry	8,998.
CRG53	5' 3"	Satin Ebony	10,298.

Model	Size	Style and Finish	List Price*
CRG53	5' 3"	Polished Ebony	9,998.
CRG53	5' 3"	Satin Walnut/Mahogany	10,398.
CRG53	5' 3"	Polished Walnut/Mahogany	10,398.
CRG53	5' 3"	French Provincial Satin Cherry	10,798.
CRG53	5' 3"	Polished Bubinga	10,798.
CRG53	5' 3"	Polished White	10,398.
CRG53L	5' 3"	Satin Ebony	10,098.
CRG53L	5' 3"	Polished Ebony	9,798.
CRG53L	5' 3"	Polished Mahogany	10,198.
CRG53L	5' 3"	Polished Bubinga	10,598.
CRG57	5' 7"	Satin Ebony	11,098.
CRG57	5' 7"	Polished Ebony	10,798.
CRG57	5' 7"	Satin Walnut/Mahogany	11,198.
CRG57	5' 7"	Polished Walnut/Mahogany	11,198.
CRG57	5' 7"	French Provincial Satin Cherry	11,598.
CRG57	5' 7"	Polished Bubinga	11,598.
CRG57	5' 7"	Polished White	11,198.
CRG57L	5' 7"	Satin Ebony	10,898.
CRG57L	5' 7"	Polished Ebony	10,598.
CRG57L	5' 7"	Polished Mahogany	10.998.
CRG57L	5' 7"	Polished Bubinga	11,398.
CRG62	6' 2"	Satin Ebony	12,498.
CRG62	6' 2"	Polished Ebony	12,198.
CRG62	6' 2"	Polished Mahogany	12,598.
CRG62L	6' 2"	Polished Ebony	11,998.

Disklavier — see "Yamaha"

Ebel, Carl

Verticals

115	45"	Polished Ebony	5,990.
115	45"	Polished Mahogany/Walnut/Oak	6,190.
121	48"	Polished Ebony	6,350.
121	48"	Polished Mahogany/Walnut	6,580.

Grands

G-151	4' 11½"	Polished Ebony	11,790.
G-151	4' 11½"	Polished Mahogany/Walnut/Oak/White	12,290.
G-151	4' 11½"	Satin Finishes	12,290.
G-151	4' 11½"	Polished Ebony (round leg)	12,090.
G-151	4' 11½"	Polished Mahogany/Walnut (round leg)	12,590.
G-151	4' 11½"	Satin Finishes (round leg)	12,590.
G-151	4' 11½"	Polished Ebony (curved leg)	12,090.
G-151	4' 11½"	Polished Mahogany/Walnut (curved leg)	12,590.

*For explanation of terms and prices, please see pages 117–121.

Model	Size	Style and Finish	List Price*

Ebel, Carl (continued)

Model	Size	Style and Finish	List Price
G-151	4' 11½"	Satin Finishes (curved leg)	12,590.
G-151	4' 11½"	Ebony w/Sapele Fallboard Front	12,290.
G-151	4' 11½"	Ebony w/Bubinga Fallbrd. & Lid Underside	14,290.
G-151	4' 11½"	Ebony w/Sapele Fallboard & Lid Underside	12,590.

Essex

Verticals

Model	Size	Style and Finish	List Price
EUP-108C	42"	Continental Polished Ebony	4,570.
EUP-111E	44"	Polished Ebony	4,910.
EUP-111E	44"	Polished Sapele Mahogany	5,010.
EUP-111E	44"	Polished Walnut	5,030.
EUP-111E	44"	Polished White	4,940.
EUP-111F	44"	French Provincial Satin Cherry	5,050.
EUP-111M	44"	Modern Satin Walnut	4,870.
EUP-111R	44"	English Regency Satin Sapele Mahogany	4,770.
EUP-111T	44"	Transitional Satin Ash	4,810.
EUP-116E	45"	Polished Ebony	5,290.
EUP-116E	45"	Polished Sapele Mahogany	5,390.
EUP-116E	45"	Polished Walnut	5,390.
EUP-116E	45"	Polished White	5,290.
EUP-116FC	45"	French Country Satin Cherry	5,390.
EUP-116CT	45"	Contemporary Satin Sapele Mahogany	5,590.
EUP-116IP	45"	Italian Provincial Satin Cherry	5,590.
EUP-116IP	45"	Italian Provincial Satin Walnut	5,590.
EUP-116QA	45"	Queen Anne Satin Cherry	5,590.
EUP-116ST	45"	Sheraton Traditional Satin Sapele Mahogany	5,590.
EUP-116EC	45"	English Country Satin Walnut	5,790.
EUP-116ET	45"	English Traditional Satin Sapele Mahogany	5,790.
EUP-116FF	45"	Formal French Satin Brown Cherry	5,790.
EUP-116FF	45"	Formal French Satin Red Cherry	5,790.
EUP-123E	48"	Polished Ebony	5,690.
EUP-123E	48"	Satin Sapele Mahogany	5,890.
EUP-123E	48"	Polished Sapele Mahogany	5,790.
EUP-123E	48"	Satin Walnut	5,790.
EUP-123CL	48"	French Satin Walnut	6,190.
EUP-123CL	48"	French Satin Sapele Mahogany	6,300.
EUP-123FL	48"	Empire Satin Walnut	6,190.
EUP-123FL	48"	Empire Satin Sapele Mahogany	6,300.

Grands

Model	Size	Style and Finish	List Price
EGP-155	5' 1"	Polished Ebony	11,790.
EGP-155	5' 1"	Polished Walnut	11,990.
EGP-155	5' 1"	Polished Sapele Mahogany	12,190.

Model	Size	Style and Finish	List Price*
EGP-155	5' 1"	Polished Cherry	12,390.
EGP-155	5' 1"	Polished Kewazinga Bubinga	12,590.
EGP-155T	5' 1"	Polished Ebony	12,190.
EGP-155R	5' 1"	Renaissance Polished Ebony	12,390.
EGP-155T	5' 1"	Polished Walnut	12,590.
EGP-155R	5' 1"	Renaissance Polished Sapele Mahogany	12,790.
EGP-161	5' 3"	Satin Ebony	13,190.
EGP-161	5' 3"	Polished Ebony	12,990.
EGP-161	5' 3"	Satin Sapele Mahogany	14,790.
EGP-161	5' 3"	Polished Sapele Mahogany	14,590.
EGP-161	5' 3"	Satin Walnut	14,790.
EGP-161	5' 3"	Satin Cherry	15,190.
EGP-161	5' 3"	Satin Kewazinga Bubinga	15,390.
EGP-161	5' 3"	Polished White	13,190.
EGP-161N	5' 3"	Neo-Classic Satin Sapele Mahogany	15,790.
EGP-161N	5' 3"	Neo-Classic Polished Sapele Mahogany	15,590.
EGP-161N	5' 3"	Neo-Classic Satin Cherry	16,390.
EGP-161F	5' 3"	French Provincial Satin Walnut	16,190.
EGP-161F	5' 3"	French Provincial Polished Walnut	15,990.
EGP-161F	5' 3"	French Provincial Satin Brown Cherry	16,390.
EGP-161F	5' 3"	French Provincial Satin Red Cherry	16,390.
EGP-173	5' 8"	Polished Ebony	15,190.
EGP-173	5' 8"	Polished Walnut	15,590.
EGP-173	5' 8"	Polished Sapele Mahogany	15,790.
EGP-173	5' 8"	Polished Cherry	15,990.
EGP-173	5' 8"	Polished Kewazinga Bubinga	16,590.
EGP-173	5' 8"	Polished White	16,190.
EGP-183	6'	Satin Ebony	18,900.
EGP-183	6'	Polished Ebony	18,640.
EGP-183	6'	Polished Sapele Mahogany	19,850.
EGP-183	6'	Satin Walnut	20,650.

Estonia

The Estonia factory can make custom-designed finishes with exotic veneers; prices upon request. Prices here include Jansen adjustable artist bench.

Grands

L168	5' 6"	Satin and Polished Ebony	31,100.
L168	5' 6"	Satin and Polished Mahogany	33,695.
L168	5' 6"	Satin and Polished Walnut	33,695.
L168	5' 6"	Satin and Polished Bubinga	36,625.
L168	5' 6"	"Hidden Beauty" Polished Ebony w/Bubinga	34,500.
L168	5' 6"	"Hidden Beauty" Polished Ebony w/Karelia	36,225.
L168	5' 6"	Satin and Polished White	33,695.

*For explanation of terms and prices, please see pages 117–121.

Estonia (continued)

Model	Size	Style and Finish	List Price*
L190	6' 3"	Satin and Polished Ebony	37,945.
L190	6' 3"	Satin and Polished Mahogany	40,895.
L190	6' 3"	Polished Pyramid Mahogany	49,060.
L190	6' 3"	Victorian Satin Pyramid Mahogany	54,500.
L190	6' 3"	Satin and Polished Rosewood	49,060.
L190	6' 3"	Victorian Satin Rosewood	55,500.
L190	6' 3"	Satin and Polished Walnut	40,895.
L190	6' 3"	Satin and Polished Bubinga	44,160.
L190	6' 3"	Satin or Polished White	40,895.
L190	6' 3"	"Hidden Beauty" Polished Ebony w/Bubinga	40,425.
L190	6' 3"	"Hidden Beauty" Polished Ebony w/Karelia	41,370.
L273	9'	Satin and Polished Ebony	92,000.
L273	9'	Satin and Polished Walnut	110,400.
	All models	Queen Anne, add'l	3,385.
	All models	Victorian, add'l	3,385.

Everett

Verticals

Model	Size	Style and Finish	List Price*
EV-112	44"	Continental Polished Ebony	4,380.
EV-112	44"	Continental Polished Mahogany	4,500.
EV-113	45"	Polished Ebony	4,580.
EV-113	45"	Polished Mahogany	4,700.
EV-115CB	45"	Chippendale Polished Mahogany	4,900.
EV-121	48"	Polished Ebony	5,180.
EV-121	48"	Polished Mahogany	5,300.

Grands

Model	Size	Style and Finish	List Price*
EV-146	4' 9"	Polished Ebony	10,580.
EV-146	4' 9"	Polished Mahogany/White	11,480.
EV-152	5'	Polished Ebony	11,980.
EV-152	5'	Polished Mahogany	12,480.
EV-152	5'	Polished Sapele	12,480.
EV-165	5' 5"	Polished Ebony	12,780.
EV-165	5' 5"	Polished Mahogany/Walnut	13,280.
EV-185	6' 1"	Polished Ebony	14,780.

Falcone — see "Sejung"

Fandrich & Sons

These are the prices on the Fandrich & Sons Web site. The company says they are not subject to further discount.

Model	Size	Style and Finish	List Price*
Verticals			
126V	50"	Polished Ebony	16,040.
132V	52"	Polished Ebony	17,300.
Grands			
165HGS	5' 5"	Polished Ebony	19,990.
165S	5' 5"	Polished Ebony	16,560.
185HGS	6' 1"	Polished Ebony	23,990.
185S	6' 1"	Polished Ebony	17,560.
203HGS	6' 8"	Polished Ebony	28,840.

Fazioli

Fazioli is willing to make custom-designed cases with exotic veneers, marquetry, and other embellishments. Prices on request to Fazioli.

Grands

Model	Size	Style and Finish	List Price*
F156	5' 2"	Satin and Polished Ebony	92,400.
F156	5' 2"	Satin Walnut/Palisander	102,400.
F156	5' 2"	Polished Walnut/Palisander	106,200.
F156	5' 2"	Polished Pyramid Mahogany	110,600.
F156	5' 2"	Polished Burl Woods	115,400.
F156	5' 2"	Solid Colors, Satin or Polished	93,200.
F183	6'	Satin and Polished Ebony	105,600.
F183	6'	Satin Walnut/Palisander	116,400.
F183	6'	Polished Walnut/Palisander	121,400.
F183	6'	Polished Pyramid Mahogany	125,600.
F183	6'	Polished Burl Woods	132,000.
F183	6'	Solid Colors, Satin or Polished	106,600.
F212	6' 11"	Satin and Polished Ebony	120,200.
F212	6' 11"	Satin Walnut/Palisander	132,200.
F212	6' 11"	Polished Walnut/Palisander	138,200.
F212	6' 11"	Polished Pyramid Mahogany	144,000.
F212	6' 11"	Polished Burl Woods	150,200.
F212	6' 11"	Solid Colors, Satin or Polished	120,600.
F228	7' 6"	Satin and Polished Ebony	138,000.
F228	7' 6"	Satin Walnut/Palisander	151,600.
F228	7' 6"	Polished Walnut/Palisander	158,400.
F228	7' 6"	Polished Pyramid Mahogany	165,400.
F228	7' 6"	Polished Burl Woods	172,200.
F228	7' 6"	Solid Colors, Satin or Polished	139,200.
F278	9' 2"	Satin and Polished Ebony	179,200.
F278	9' 2"	Satin Walnut/Palisander	197,000.
F278	9' 2"	Polished Walnut/Palisander	206,000.
F278	9' 2"	Polished Pyramid Mahogany	214,800.
F278	9' 2"	Polished Burl Woods	223,800.

*For explanation of terms and prices, please see pages 117–121.

Model	Size	Style and Finish	List Price*

Fazioli (continued)

Model	Size	Style and Finish	List Price*
F278	9' 2"	Solid Colors, Satin or Polished	180,800.
F308	10' 2"	Satin and Polished Ebony	196,200.
F308	10' 2"	Satin Walnut/Palisander	215,600.
F308	10' 2"	Polished Walnut/Palisander	225,600.
F308	10' 2"	Polished Pyramid Mahogany	235,400.
F308	10' 2"	Polished Burl Woods	245,000.
F308	10' 2"	Solid Colors, Satin or Polished	200,000.
F308	10' 2"	Fourth pedal and two lyres included in price of F308	
All other models		*Fourth pedal, add'l*	*12,000.*

Feurich

Prices do not include bench. Euro = $1.40

Verticals

Model	Size	Style and Finish	List Price
F 123	49"	Satin Ebony	25,200.
F 123	49"	Polished Ebony	26,800.
F 123	49"	Polished Mahogany/Walnut	31,240.
F 123	49"	With Fandrich Action, add'l	3,100.

Grands

Model	Size	Style and Finish	List Price
F 172	5' 8"	Satin Ebony	68,500.
F 172	5' 8"	Polished Ebony	73,640.
F 172	5' 8"	Polished Ebony w/Pyramid Mahog.	81,300.
F 172	5' 8"	Polished Mahogany	80,440.
F 172	5' 8"	Polished Sapele Mahogany/Walnut	78,300.
F 172	5' 8"	Satin Cherry	69,720.
F 172 ADF	5' 8"	"Old German Style" Satin Ebony	75,160.
F 172 ADF	5' 8"	"Old German Style" Polished Ebony	84,380.
F 172 ADF	5' 8"	"Old German Style" Satin Cherry	75,160.
F 172 C	5' 8"	Classic Polished Ebony	77,530.
F 172 C	5' 8"	Classic Polished Ebony w/Pyramid Mahog.	81,240.
F 172 R	5' 8"	Rococco Polished Walnut	105,840.
F 172 S	5' 8"	Sheraton Polished Mahogany	90,720.
F 227	7' 5"	Satin Ebony	89,100.
F 227	7' 5"	Polished Ebony	98,952.
F 227	7' 5"	Polished Ebony w/Pyramid Mahog.	101,900.
F 227	7' 5"	Polished Mahogany	106,366.
F 227	7' 5"	Polished Walnut	106,344.
F 227 ADF	7' 5"	"Old German Style" Satin Ebony	97,534.
F 227 ADF	7' 5"	"Old German Style" Polished Ebony	107,940.
F 227 R	7' 5"	Rococco Polished Walnut	136,354.

Förster, August

Prices do not include bench. Euro=$1.60

Verticals

Model	Size	Style and Finish	List Price
116C	46"	Chippendale Polished Ebony	29,309.
116C	46"	Chippendale Satin and Polished Walnut	29,754.
116C	46"	Chippendale Satin and Polished Mahogany	28,410.
116C	46"	Chippendale Polished White	29,149.
116D	46"	Continental Polished Ebony	22,932.
116D	46"	Continental Satin and Polished Walnut	24,411.
116D	46"	Continental Satin and Polished Mahogany	23,050.
116D	46"	Continental Polished White	23,790.
116E	46"	Polished Ebony	26,780.
116E	46"	Satin and Polished Walnut	28,225.
116E	46"	Satin and Polished Mahogany	26,880.
116E	46"	Polished White	27,620.
125G	49"	Polished Ebony	29,854.
125G	49"	Satin and Polished Walnut	31,870.
125G	49"	Satin and Polished Mahogany	29,955.
125G	49"	Polished White	30,745.

Grands

Model	Size	Style and Finish	List Price
170	5' 8"	Polished Ebony	61,792.
170	5' 8"	Satin and Polished Walnut	64,043.
170	5' 8"	Satin and Polished Mahogany	61,893.
170	5' 8"	Polished White	64,514.
170	5' 8"	"Classic" Polished Ebony	68,915.
170	5' 8"	"Classic" Polished Walnut	78,374.
170	5' 8"	"Classic" Polished Mahogany	70,226.
170	5' 8"	"Classic" Polished White	72,678.
190	6' 4"	Polished Ebony	69,520.
190	6' 4"	Satin and Polished Walnut	71,838.
190	6' 4"	Satin and Polished Mahogany	69,654.
190	6' 4"	Polished White	71,502.
190	6' 4"	"Classic" Polished Ebony	76,643.
190	6' 4"	"Classic" Polished Walnut	86,118.
190	6' 4"	"Classic" Polished Mahogany	77,920.
190	6' 4"	"Classic" Polished White	81,011.
215	7' 2"	Polished Ebony	78,390.
275	9' 1"	Polished Ebony	145,876.
170 or 190		*Pyramid Mahogany, add'l*	8,702.
170 or 190		*Chippendale, add'l*	13,978.

*For explanation of terms and prices, please see pages 117–121.

Model	Size	Style and Finish	List Price*

Grotrian

Prices do not include bench. Other woods available on request. Euro = $1.60

Verticals

Model	Size	Style and Finish	List Price
Fried. Grotrian	43½"	Polished Ebony	18,867.
Cristal	44"	Satin Ebony	21,854.
Cristal	44"	Polished Ebony	22,711.
Cristal	44"	Open-pore Oak/Walnut/Beech	21,854.
Cristal	44"	Polished Walnut/White	23,541.
Canto	45"	Satin Ebony, Open-pore Beech	23,541.
Canto	45"	Polished Ebony	25,379.
Carat	45½"	Polished Ebony	28,047.
Carat	45½"	Open-pore Oak/Walnut	27,287.
Carat	45½"	Polished Walnut/White	30,335.
College	48"	Satin Ebony	30,838.
College	48"	Polished Ebony	31,985.
College	48"	Open-pore Beech	30,838.
Classic	49"	Polished Ebony	37,035.
Classic	49"	Open-pore Oak/Walnut	35,795.
Classic	49"	Polished Walnut/White	40,180.
Concertino	52"	Polished Ebony	44,323.
	48"–52"	*Sostenuto pedal, add'l*	1,345.

Grands

Model	Size	Style and Finish	List Price
Chambre	5' 5"	Satin Ebony	66,197.
Chambre	5' 5"	Polished Ebony	72,870.
Chambre	5' 5"	Open-pore Oak/Walnut	68,485.
Chambre	5' 5"	Polished Walnut/White	78,968.
Cabinet	6' 3"	Satin Ebony	76,300.
Cabinet	6' 3"	Polished Ebony	84,496.
Cabinet	6' 3"	Open-pore Oak/Walnut	79,348.
Cabinet	6' 3"	Polished Walnut/White	91,928.
Charis	6' 3"	Satin Ebony	85,124.
Charis	6' 10"	Polished Ebony	94,018.
Concert	7' 4"	Satin Ebony	101,527.
Concert	7' 4"	Polished Ebony	113,583.
Concert Royal	9' 1"	Polished Ebony	137,943.
All models		*Chippendale/Empire, add'l*	4,704.
All models		*CS Style, add'l*	5,712.
All models		*Rococo, add'l*	14,448.

Gulbransen

Verticals

Model	Size	Style and Finish	List Price
120	47"	Polished Ebony	4,790.
120	47"	Polished Mahogany	4,790.

Model	Size	Style and Finish	List Price*
140	55"	Polished Ebony	6,390.
All verticals		With Pianomation CD Player Installed, add'l	4,140.

Grands

80462	4' 11"	Polished Ebony	7,790.
80470	4' 11"	Polished Mahogany	7,990.
80662	5' 2"	Polished Ebony	7,990.
80670	5' 2"	Polished Mahogany	8,390.
All Grands		With Pianomation CD Player Installed, add'l	4,140.

Haessler

Prices do not include bench.

Verticals

115 K	45"	Satin and Polished Ebony	17,590.
115 K	45"	Satin Beech/Ash/Waxed Alder	17,304.
115 K	45"	Satin and Polished White	18,272.
118 K	47"	Satin and Polished Ebony	19,306.
118 K	47"	Satin Ebony with Walnut Accent	20,780.
118 K	47"	Satin and Polished Mahogany	20,362.
118 K	47"	Satin and Polished Walnut	20,362.
118 K	47"	Satin and Polished Cherry	21,824.
118 K	47"	Cherry with Yew Inlay, Satin and Polish	21,824.
118 K	47"	Satin Oak	18,458.
118 K	47"	Polished Bubinga	22,066.
118 K	47"	Satin and Polished White	20,120.
118 KM	47"	Satin and Polished Ebony	20,274.
118 KM	47"	Satin and Polished White	21,032.
118 CH	47"	Chippendale Satin and Polished Mahogany	21,770.
118 CH	47"	Chippendale Satin and Polished Walnut	21,770.
124 K	49"	Satin and Polished Ebony	22,144.
124 K	49"	Satin Ebony with Walnut Accent	21,572.
124 K	49"	Satin and Polished Mahogany	22,056.
124 K	49"	Satin and Polished Walnut	22,056.
124 K	49"	Satin and Polished Cherry	22,594.
124 K	49"	Cherry with Yew Inlay, Satin and Polish	23,618.
124 K	49"	Satin and Polished White	21,286.
124 KM	49"	Satin and Polished Ebony	20,978.
124 KM	49"	Satin and Polished White	21,736.
132	52"	Satin and Polished Ebony	27,886.

Grands

175	5' 8"	Satin and Polished Ebony	53,132.
175	5' 8"	Satin and Polished Mahogany	55,254.
175	5' 8"	Satin and Polished Walnut	55,782.
175	5' 8"	Satin and Polished Cherry	55,518.

*For explanation of terms and prices, please see pages 117–121.

Haessler (continued)

Model	Size	Style and Finish	List Price*
175	5' 8"	Polished Bubinga	58,444.
175	5' 8"	Satin and Polished White	62,502.
175	5' 8"	Saxony Polished Pyramid Mahogany	70,104.
175	5' 8"	Saxony Polished Burl Walnut	70,780.
175	5' 8"	"President" Polished Ebony	59,316.
175	5' 8"	"President" Polished Mahogany	61,692.
175	5' 8"	"President" Polished Walnut	62,282.
175	5' 8"	"President" Polished Bubinga	65,244.
175	5' 8"	Louis XV Ebony, Satin and Polished	62,014.
175	5' 8"	Louis XV Mahogany, Satin and Polished	65,114.
175	5' 8"	Louis XV Walnut, Satin and Polished	64,496.
175	5' 8"	Kaiser Wilhelm II Polished Ebony	62,546.
175	5' 8"	Kaiser Wilhelm II Polished Mahogany	65,054.
175	5' 8"	Kaiser Wilhelm II Polished Walnut	65,684.
175	5' 8"	Kaiser Wilhelm II Polished Cherry	65,364.
175	5' 8"	Ambassador Satin East Indian Rosewood	72,800.
175	5' 8"	Ambassador Satin Walnut	67,408.
175	5' 8"	Nicolas II Satin Walnut w/Burl Inlay	72,800.
175	5' 8"	Louis XVI Rococo Satin White w/Gold	78,194.
175	5' 8"	Classic Alexandra Polished Ebony	60,398.
175	5' 8"	Classic Alexandra Polished Mahogany	63,414.
175	5' 8"	Classic Alexandra Polished Walnut	62,812.
186	6' 1"	Satin and Polished Ebony	59,862.
186	6' 1"	Satin and Polished Mahogany	62,248.
186	6' 1"	Satin and Polished Walnut	62,854.
186	6' 1"	Satin and Polished Cherry	62,558.
186	6' 1"	Polished Bubinga	65,846.
186	6' 1"	Satin and Polished White	62,854.
186	6' 1"	Saxony Polished Pyramid Mahogany	78,980.
186	6' 1"	Saxony Polished Burl Walnut	79,740.
186	6' 1"	"President" Polished Ebony	66,824.
186	6' 1"	"President" Polished Mahogany	69,498.
186	6' 1"	"President" Polished Walnut	70,168.
186	6' 1"	"President" Polished Bubinga	73,504.
186	6' 1"	Louis XV Ebony, Satin and Polished	69,862.
186	6' 1"	Louis XV Mahogany, Satin and Polished	73,360.
186	6' 1"	Louis XV Walnut, Satin and Polished	72,666.
186	6' 1"	Kaiser Wilhelm II Polished Ebony	70,466.
186	6' 1"	Kaiser Wilhelm II Polished Mahogany	73,294.
186	6' 1"	Kaiser Wilhelm II Polished Walnut	73,996.
186	6' 1"	Kaiser Wilhelm II Polished Cherry	73,644.
186	6' 1"	Ambassador Satin East Indian Rosewood	82,016.
186	6' 1"	Ambassador Satin Walnut	75,944.

Model	Size	Style and Finish	List Price*
186	6' 1"	Nicolas II Satin Walnut w/Burl Inlay	82,016.
186	6' 1"	Louis XVI Rococo Satin White w/Gold	88,088.
186	6' 1"	Classic Alexandra Polished Ebony	68,046.
186	6' 1"	Classic Alexandra Polished Mahogany	71,446.
186	6' 1"	Classic Alexandra Polished Walnut	70,764.

Hailun

Verticals

HU116	45½"	Satin Ebony/Walnut (school piano)	4,780.
HL121	48"	Polished Ebony	4,990.
HL121	48"	Polished Mahogany	5,390.
HU121C	48"	Polished Ebony (curved legs)	5,190.
HU121C	48"	Polished Mahogany/Walnut (curved legs)	5,390.
H1	48"	"Estate" Polished Ebony with Mahogany Trim	5,390.
HU125	50"	Polished Ebony	5,590.
HU125	50"	Polished Mahogany/Walnut	5,990.
H5	50"	Polished Ebony	5,790.
H5	50"	Polished Mahogany/Walnut	6,190.
H31P	52"	Polished Ebony	7,790.

Grands

HG151	4' 11½"	Polished Ebony	9,990.
HG151	4' 11½"	Polished Mahogany/Walnut	10,390.
HG151C	4' 11½"	Polished Ebony (curved legs)	10,790.
HG151C	4' 11½"	Polished Mahogany/Walnut (curved legs)	11,190.
HG161	5' 4"	Polished Ebony	11,390.
HG161	5' 4"	Polished Mahogany/Walnut	11,790.
HG161	5' 4"	"Georgian" Polished Ebony	12,190.
HG161	5' 4"	"Georgian" Polished Mahogany/Walnut	12,590.
HG178	5' 10"	Polished Ebony	13,390.
HG178	5' 10"	Polished Mahogany/Walnut	13,990.
HG178	5' 10"	"Baroque" Polished Ebony w/Birds-Eye Maple	14,590.
HG198	6' 5"	Polished Ebony	18,790.
HG198	6' 5"	Polished Mahogany/Walnut	19,390.
HG218	7' 2"	Polished Ebony	24,790.
HG277	9' 1"	Polished Ebony	53,790.

Hallet, Davis & Co.

Model numbers ending in "I" use imported veneers from around the world.

Verticals

H-C43R	43"	Satin Cherry/Oak (Roung Leg)	3,900.
H-C43F	43"	French Provincial Satin Cherry/Oak	3,900.
H-111GD	44"	Continental Polished Ebony	3,510.
H-111GD	44"	Continental Polished Mahogany/Walnut/White	3,590.

*For explanation of terms and prices, please see pages 117–121.

Hallet, Davis & Co. (continued)

Model	Size	Style and Finish	List Price*
H-111GD I	44"	Continental Polished American Walnut	3,790.
H-115GC	45"	Chippendale Polished Ebony	3,880.
H-115GC	45"	Chippendale Polished Mahogany/Walnut/White	3,920.
H-115GC I	45"	Chippendale Polished American Walnut	4,120.
H-115WH	46"	Polished Ebony	3,920.
H-115WH	46"	Polished Mahogany/Walnut	3,970.
H-115WH I	46"	Polished Walnut	4,170.
H-121WH	48"	Polished Ebony	4,140.
H-121WH	48"	Polished Mahogany/Walnut	4,250.
H-121WH I	48"	Polished American Walnut	4,450.
H-126WH	50"	Polished Ebony	4,790.
H-126WH	50"	Polished Mahogany	4,900.
H-131WH	52"	Polished Ebony	6,000.

Grands

Model	Size	Style and Finish	List Price*
H-146C	4' 9"	Satin Ebony	8,190.
H-146C	4' 9"	Polished Ebony	7,790.
H-146C	4' 9"	Polished Mahogany/White	8,190.
H-146C I	4' 9"	"Metropolitan" Polished Ebony/Silver Plate	8,190.
H-146C I	4' 9"	Satin Mahogany	8,590.
H-146C I	4' 9"	Polished Walnut	8,590.
H-146S	4' 9"	Queen Anne Polished Ebony	8.190.
H-146S	4' 9"	Queen Anne Polished Mahogany	8,590.
H-146S	4' 9"	Queen Anne Polished Walnut	8,790.
H-152C	5'	Satin Ebony	9,590.
H-152C	5'	Polished Ebony	9,190.
H-152C	5'	Polished Mahogany/White	9,590.
H-152C	5'	Polished Brown Sapele Mahogany	9,590.
H-152C I	5'	"Metropolitan" Polished Ebony/Silver Plate	9,790.
H-152C I	5'	Satin Mahogany/Walnut	10,190.
H-152C I	5'	Polished Mahogany/Walnut	9,990.
H-152D	5'	Victorian Polished Ebony	9,990.
H-152D	5'	Victorian Polished Mahogany	10,390.
H-152D	5'	Victorian Polished Brown Sapele Mahogany	10,390.
H-152D I	5'	Victorian Satin Mahogany/Walnut	10,990.
H-152D I	5'	Victorian Polished Mahogany/Walnut	10,790.
H-152S	5'	Queen Anne Polished Ebony	9,990.
H-152S I	5'	Queen Anne Satin Mahogany/Walnut	10,990.
H-152S I	5'	Queen Anne Polished Mahogany/Walnut	10,790.
H-165C	5' 5"	Satin Ebony	10,590.
H-165C	5' 5"	Polished Ebony	10,190.
H-165C	5' 5"	Polished Mahogany/White	10,590.
H-165C	5' 5"	Polished Brown Sapele Mahogany	10,590.
H-165C I	5' 5"	"Metropolitan" Polished Ebony/Silver Plate	10,790.

Model	Size	Style and Finish	List Price*
H-165C I	5' 5"	Satin Mahogany/Walnut	11,190.
H-165C I	5' 5"	Polished Mahogany/Walnut	10,990.
H-165D	5' 5"	"Period" Polished Ebony	10,990.
H-165D	5' 5"	"Period" Polished Brown Sapele Mahogany	11,190.
H-165D I	5' 5"	"Period" Satin Mahogany/Walnut	11,990.
H-165D I	5' 5"	"Period" Polished Mahogany	11,070.
H-165D I	5' 5"	"Period" Polished Walnut	11,790.
H-185C	6' 1"	Satin Ebony	12,390.
H-185C	6' 1"	Polished Ebony	11,990.
H-185C	6' 1"	Polished Mahogany/Sapele Mahog./Walnut	12,390.
H-185C I	6' 1"	"Metropolitan" Polished Ebony/Silver Plate	12,390.
H-185C I	6' 1"	Satin Mahogany/Walnut	12,990.
H-185C I	6' 1"	Polished Mahogany/Walnut	12,790.
H-185D	6' 1"	"Period" Polished Ebony	12,590.
H-215C	7' 1"	Polished Ebony	18,790.

Hardman, Peck & Co.

Verticals

R112	44"	Continental Polished Ebony	3,510.
R112	44"	Continental Polished Mahogany/Walnut/White	3,510.
R110F	44"	French Provincial Satin Mahogany/Oak	4,090.
R110R	44"	Satin Mahogany/Oak (round legs)	4,090.
R115LS	45"	Polished Ebony	3,690.
R115LS	45"	Polished Dark Mahogany	3,790.
R115F	45"	French Provincial Satin Imported Mahogany	4,290.
R115R	45"	Satin Imported Mahogany (round legs)	4,290.
R116	46"	School Polished Ebony	3,690.
R116	46"	School Satin Cherry	3,790.
R117XK	46"	Chippendale Polished Dark Mahogany	3,990.
R120LS	48"	Polished Ebony	3,990.
R120LS	48"	Polished Dark Mahogany	4,090.
R132HA	52"	Polished Ebony	5,590.

Grands

R143S	4' 8"	Polished Ebony	7,590.
R143S	4' 8"	Polished Dark Mahogany, White	7,990.
R143F	4' 8"	French Provincial Satin Mahogany, Cherry	8,390.
R143R	4' 8"	Polished Ebony/Dark Mahogany (round legs)	8,390.
R150S	5'	Polished Ebony	7,990.
R150S	5'	Polished Dark Mahogany/White	8,390.
R150F	5'	French Provincial Satin Mahogany, Cherry	8,790.
R150R	5'	Polished Ebony/Dark Mahogany (round legs)	8,790.
R158S	5' 3"	Polished Ebony	8,390.
R158S	5' 3"	Polished Dark Mahogany	8,790.

*For explanation of terms and prices, please see pages 117–121.

Model	Size	Style and Finish	List Price*

Hardman, Peck & Co. (continued)

Model	Size	Style and Finish	List Price*
R158F	5' 3"	French Provincial Satin Mahogany, Cherry	9,190.
R158R	5' 3"	Polished Ebony/Dark Mahogany (round legs)	9,190.
R168S	5' 7"	Polished Ebony	8,990.
R168S	5' 7"	Polished Dark Mahogany	9,390.
R168F	5' 7"	French Provincial Satin Mahogany, Cherry	9,790.
R168R	5' 7"	Polished Ebony/Dark Mahogany (round legs)	9,790.
R185S	6' 1"	Polished Ebony	10,390.
R185S	6' 1"	Polished Dark Mahogany	10,790.

Heintzman & Co.

Verticals

Model	Size	Style and Finish	List Price*
121D	47½"	Polished Ebony	5,900.
121D	47½"	Polished White	5,900.
121D	47½"	Polished Mahogany/Walnut/Cherry	5,970.
121DL	47½"	Satin Ebony	5,970.
121DL	47½"	Polished Ebony	5,900.
121DL	47½"	Satin White	5,970.
121DL	47½"	Polished White	5,900.
121DL	47½"	Satin Mahogany/Walnut/Cherry	5,970.
121DL	47½"	Polished Mahogany/Walnut/Cherry	5,970.
123B	48½"	Satin Ebony	6,520.
123B	48½"	Polished Ebony	6,420.
123B	48½"	Satin White	6,520.
123B	48½"	Polished White	6,420.
123B	48½"	Satin Mahogany/Walnut/Cherry	6,520.
123B	48½"	Polished Mahogany/Walnut/Cherry	6,520.
123E	48½"	Polished Ebony/White	6,040.
123E	48½"	Polished Mahogany/Walnut/Cherry	6,110.
123F	48½"	French Provincial Polished Ebony	6,040.
123F	48½"	French Provincial Polished Mahogany	6,110.
126C	50"	Satin Ebony	6,700.
126C	50"	Polished Ebony	6,500.
126C	50"	Polished Mahogany	6,510.
130A	51"	Polished Ebony	6,790.
130A	51"	Polished Mahogany	6,850.
132C	52"	Satin Ebony	7,170.
132C	52"	Polished Ebony	7,100.
132C	52"	Satin Mahogany	7,170.
132C	52"	Polished Mahogany/Walnut/Cherry	7,170.
132D	52"	Satin Ebony, Decorative Panel	7,300.
132D	52"	Polished Ebony, Decorative Panel	7,100.
132D	52"	Satin Mahog./Wal./Cherry, Decorative Panel	7,300.

Model	Size	Style and Finish	List Price*
132D	52"	Polished Mahog./Wal./Cherry, Décor. Panel	7,170.
132E	52"	French Provincial Satin Ebony	7,260.
132E	52"	French Provincial Polished Ebony	7,190.
132E	52"	French Provincial Satin Mahogany	7,260.
132E	52"	French Provincial Polished Mahogany/Cherry	7,260.
140CK	52"	Satin Ebony	8,990.
140CK	55"	Polished Ebony	8,790.
140CK	55"	Satin Mahogany/Walnut/Cherry	8,990.
140CK	55"	Polished Mahogany/Walnut/Cherry	8,860.

Grands

Model	Size	Style and Finish	List Price*
168	5' 6"	Hand-rubbed Satin Ebony	15,650.
168	5' 6"	Polished Ebony	15,250.
168	5' 6"	Polished White	15,250.
168	5' 6"	Satin Mahogany	15,650.
168	5' 6"	Polished Mahogany	15,650.
168	5' 6"	Sapele Mahogany	15,850.
186	6' 1"	Hand-rubbed Satin Ebony	17,190.
186	6' 1"	Polished Ebony	16,790.
186	6' 1"	Polished White	16,790.
186	6' 1"	Satin Mahogany	17,190.
186	6' 1"	Polished Mahogany	17,190.
186	6' 1"	Sapele Mahogany	17,390.
203	6' 8"	Hand-rubbed Satin Ebony	18,400.
203	6' 8"	Polished Ebony	18,000.
203	6' 8"	Polished White	18,000.
203	6' 8"	Satin Mahogany	18,400.
203	6' 8"	Polished Mahogany	18,400.
203	6' 8"	Sapele Mahogany	18,600.
274	*9'*	*Satin and Polished Ebony*	*on request*

Hoffmann, W.

Verticals

Model	Size	Style and Finish	List Price*
H120	47"	Polished Ebony	11,700.
H120	47"	Satin Cherry/Beech/Alder	11,700.
H120	47"	Polished Mahogany/Walnut/White	11,700.
H128	50"	Polished Ebony	12,400.
H128	50"	Satin Cherry/Beech/Alder	12,400.
H128	50"	Polished Mahogany/Walnut/White	12,400.

Grands

Model	Size	Style and Finish	List Price*
158	*5' 2"*	*Polished Ebony*	*on request*
175	5' 8"	Polished Ebony	16,790.
175	5' 8"	Polished Mahogany/Walnut/White	35,800.
175	5' 8"	Chrome	34,600.
188	*6' 2"*	*Polished Ebony*	*on request*

*For explanation of terms and prices, please see pages 117–121.

Model	Size	Style and Finish	List Price*
Kawai			
Verticals			
K-15	44"	Continental Polished Ebony	4,190.
K-15	44"	Continental Polished Mahogany	4,790.
506N	44½"	Satin Ebony	4,390.
506N	44½"	Satin Mahogany/Oak	4,390.
508	44½"	Satin Mahogany/Oak	4,990.
607	44½"	Satin American Oak	5,390.
607	44½"	French Provincial Satin Cherry	5,490.
607	44½"	Queen Anne Satin Mahogany	5,490.
K-2	45"	Satin and Polished Ebony	5,390.
K-2	45"	Satin and Polished Mahogany	5,990.
UST-9	46"	Satin Ebony/Oak/Walnut/Cherry	6,590.
907N	46½"	English Regency Satin Mahogany	7,990.
907N	46½"	French Provincial Satin Cherry	7,990.
K-3	48"	Satin and Polished Ebony	7,190.
K-3	48"	Satin and Polished Mahogany	7,790.
K-3	48"	Polished White	7,590.
K-5	49"	Satin and Polished Ebony	9,390.
K-5	49"	Polished Sapele Mahogany	10,590.
K-5	49"	French Provincial Polished Mahogany	10,790.
K-6	52"	Polished Ebony	12,390.
K-8	52"	Satin and Polished Ebony	14,790.
Grands			
GM-10K	5'	Satin and Polished Ebony	11,190.
GM-10K	5'	Polished Mahogany	12,190.
GM-10K	5'	French Provincial Polished Mahogany	13,190.
GM-12	5'	Satin and Polished Ebony	13,790.
GM-12	5'	Polished Mahogany/Snow White	14,990.
GE-20	5' 1"	Satin and Polished Ebony	15,990.
GE-20	5' 1"	Satin Walnut	17,590.
GE-20	5' 1"	Polished Mahogany/Sapele Mahogany	17,590.
GE-20	5' 1"	Polished Snow White	17,190.
GE-20	5' 1"	French Provincial Polished Mahogany	19,190.
GE-30	5' 5"	Satin and Polished Ebony	18,190.
GE-30	5' 5"	Polished Mahogany	20,390.
GE-30	5' 5"	Polished Sapele Mahogany	20,390.
GE-30	5' 5"	Satin Walnut	19,990.
GE-30	5' 5"	Polished Snow White	19,590.
RX-1	5' 5"	Satin and Polished Ebony	21,190.
RX-1	5' 5"	Satin Walnut	24,590.
RX-1	5' 5"	Polished Walnut/Sapele Mahogany	25,390.
RX-1	5' 5"	Polished Snow White	24,590.
RX-2	5' 10"	Satin and Polished Ebony	24,790.

Model	Size	Style and Finish	List Price*
RX-2	5' 10"	Satin Mahogany/Walnut/Cherry/Oak	27,790.
RX-2	5' 10"	Polished Walnut/Mahogany	28,790.
RX-2	5' 10"	Polished Sapele Mahogany	28,790.
RX-2	5' 10"	Polished Rosewood	31,990.
RX-2	5' 10"	Polished Snow White	26,790.
RX-2	5' 10"	French Provincial Polished Mahogany	31,990.
RX-3	6' 1"	Satin and Polished Ebony	31,990.
RX-3	6' 1"	Satin Walnut	36,390.
RX-3	6' 1"	Polished Sapele Mahogany	38,390.
RX-3	6' 1"	Polished Snow White	34,190.
CR40N	6' 1"	Plexiglass	110,790.
RX-5	6' 6"	Satin and Polished Ebony	36,190.
RX-5	6' 6"	Satin Walnut	40,390.
RX-5	6' 6"	Polished Sapele Mahogany	42,390.
RX-5	6' 6"	Polished Snow White	38,390.
RX-6	7'	Satin and Polished Ebony	40,390.
RX-7	7' 6"	Satin and Polished Ebony	46,590.
EX	9'	Polished Ebony	109,990.
EXG	9'	Polished Ebony	116,790.

Kawai, Shigeru

Grands

Model	Size	Style and Finish	List Price*
SK2	5' 10"	Polished Ebony	37,500.
SK2	5' 10"	Polished Sapele Mahogany	39,500.
SK2	5' 10"	Polished Pyramid Mahogany	59,500.
SK2	5' 10"	Polished Honduran Mahogany	44,700.
SK2	5' 10"	"Classic Noblesse" w/Burl Walnut Inlay	57,300.
SK3	6' 1"	Satin Ebony	45,700.
SK3	6' 1"	Polished Ebony	43,700.
SK3	6' 1"	Polished Sapele Mahogany	46,100.
SK5	6' 6"	Polished Ebony	50,100.
SK5	6' 6"	Polished Sapele Mahogany	53,100.
SK6	7'	Satin Ebony	58,500.
SK6	7'	Polished Ebony	56,500.
SK7	7' 6"	Polished Ebony	62,500.
SK7	7' 6"	Polished Pyramid Mahogany	93,700.
SK7	7' 6"	"Classic Noblesse" w/Burl Walnut Inlay	85,700.
SK-EX	9'	Polished Ebony	144,800.

Kemble

Verticals

Model	Size	Style and Finish	List Price*
Cambridge	44"	Continental Polished Ebony	9,940.
Oxford-CT	44"	Polished Ebony	10,140.

*For explanation of terms and prices, please see pages 117–121.

Kemble (continued)

Oxford-CT	44"	Polished Ebony and Chrome	10,440.
Classic-T	45"	Polished Ebony	10,540.
Classic-T	45"	Polished Ebony and Chrome	10,840.
Classic-T	45"	Satin Mocha Oak	10,440.
Empire	46½"	Empire Polished Mahogany	12,540.
Prestige	46½"	Satin Cherry with Yew Inlay	12,540.
K121CL	48"	Polished Ebony/Mahogany	11,740.
K121CL	48"	Satin American Walnut	11,540.
K121CLM	48"	"Mozart" Polished Ebony with Oval	12,740.
K121CLM	48"	"Mozart" Polished Mahogany with Inlay	12,740.
Vermont	48"	Satin Cherry/Mocha Oak	13,940.
Conservatoire	49"	Polished Ebony	12,740.
Conservatoire	49"	Satin American Walnut	12,540.
K132SN	52"	Polished Ebony/Mahogany	15,940.

Grands

KC173	5' 8"	Polished Ebony	29,540.

Kimball

Verticals

K44	44"	French Provincial Cherry/Oak	7,380.
K49	49"	Polished Ebony	13,380.

Grands

K1	5' 1"	Polished Ebony	16,790.
K1	5' 1"	Polished Mahogany	17,590.
K2	5' 9"	Polished Ebony	18,790.
K2	5' 9"	Polished Mahogany	19,590.
K3	6' 2"	Polished Ebony	20,790.

Knabe, Wm.

Verticals

WKV-118F	46½"	French Prov. Lacquer Semi-Gloss Cherry	9,200.
WKV-118R	46½"	Renaissance Lacquer Polished Ebony	9,100.
WKV-118R	46½"	Renaissance Lacquer Semi-Gloss Walnut	9,200.
WKV-118R	46½"	Renaissance Lacquer Satin American Oak	8,900.
WKV-118T	46½"	Lacquer Semi-Gloss Mahogany	9,200.
WKV-121	48"	Satin Ebony	9,500.
WKV-121	48"	Polished Ebony	9,100.
WKV-121	48"	Polished Mahogany	10,400.
WKV-121A	48"	170th Anniv. Lacquer Semi-Gloss Dark Walnut	12,190.
WKV-131	52"	Satin Ebony	10,400.
WKV-131	52"	Polished Ebony	10,000.

Model	Size	Style and Finish	List Price*
WKV-131	52"	Polished Mahogany	11,400.
Grands			
WKG-53	5' 3"	Satin Ebony	21,200.
WKG-53	5' 3"	Polished Ebony	20,600.
WKG-53	5' 3"	Lacquer Semi-Gloss Wood Finishes	22,600.
WKG-53	5' 3"	Polished Wood Finishes	22,200.
WKG-53	*5' 3"*	*Polished Bubinga/Pommele*	*22,600.*
WKG-58	5' 8"	Satin Ebony	24,600.
WKG-58	5' 8"	Polished Ebony	23,900.
WKG-58	5' 8"	Lacquer Semi-Gloss Wood Finishes	26,000.
WKG-58	5' 8"	Polished Wood Finishes	25,400.
WKG-58	*5' 8"*	*Polished Bubinga/Pommele*	*26,000.*
WKG-58A	5' 8"	170th Anniv. Lacquer Semi-Gloss Walnut	30,800.
WKG-58F	5' 8"	French Provincial Satin Ebony	27,800.
WKG-58F	5' 8"	French Provincial Polished Ebony	27,200.
WKG-58F	5' 8"	French Prov. Lacquer Semi-Gloss Woods	29,200.
WKG-58F	5' 8"	French Provincial Polished Woods	28,600.
WKG-58M	5' 8"	Empire Satin Ebony	25,300.
WKG-58M	5' 8"	Empire Polished Ebony	24,600.
WKG-58M	5' 8"	Empire Lacquer Semi-Gloss Wood Finishes	26,700.
WKG-58M	5' 8"	Empire Polished Wood Finishes	26,200.
WKG-58M	*5' 8"*	*Empire Polished Bubinga/Pommele*	*26,700.*
WKG-64	6' 4"	Satin Ebony	29,700.
WKG-64	6' 4"	Polished Ebony	29,000.
WKG-64	6' 4"	Lacquer Semi-Gloss Wood Finishes	31,100.
WKG-64	6' 4"	Polished Wood Finishes	30,700.
WKG-70	7'	Satin Ebony	37,600.
WKG-70	7'	Polished Ebony	36,800.
WKG-70	7'	Lacquer Semi-Gloss Wood Finishes	37,000.
WKG-76	7' 6"	Satin Ebony	38,600.
WKG-76	7'6"	Polished Ebony	37,600.

Kohler & Campbell

Verticals

Model	Size	Style and Finish	List Price*
KC-142	42"	Continental Polished Ebony	4,190.
KC-142	42"	Continental Satin Cherry/Walnut	4,190.
KC-142	42"	Continental Polished Mahogany/Walnut/Ivory	4,190.
KC-244F	44"	French Provincial Satin Cherry	5,250.
KC-244M	44"	Mediterranean Satin Brown Oak	5,250.
KC-244T	44"	Satin Mahogany	5,250.
KC-245	45"	Polished Ebony	4,790.
KC-245	45"	Satin Cherry/Walnut	4,790.
KC-245	45"	Polished Mahogany/Walnut/Ivory	4,890.

*For explanation of terms and prices, please see pages 117–121.

Model	Size	Style and Finish	List Price*

Kohler & Campbell (continued)

Model	Size	Style and Finish	List Price*
KC-247	46½"	Satin and Polished Ebony	6,790.
KC-247	46½"	Satin Mahogany/Walnut	6,790.
KC-247	46½"	Polished Mahogany/Walnut	6,790.
KC-647F	46½"	French Provincial Satin Cherry	6,190.
KC-647R	46½"	Renaissance Satin Walnut	6,190.
KC-647T	46½"	Satin Mahogany	6,190.
KC-118C	46½"	Polished Ebony	5,190.
KC-118C	46½"	Polished Mahogany/Walnut	5,390.
KM-647F	46½"	French Provincial Satin Cherry	6,700.
KM-647R	46½"	Renaissance Satin Walnut	6,700.
KM-647T	46½"	Satin Mahogany	6,700.
KC-121M	48"	Satin Ebony	5,590.
KC-121M	48"	Polished Ebony	5,390.
KC-121M	48"	Polished Mahogany	5,590.
KMV-48SD	48"	Satin Ebony	10,100.
KMV-48SD	48"	Polished Ebony	9,700.
KMV-48SD	48"	Polished Mahogany	11,200.
KC-131	52"	Polished Ebony	5,890.
KC-131	52"	Polished Mahogany	5,990.
KMV-52MD	52"	Satin Ebony	11,200.
KMV-52MD	52"	Polished Ebony	10,800.
KMV-52MD	52"	Polished Mahogany	11,800.

Grands

Model	Size	Style and Finish	List Price*
KIG-47	4' 7"	Polished Ebony	10,090.
KIG-47	4' 7"	Polished Mahogany	10,790.
KIG-48	4' 8"	Polished Ebony	10,090.
KIG-48	4' 8"	Polished Mahogany/Walnut	10,790.
KCG-450	4' 9"	Satin Ebony	11,590.
KCG-450	4' 9"	Polished Ebony	10,790.
KCG-450	4' 9"	Lacquer Satin Mahogany/Walnut	11,590.
KCG-450	4' 9"	Polished Mahogany/Walnut	11,590.
KCG-450KAF	4' 9"	Queen Anne Lacquer Satin Cherry	13,990.
KCG-450KAF	4' 9"	Queen Anne Polished Mahogany	13,990.
KCG450KBF	4' 9"	French Provincial Satin Mahogany/Cherry	14,790.
KCG450KBF	4' 9"	French Provincial Polished Mahogany/Cherry	14,790.
KCG-500	5' 1½"	Satin Ebony	12,790.
KCG-500	5' 1½"	Polished Ebony	12,090.
KCG-500	5' 1½"	Lacquer Satin Mahogany and Pol. Mahogany	12,790.
KCG-500	5' 1½"	Lacquer Satin Walnut and Polished Walnut	12,790.
KCG-500KAF	5' 1½"	Queen Anne Satin Mahogany/Cherry	15,190.
KCG-500KAF	5' 1½"	Queen Anne Polished Mahogany/Cherry	15,190.
KCG-500KBF	5' 1½"	French Provincial Polished Mahogany/Cherry	15,790.
KCM-500	5' 1½"	Satin Ebony	15,000.

Model	Size	Style and Finish	List Price*
KCM-500	5' 1½"	Polished Ebony	14,300.
KCM-500	5' 1½"	Lacquer Satin Mahogany/Walnut	15,000.
KCM-500	5' 1½"	Polished Mahogany/Walnut	15,000.
KCG-600	5' 9"	Satin Ebony	14,690.
KCG-600	5' 9"	Polished Ebony	13,790.
KCG-600	5' 9"	Lacquer Satin Mahogany and Pol. Mahogany	13,790.
KCG-600	5' 9"	Lacquer Satin Walnut and Polished Walnut	13,790.
KCG-600KBF	5' 9"	French Provincial Lacquer Semi-Gloss Cherry	17,090.
KCG-600SKAF	5' 9"	Louis XV Lacquer Semi-Gloss Cherry/Walnut	18,190.
KCG-600L	5' 9"	Empire Polished Ebony	15,590.
KCM-600	5' 9"	Satin Ebony	16,300.
KCM-600	5' 9"	Polished Ebony	15,400.
KCM-600	5' 9"	Lacquer Satin Mahogany/Walnut	16,300.
KCM-600	5' 9"	Polished Mahogany/Walnut	16,300.
KCM-600 KBF	5' 9"	French Provincial Lacquer Semi-Gloss Cherry	18,590.
KCG-650	6' 1"	Satin Ebony	15,990.
KCG-650	6' 1"	Polished Ebony	15,090.
KCG-650	6' 1"	Lacquer Satin Mahogany/Walnut	15,990.
KCG-650	6' 1"	Polished Mahogany/Walnut	15,990.
KCM-650	6' 1"	Satin Ebony	17,400.
KCM-650	6' 1"	Polished Ebony	16,500.
KCM-650	6' 1"	Lacquer Satin Mahogany/Walnut	17,400.
KCM-650	6' 1"	Polished Mahogany/Walnut	17,400.
KFM-700	6' 10"	Polished Ebony	32,800.
KFM-850	7' 6"	Polished Ebony	34,800.

Mason & Hamlin

Verticals

Model	Size	Style and Finish	List Price*
50	50"	Satin and Polished Ebony	19,692.
50	50"	Satin Mahogany	20,030.

Grands

Model	Size	Style and Finish	List Price*
B	5' 4"	Satin Ebony	43,838.
B	5' 4"	Polished Ebony	46,420.
B	5' 4"	Satin Mahogany/Walnut	46,852.
B	5' 4"	Polished Pyramid Mahogany	53,488.
A	5' 8"	Satin Ebony	50,018.
A	5' 8"	Polished Ebony	53,488.
A	5' 8"	Satin Mahogany/Walnut	53,780.
A	5' 8"	Satin Rosewood	59,694.
A	5' 8"	Polished Pyramid Mahogany	65,376.
A	5' 8"	Polished Bubinga	61,782.
A	5' 8"	Satin Macassar Ebony	63,164.
A	5' 8"	Polished Macassar Ebony	65,376.

*For explanation of terms and prices, please see pages 117–121.

Mason & Hamlin (continued)

Model	Size	Style and Finish	List Price*
A	5' 8"	"Monticello" Polished Ebony	56,980.
A	5' 8"	"Monticello" Satin Mahogany	57,252.
A	5' 8"	"Monticello" Satin Walnut/Rosewood	69,406.
AA	6' 4"	Satin Ebony	57,710.
AA	6' 4"	Polished Ebony	59,582.
AA	6' 4"	Satin Mahogany/Walnut	60,748.
AA	6' 4"	Polished Pyramid Mahogany	66,462.
AA	6' 4"	Satin Rosewood	64,104.
AA	6' 4"	Polished Bubinga	66,192.
AA	6' 4"	Satin Macassar Ebony	67,574.
AA	6' 4"	Polished Macassar Ebony	69,786.
AA	6' 4"	"Monticello" Polished Ebony	63,738.
AA	6' 4"	"Monticello" Satin Mahogany	64,220.
AA	6' 4"	"Monticello" Satin Rosewood	78,388.
BB	7'	Satin Ebony	65,402.
BB	7'	Polished Ebony	67,284.
BB	7'	Satin Mahogany/Walnut	67,718.
BB	7'	Polished Pyramid Mahogany	80,626.
BB	7'	Satin Rosewood	75,806.
BB	7'	Polished Bubinga	77,686.
BB	7'	Satin Macassar Ebony	78,674.
BB	7'	Polished Macassar Ebony	80,626.
BB	7'	"Monticello" Polished Ebony	70,496.
BB	7'	"Monticello" Satin Mahogany	71,190.
BB	7'	"Monticello" Satin Rosewood	87,368.
CC	9' 4"	Satin Ebony	97,240.
CC	9' 4"	Polished Ebony	101,650.
CC	9' 4"	Satin Rosewood	110,000.

May Berlin

Verticals

Model	Size	Style and Finish	List Price*
M 114 T	45"	Polished Ebony	5,180.
M 121 M	47½"	Continental Polished Ebony	5,580.
M 121 T	47½"	Polished Ebony	5,380.
M 121 T	47½"	Satin Beech/Cherry/Walnut	5,380.
M 121 T	47½"	Polished White	5,380.
M 126 N	49½"	"Noblesse" Polished Ebony	5,780.

Grands

Model	Size	Style and Finish	List Price*
M 162 T	5' 4"	Polished Ebony	14,780.
M 187 T	6' 2"	Polished Ebony	17,180.

Model	Size	Style and Finish	List Price*

Meister, Otto

Verticals

Model	Size	Style and Finish	List Price
C-45	45"	French Provincial Satin Cherry	3,770.
C-45	45"	American Country Satin Oak	3,770.
XU-26B	49"	Polished Ebony	5,580.
OU-132HA	52"	Polished Ebony	5,790.

Grands

Model	Size	Style and Finish	List Price
G-143	4' 8"	Polished Ebony	7,580.
G-143	4' 8"	Polished Mahogany	7,780.
G-143	4' 8"	French Provincial Polished Mahogany	7,780.
G-150	5'	Polished Ebony	7,910.
G-158	5' 2"	Polished Ebony	8,130.
G-168	5' 7"	Polished Ebony	8,560.
G-168	5' 7"	Polished Mahogany	8,280.

Miller, Henry F.

Verticals

Model	Size	Style and Finish	List Price
HMV-043	42½"	Continental Polished Ebony	4,100.
HMV-043	42½"	Continental Polished Mahogany	4,200.
HMV-045	43½"	French Provincial Satin Cherry	5,000.
HMV-045	43½"	Italian Provincial Satin Cherry	5,020.
HMV-045	43½"	Mediterranean Satin Oak	5,020.
HMV-047	46½"	Satin Ebony	4,832.
HMV-047	46½"	Polished Ebony	4,738.
HMV-047	46½"	Polished Mahogany	4,832.
HMV-048	48"	Satin Cherry	5,520.

Grands

Model	Size	Style and Finish	List Price
HMG-058S	4' 10"	Satin Ebony	10,410.
HMG-058S	4' 10"	Polished Ebony	10,310.
HMG-058S	4' 10"	Polished Mahogany	10,610.
HMG-063S	5' 3"	Satin Ebony	11,830.
HMG-063S	5' 3"	Polished Ebony	11,580.
HMG-063S	5' 3"	Polished Mahogany	12,030.

Nordiska

Verticals

Model	Size	Style and Finish	List Price
109-CM	43"	Continental Polished Ebony/Mahogany	3,480.
114-MC	45"	French Satin Walnut/Mahogany	4,580.
114-MCH	45"	Satin Walnut/Mahogany	4,580.
116-CB	46"	Chippendale Polished Ebony	4,580.
116-CB	46"	Chippendale Polished Walnut/Mahogany	4,780.

*For explanation of terms and prices, please see pages 117–121.

Model	Size	Style and Finish	List Price*

Nordiska (continued)

Model	Size	Style and Finish	List Price*
116-MC	46"	Satin Ebony/Walnut	4,580.
118-C GT	47"	Polished Ebony	4,480.
118-MC	47"	Satin Walnut/Mahogany/Oak	4,780.
120-CA	47"	Polished Ebony	4,780.
120-CA	47"	Polished Walnut/Mahogany	4,980.
126-PRO	50"	Polished Ebony	5,580.
126-PRO	50"	Satin Walnut	5,580.
126-PRO	50"	Satin Mahogany	5,780.
131	52"	Polished Ebony	6,180.
131	52"	Satin Mahogany	6,380.

Grands

Model	Size	Style and Finish	List Price*
B	4' 8"	Polished Ebony	8,980.
B	4' 8"	Polished Walnut/Mahogany	9,390.
D	5'	Satin and Polished Ebony	9,590.
D	5'	Satin Walnut	10,180.
D	5'	Polished Walnut/Mahogany	10,180.
D	5'	Polished Sapele Mahogany/White	9,980.
D	5'	Demi-Chippendale Polished Ebony	10,500.
D	5'	Demi-Chippendale Satin Mahogany	11,100.
D	5'	Demi-Chippendale Polished Mahogany/Walnut	11,100.
D	5'	Demi-Chippendale Polished Sapele Mahogany	10,780.
G	5' 5"	Polished Ebony	10,780.
G	5' 5"	Polished Sapele Mahogany	11,100.
G	5' 5"	Polished Walnut/Mahogany	11,380.
G	5' 5"	Demi-Chippendale Polished Ebony	11,780.
G	5' 5"	Demi-Chippendale Polished Walnut/Mahogany	12,380.
G	5' 5"	Regency Polished Ebony	11,380.
G	5' 5"	Regency Polished Walnut/Mahogany	11,980.
G	5' 5"	Satin Ebony with Acrylic	24,600.
K	6' 1"	Polished Ebony	12,580.
K	6' 1"	Polished Walnut/Mahogany	13,180.
K	6' 1"	Empire Polished Ebony	13,980.
K	6' 1"	Empire Polished Walnut/Mahogany	14,580.
K	6' 1"	Imperial Polished Ebony	13,180.
K	6' 1"	Imperial Polished Walnut/Mahogany	13,780.
O	7'	Polished Ebony	21,180.
Y	9'	Polished Ebony	53,000.

Palatino

Verticals

Model	Size	Style and Finish	List Price*
PUP-110TS	43½"	Polished Ebony	4,790.
PUP-110TS	43½"	Polished Brown Mahogany	4,490.

Model	Size	Style and Finish	List Price*
PUP-121T	48"	Satin Ebony	5,798.
PUP-121T	48"	Polished Ebony	5,798.
PUP-121T	48"	Satin Brown Mahogany	5,998.
PUP-121T	48"	Polished Brown Mahogany/Cherry/Ivory	5,998.
PUP-121Y	48"	Satin Cherry	4,998.
PUP-123F	48½"	French Polished Ebony	5,598.
PUP-123F	48½"	French Polished Mahogany/Cherry/Ivory	5,798.
PUP-123C-JH	48½"	Satin Ebony/Brown Mahogany	5,690.
PUP-123C-JH	48½"	Satin White	5,890.
PUP-123T	48½"	Satin Ebony	5,598.
PUP-123T	48½"	Polished Ebony	5,598.
PUP-123T	48½"	Satin Brown Mahogany	5,798.
PUP-123T	48½"	Polished Brown Mahogany/Cherry/Red/Ivory	5,798.
PUP-123TU-A	48½"	Polished Ebony w/Decorated Wood Panel	5,990.
PUP-123Y	48½"	Polished Ebony	5,598.
PUP-123Y	48½"	Polished Brown Mahogany/Cherry/Ivory/Red	5,798.
PUP-124	49"	Polished Ebony	6,198.
PUP-124T1	49"	Polished Ebony	5,998.
PUP-124T2	49"	Polished Ebony	5,998.
PUP-126T	50"	Polished Ebony	5,998.

Grands

Model	Size	Style and Finish	List Price*
PGD-46F	4' 6"	French Satin Ebony	9,540.
PGD-46F	4' 6"	French Polished Ebony	9,540.
PGD-46F	4' 6"	French Polished Brown Mahogany	9,940.
PGD-46T	4' 6"	Satin Ebony	9,290.
PGD-46T	4' 6"	Polished Ebony	9,290.
PGD-46T	4' 6"	Polished Brown Mahogany/Ivory/Red	9,690.
PGD-50F	5'	French Satin Ebony	10,290.
PGD-50F	5'	French Polished Ebony	10,290.
PGD-50F	5'	French Polished Brown Mahogany	10,690.
PGD-50T	5'	Satin Ebony	10,090.
PGD-50T	5'	Polished Ebony	10,090.
PGD-50T	5'	Polished Brown Mahogany/Ivory/Red	10,490.
PGD-59F	5' 9"	French Satin Ebony	12,340.
PGD-59F	5' 9"	French Polished Ebony	12,340.
PGD-59F	5' 9"	French Polished Brown Mahogany	12,740.
PGD-59T	5' 9"	Satin Ebony	12,090.
PGD-59T	5' 9"	Polished Ebony	12,090.
PGD-59T	5' 9"	Polished Brown Mahogany	12,490.
PGD-90T	9'	Polished Ebony	70,200.

Pearl River

Verticals

Model	Size	Style and Finish	List Price*
UP-108D3	42½"	Continental Polished Ebony	3,140.

*For explanation of terms and prices, please see pages 117–121.

Model	Size	Style and Finish	List Price*

Pearl River (continued)

Model	Size	Style and Finish	List Price*
UP-108D3	42½"	Continental Polished Mahogany/Walnut	3,220.
UP-108D3	42½"	Continental Polished White	2,780.
UP-108M2	42½"	Demi-Chippendale Polished Ebony	3,480.
UP-108M2	42½"	Demi-Chippendale Polished Mahogany	3,580.
UP-108M2	42½"	Demi-Chippendale Polished Walnut/White	2,980.
UP-108T2	42½"	Polished Ebony	3,100.
UP-108T2	42½"	Polished Mahogany/Walnut	2,980.
UP-108T2	42½"	Polished White	3,220.
UP-110P1	43½"	Satin Walnut/Cherry/Oak	3,240.
UP-110P2	43½"	French Provincial Satin Cherry	3,960.
UP-110P2	43½"	Satin Oak	3,440.
UP-110P5	43½"	Italian Provincial Satin Walnut/Cherry	3,960.
UP-110P6	43½"	French Classic Satin Cherry	4,280.
UP-115E	45"	Satin Ebony/Oak/Walnut	3,860.
UP-115M	45"	Polished Ebony	3,660.
UP-115M	45"	Polished Dark Mahogany	3,740.
UP-115P1	45"	Satin Walnut	4,580.
UP-115P1	45"	Satin Cherry	4,140.
UP-118E	47"	Polished Ebony	3,980.
UP-118E	47"	Polished Mahogany	3,980.
UP-118E	47"	Polished Walnut/White	3,380.
UP-120S	48"	Polished Ebony	4,440.
UP-120S	48"	Polished Mahogany	4,540.
UP-125M1	49"	Polished Ebony (with Yamaha)	5,200.
UP-130T	51½"	Polished Ebony	4,590.
UP-130T2	51½"	Polished Mahogany w/Burl Oval Inlay	5,780.

Grands

Model	Size	Style and Finish	List Price*
GP-142	4' 7"	Polished Ebony	7,190.
GP-142	4' 7"	Polished Mahogany	7,390.
GP-142D	4' 7"	French Provincial Satin Cherry	8,190.
GP-142P1	4' 7"	Satin Walnut	8,590.
GP-150	5'	Hand-rubbed Satin Ebony	7,790.
GP-150	5'	Polished Ebony	7,590.
GP-150	5'	Satin Cherry	7,790.
GP-150D	5'	Satin Walnut	8,390.
GP-159	5' 3"	Hand-rubbed Satin Ebony	8,990.
GP-159	5' 3"	Polished Ebony	8,790.
GP-159	5' 3"	Satin and Polished Mahogany	9,190.
GP-159H	5' 3"	Polished Walnut	9,790.
GP-170	5' 7"	Hand-rubbed Satin Ebony	10,990.
GP-170	5' 7"	Polished Ebony	10,790.
GP-170	5' 7"	Satin Mahogany	10,790.
GP-170	5' 7"	Polished Mahogany	11,190.

Model	Size	Style and Finish	List Price*
GP-170D	5' 7"	French Provincial Satin Cherry	11,390.
GP-183	6'	Polished Ebony	11,790.
GP-186	6' 1"	Euro-style Polished Ebony (Silver Plate & Trim)	12,790.
GP-188	6' 4"	Polished Ebony	15,790.
GP-198	6' 6"	Butterfly Lid Satin Blue & Pink/Silver	26,790.
GP-213	7'	Polished Ebony	17,200.
GP-275	9'	Polished Ebony	56,790.
GP-275F	9'	Polished Ebony	57,910.

Perzina, Gebr.

Verticals

Model	Size	Style and Finish	List Price*
GP-112	44"	Continental Polished Ebony	6,190.
GP-112	44"	Continental Polished Mahogany/Walnut/Oak	6,350.
GP-112	44"	Continental Polished White	6,350.
GP-112	44"	Continental Satin Finishes	6,350.
GP-112	44"	Polished Ebony	6,350.
GP-112	44"	Polished Mahogany/Walnut/Oak	6,550.
GP-112	44"	Polished White	6,550.
GP-112	44"	Satin Finishes	6,550.
GP-112	44"	Queen Anne Polished Ebony	6,550.
GP-112	44"	Queen Anne Polished Mahogany/Walnut	6,640.
GP-112	44"	Queen Anne Satin Walnut	6,640.
GP-118	46½"	Satin Ebony	8,590.
GP-118	46½"	Polished Ebony	8,190.
GP-118	46½"	Polished Mahogany/Walnut	8,590.
GP-122	48"	Polished Ebony	8,130.
GP-122	48"	Polished Ebony with Pommele Center	8,540.
GP-122	48"	Polished Mahogany/Walnut/Oak/White	8,670.
GP-122	48"	Satin Finishes	8,670.
GP-122	48"	Deco Leg Polished Ebony	8,570.
GP-122	48"	Deco Leg Polished Ebony w/Oak Trim	8,950.
GP-122	48"	Deco Leg Polished Mahogany/Oak/White	8,950.
GP-122	48"	Deco Leg Polished Ebony w/Bubinga Front	9,190.
GP-122	48"	Deco Leg Polished Bubinga	9,390.
GP-122	48"	Queen Anne Polished Ebony	8,570.
GP-122	48"	Queen Anne Polished Mahogany/Walnut	8,950.
GP-122	48"	Queen Anne Satin Walnut	8,950.
GP-122	48"	Queen Anne Polished Ebony w/Molding	8,670.
GP-122	48"	Queen Anne Pol. Mahogany/Walnut w/Molding	9,190.
GP-122	48"	Queen Anne Satin Walnut w/Molding	9,190.
GP-129	51"	Polished Ebony	9,290.
GP-129	51"	Polished Ebony w/Pommele Center	9,620.
GP-129	51"	Polished Mahogany/Walnut/Oak/White	9,920.
GP-129	51"	Satin Finishes	9,920.

*For explanation of terms and prices, please see pages 117–121.

Model	Size	Style and Finish	List Price*

Perzina, Gebr. (continued)

Model	Size	Style and Finish	List Price*
GP-129	51"	Queen Anne Polished Ebony	9,620.
GP-129	51"	Queen Anne Polished Mahogany/Walnut	10,190.
GP-129	51"	Queen Anne Satin Walnut	10,190.
GP-129	51"	Queen Anne Pol. Mahogany/Walnut w/Molding	10,560.
GP-129	51"	Queen Anne Satin Walnut w/Molding	10,560.
All models		With German slow-fall fallboard, add'l	290.

Grands

On E-series grands, other leg styles and finishes available by special order.

Model	Size	Style and Finish	List Price*
E-160	5' 3"	Polished Ebony	25,790.
E-160	5' 3"	Polished Mahogany/Walnut	27,160.
EX-160	5' 3"	Upgrade to Renner AA hammers, etc., add'l	1,200.
G-160	5' 3"	Polished Ebony	18,790.
G-160	5' 3"	Polished Mahogany/Walnut/Oak/White	19,520.
G-160	5' 3"	Satin Finishes	19,520.
G-160	5' 3"	Polished Ebony (round leg)	19,190.
G-160	5' 3"	Satin Mahogany/Walnut (round leg)	19,790.
G-160	5' 3"	Polished Mahogany/Walnut (round leg)	19,790.
G-160	5' 3"	Queen Anne Polished Ebony	19,190.
G-160	5' 3"	Queen Anne Satin Mahogany/Walnut	19,790.
G-160	5' 3"	Queen Anne Polished Mahogany/Walnut	19,790.
G-160	5' 3"	Designer Ebony w/Sapele Fallboard/Lid	20,220.
G-160	5' 3"	Designer Ebony w/Bubinga Fallboard/Lid	20,220.
G-160	5' 3"	Designer Satin Bubinga	21,690.
GX-160	5' 3"	Upgrade to Renner AA hammers, etc., add'l	1,200.
E-187	6' 1"	Polished Ebony	28,130.
E-187	6' 1"	Polished Mahogany/Walnut	29,510.
EX-187	6' 1"	Upgrade to Renner AA hammers, etc., add'l	1,200.
G-187	6' 1"	Polished Ebony	20,920.
G-187	6' 1"	Polished Mahogany/Walnut/Oak/White	21,960.
G-187	6' 1"	Satin Finishes	21,960.
G-187	6' 1"	Polished Ebony (round leg)	21,270.
G-187	6' 1"	Satin Mahogany/Walnut (round leg)	22,300.
G-187	6' 1"	Polished Mahogany/Walnut (round leg)	22,300.
G-187	6' 1"	Queen Anne Polished Ebony	21,270.
G-187	6' 1"	Queen Anne Satin Mahogany/Walnut	22,300.
G-187	6' 1"	Queen Anne Polished Mahogany/Walnut	22,300.
G-187	6' 1"	Designer Ebony w/Sapele Fallboard/Lid	22,640.
G-187	6' 1"	Designer Ebony w/Bubinga Fallboard/Lid	22,640.
G-187	6' 1"	Designer Satin Bubinga	24,660.
GX-187	6' 1"	Upgrade to Renner AA hammers, etc., add'l	1,200.

Petrof

Prices below do not include bench. Add from $220 to $630 (most are under $400), depending on choice of bench.

Verticals

Model	Size	Style and Finish	List Price
P 116 E1	45"	Continental Polished Ebony	10,290.
P 118 C1	46"	Chippendale Polished Mahogany/Walnut	12,448.
P 118 D1	46"	Demi-Chip. Designer Pol. Mahogany/Walnut	11,694.
P 118 G1	46"	Polished Ebony/Mahogany/Walnut	11,980.
P 118 M1	46"	Polished Ebony/Mahogany/Walnut	11,408.
P 118 P1	46"	Satin Mahogany	11,148.
P 118 P1	46"	Classic Polished Ebony/Mahogany/Walnut	11,148.
P 118 R1	46"	Rococo Satin White	13,202.
P 125 F1	49½"	Satin Mahogany	12,942.
P 125 F1	49½"	Polished Ebony/Mahogany/Walnut	12,942.
P 125 G1	49½"	Polished Ebony/Mahogany/Walnut	13,384.
P 125 M1	49½"	Polished Ebony/Mahogany/Walnut	13,150.
P 131 M1	51"	Polished Ebony/Mahogany/Walnut	16,660.
P 135 K1	53"	"Classic" Polished Ebony	20,040.

Grands

Model	Size	Style and Finish	List Price
VI	4' 8½"	Polished Ebony/Mahogany/Walnut	28,100.
VI DC	4' 8½"	Demi-Chip. Polished Ebony/Mahogany/Walnut	29,140.
V	5' 2"	Polished Ebony/Mahogany/Walnut	29,920.
V	5' 2"	Satin Walnut	29,920.
V DC	5' 2"	Demi-Chip. Polished Ebony/Mahogany/Walnut	31,220.
IV	5' 7"	"Classic" Polished Ebony/Mahogany/Walnut	36,680.
IV	5' 7"	Satin Walnut	31,480.
IV C	5' 7"	Chippendale Polished Ebony/Mahogany/Walnut	37,980.
IV DC	5' 7"	Demi-Chip. Polished Ebony/Mahogany/Walnut	35,640.
IV	5' 7"	Rococo Satin White	40,320.
III S	6' 3"	Polished Ebony	32,780.
III	6' 3"	"Majestic" Polished Ebony/Mahogany/Walnut	36,940.
210	6' 10"	"Pasat" Polished Ebony	58,000.
II	7' 5"	Polished Ebony/Walnut	66,000.
I	9' 2"	"Mistral" Polished Ebony	91,800.

PianoDisc

Prices for PianoDisc and QuietTime systems vary by piano manufacturer and installer. The following are suggested retail prices from PianoDisc. The usual dealer discounts may apply, especially as an incentive to purchase a piano.

Opus7 "Opulence," factory-installed or retrofitted		19,295.
Opus7 "Luxury," factory-installed or retrofitted		15,295.
Opus7 Performance Package option		3,435.

*For explanation of terms and prices, please see pages 117–121.

Model	Size	Style and Finish	List Price*

PianoDisc (continued)

228CFX System, factory-installed or retrofitted:

Playback only		7,695.
Add for MX (Music Expansion) Platinum (64 MB w/35 hrs. of music included)		2,069.
Add for MX (Music Expansion) Basic (32 MB w/25 hrs. of music included)		1,448.
Add for SymphonyPro Sound Module		1,345.
Add for TFT MIDI Record system		1,868.
Add for PianoMute Rail		688.
Add for amplified speakers, pair		764.

PianoCD System	6,895.
iQ Extreme (w/Apple iPod included)	7,295.
iQ Alone (without control unit)	6,395.
QuietTime GT-2 (Control unit w/ Piano and Organ sounds, MIDI Strip, MIDI interface board, pedal switches, cable, headphones, power supply, PianoMute rail)	2,995.
QuietTime MagicStar (Same as above but with full General MIDI sound set)	3,395.
MIDI Controller (TFT MIDI Strip, MIDI interface board, pedal switches, cable, power supply)	2,055.

Pramberger

Pramberger Legacy Series Verticals

Model	Size	Style and Finish	List Price
LV-108	42"	Continental Polished Ebony	4,090.
LV-108	42"	Continental Polished Mahogany/Ivory	4,190.
LV-43F	43"	French Provincial Satin Cherry/Brown Oak	4,990.
LV-43T	43"	Satin Mahogany/Walnut	4,990.
LV-118	46½"	Polished Ebony	4,990.
LV-118	46½"	Satin Ebony/Polished Mahogany	5,190.

Pramberger Signature Series Verticals

Model	Size	Style and Finish	List Price
PV-110F	43"	French Provincial Satin Cherry	5,790.
PV-110R	43"	Renaissance Satin Walnut	5,590.
PV-110T	43"	Satin Mahogany	5,590.
PV-118F	46½"	French Provincial Satin Cherry	6.700.
PV-118R	46½"	Renaissance Satin Walnut	6,700.
PV-118T	46½"	Satin Mahogany	6,700.
PV-118S	46½"	Satin and Polished Ebony	6,790.
PV-118S	46½"	Lacquer Satin Mahogany/Walnut	6,790.
PV-121	48"	Polished Ebony	6,890.
PV-121	48"	Polished Mahogany	6,890.
PV-131	52"	Polished Ebony	6,990.
PV-131	52"	Polished Mahogany	7,190.

Model	Size	Style and Finish	List Price*

J.P. Pramberger Platinum Series Verticals

Model	Size	Style and Finish	List Price*
JP-116	45"	Satin Ebony	10,700.
JP-116	45"	Polished Ebony	10,400.
JP-116	45"	Lacquer Semi-Gloss Mahogany/Walnut	11,600.
JP-118F	46½"	French Provincial Lacquer Semi-Gloss Cherry	8,900.
JP-118T	46½"	Lacquer Semi-Gloss Mahogany	8,900.
JP-125	49"	Satin Ebony	11,100.
JP-125	49"	Polished Ebony	10,700.
JP-125	49"	Lacquer Semi-Gloss Mahogany/Walnut	12,000.
JP-125	49"	Polished Mahogany/Walnut	12,000.
JP-125	49"	Lacquer Semi-Gloss Bubinga/Rosewood	12,300.
JP-131	52"	Satin Ebony	12,200.
JP-131	52"	Polished Ebony	11,800.
JP-131	52"	Lacquer Semi-Gloss Mahogany/Walnut	13,200.
JP-131	52"	Polished Mahogany/Walnut	13,200.
JP-131	52"	Lacquer Semi-Gloss Bubinga/Rosewood	13,600.

Pramberger Legacy Series Grands

Model	Size	Style and Finish	List Price*
LG-140	4' 7"	Polished Ebony	10,090.
LG-140	4' 7"	Polished Mahogany/Walnut	10,790.
LG-145	4' 8"	Polished Ebony	10,090.
LG-145	4' 8"	Polished Mahogany/Walnut	10,790.
LG-150	4' 11½"	Satin Ebony	11,790.
LG-150	4' 11½"	Polished Ebony	11,090.
LG-150	4' 11½"	Polished Mahogany/Walnut	11,790.
LG-157	5' 2"	Satin Ebony	12,490.
LG-157	5' 2"	Polished Ebony	11,790.
LG-157	5' 2"	Polished Mahogany/Walnut	12,490.

Pramberger Signature Series Grands

Model	Size	Style and Finish	List Price*
PS-150	5'	Satin Ebony	14,390.
PS-150	5'	Polished Ebony	13,790.
PS-150	5'	Lacquer Satin Mahogany/Walnut	14,390.
PS-150	5'	Polished Mahogany/Walnut	14,390.
PS-157	5' 2"	Satin Ebony	14,990.
PS-157	5' 2"	Polished Ebony	14,390.
PS-157	5' 2"	Lacquer Satin Mahogany/Walnut	14,990.
PS-157	5' 2"	Polished Satin Mahogany/Walnut	14,990.
PS-175	5' 9"	Satin Ebony	15,990.
PS-175	5' 9"	Polished Ebony	15,090.
PS-175	5' 9"	Lacquer Satin Mahogany/Walnut	16,290.
PS-175	5' 9"	Polished Mahogany/Walnut	15,990.
PS-175KBF	5' 9"	French Provincial Lacquer Satin Cherry	17,990.
PS-175SKAF	5' 9"	Louis XV Lacquer Satin Dark Walnut/Cherry	18,790.
PS-185	6' 1"	Satin Ebony	16,890.
PS-185	6' 1"	Polished Ebony	15,990.

*For explanation of terms and prices, please see pages 117–121.

Model	Size	Style and Finish	List Price*

Pramberger (continued)

PS-185	6' 1"	Lacquer Satin Mahogany/Walnut	16,890.
PS-185	6' 1"	Polished Mahogany/Walnut	16,890.

J.P. Pramberger Platinum Series Grands

JP-160S	5' 3"	Satin Ebony	24,300.
JP-160S	5' 3"	Polished Ebony	23,600.
JP-160S	5' 3"	Lacquer Semi-Gloss Mahogany/Walnut	25,600.
JP-179F	5' 10"	Fr. Prov. Lacquer S-G Mahogany/Wal./Cherry	32,400.
JP-179L	5' 10"	Satin Ebony	27,700.
JP-179L	5' 10"	Polished Ebony	27,000.
JP-179L	5' 10"	Lacquer Semi-Gloss Mahogany/Walnut	29,000.
JP-179L	*5' 10"*	*Polished Bubinga/Pommele*	*29,000.*
JP-190A	6' 3"	Satin Ebony	31,900.
JP-190A	6' 3"	Polished Ebony	31,200.
JP-190A	6' 3"	Lacquer Semi-Gloss Mahogany/Walnut	33,200.
JP-190A	*6' 3"*	*Polished Bubinga/Pommele*	*33,600.*
JP-208B	6' 10"	Satin Ebony	34,500.
JP-208B	6' 10"	Polished Ebony	33,800.
JP-208B	6' 10"	Lacquer Semi-Gloss Mahogany/Walnut	35,800.
JP-228C	7' 6"	Satin Ebony	38,600.
JP-228C	7' 6"	Polished Ebony	37,400.
JP-280E	9' 2"	Polished Ebony	90,800.

QRS / Pianomation

Prices for Pianomation systems vary by piano manufacturer, installer, and accessories. The following are approximate retail prices for installed systems and accessories from QRS. The usual dealer discounts may apply, especially as an incentive to purchase a piano.

Pianomation 2000C with pedal solenoid and sostenuto trapwork	5,995.
Pianomation Petine with pedal solenoid, sostenuto trapwork, and amplified speaker	7,130.
Pianomation Ancho with pedal solenoid, sostenuto trapwork, and amplified speaker	7,470.
Amplified Speaker, each	350.
PNOscan, installed	1,995.
SilentPNO, installed	2,995.
Grand Piano Mute Rail (alone), installed	399.
NetPiano, Lifetime Subscription, Pianomation Owner	2,280.
Qsync	1,398.
Playola with 2000C	6,000.

Model	Size	Style and Finish	List Price*

Remington

Verticals

Model	Size	Style and Finish	List Price
RV-108	42"	Continental Polished Ebony	4,090.
RV-108	42"	Continental Polished Mahogany/Ivory	4,190.
RV-43F	43"	French Provincial Satin Cherry/Brown Oak	4,990.
RV-43T	43"	Satin Mahogany/Walnut	4,990.
RV-118	45"	Polished Ebony	4,990.
RV-118	45"	Polished Mahogany	5,190.
RV-121	48"	Polished Ebony	5,390.
RV-121	48"	Polished Mahogany	5,590.
RV-131	52"	Polished Ebony	5,790.
RV-131	52"	Polished Mahogany	5,890.

Grands

Model	Size	Style and Finish	List Price
RG-140	4' 7"	Polished Ebony	10,290.
RG-140	4' 7"	Polished Mahogany	10,790.
RG-150	4' 11½"	Polished Ebony	11,090.
RG-150	4' 11½"	Polished Mahogany	11,790.
RG-157	5' 2"	Polished Ebony	11,790.
RG-157	5' 2"	Polished Mahogany	12,490.
RG-175	5' 9"	Polished Ebony	13,990.
RG-175	5' 9"	Polished Mahogany	14,790.
RG-185	6' 1"	Polished Ebony	15,190.
RG-185	6' 1"	Polished Mahogany	15,990.

Ritmüller

Verticals

Model	Size	Style and Finish	List Price
UP-110R2	43½"	Continental Polished Ebony	3,760.
UP-110R2	43½"	Continental Polished Dark Mahogany/Walnut	3,780.
UP-110R4	43½"	French Provincial Satin Cherry	3,960.
UP-110R5	43½"	Satin Walnut	3,960.
UP-110R6	43½"	Satin American Country Oak	3,960.
UP-118R2	46½"	"Scandinavian Design" Polished Ebony	4,300.
UP-118R2	46½"	"Scandinavian Design" Polished Dark Mahogany	4,360.
UP-118R3	46½"	Satin Cherry	5,100.
UP-120R	48"	Polished Ebony	4,800.
UP-120R	48"	Polished Dark Mahogany/Walnut/White	4,840.
UP-120R1	48"	"European Decorator" Pol. Ebony w/Mahogany	4,900.
UP-120R2	48"	Chippendale Satin Walnut/Mahogany	5,020.
UP-120R3	48"	"Euro-Modern" Continental Polished Ebony	5,300.
UP-120R4	48"	French Provincial Satin Cherry	5,180.
UP-120R6	48"	Queen Anne Satin Cherry	5,440.
UP-120R7	48"	Italian Provincial Satin Walnut	5,440.
UP-120R8	48"	American Classic Satin Walnut	5,440.

*For explanation of terms and prices, please see pages 117–121.

Ritmüller (continued)

Model	Size	Style and Finish	List Price*
UP-123R	48"	"Classic Euro" Polished Ebony	5,780.
UP-123R	48"	"Classic Euro" Polished Dark Mahogany/Walnut	5,820.
UP-123R1	48"	"Deluxe European" Polished Ebony	5,780.
UP-125R	49"	"European" Polished Ebony w/Mahogany Trim	6,160.
UP-125R2	49"	"Deluxe Euro." Pol. Ebony w/Mahogany Side	6,320.
UP-126R	49"	Polished Ebony	6,180.
UP-130R	51"	Polished Ebony (movable front)	6,320.
UP-130R	51"	Satin Walnut (movable front)	6,380.
UP-130R	51"	Polished Dark Mahogany (movable front)	6,380.
UP-130R1	51"	Polished Ebony	6,280.
UP-130R2	51"	Polished Ebony	6,580.
UP-132R	52"	Polished Ebony	6,580.

Grands

Model	Size	Style and Finish	List Price*
GP-148R	4' 10"	Hand-rubbed Satin Ebony (round leg, brass trim)	8,790.
GP-148R	4' 10"	Polished Ebony (round leg, brass trim)	8,590.
GP-148R	4' 10"	Polished Mahogany (round leg, brass trim)	8,990.
GP-148R1	4' 10"	Polished Ebony (tapered leg, brass trim)	8,190.
GP-159R	5' 3"	Hand-rubbed Satin Ebony (round leg, brass trim)	10,790.
GP-159R	5' 3"	Polished Ebony (round leg, brass trim)	10,590.
GP-159R	5' 3"	Satin Mahogany (round leg, brass trim)	10,990.
GP-159R	5' 3"	Pol. Mahogany/Walnut (round leg, brass trim)	10,990.
GP-159R1	5' 3"	Hand-rubbed Sat. Ebony (tapered leg, brass trim)	10,390.
GP-159R1	5' 3"	Polished Ebony (tapered leg, brass trim)	10,190.
GP-159R1	5' 3"	Polished Dark Mahog. (tapered leg, brass trim)	10,590.
GP-159R2	5' 3"	Louis XV Satin Cherry	11,390.
GP-183R	6'	Hand-rubbed Satin Ebony (round leg, brass trim)	14,390.
GP-183R	6'	Polished Ebony (round leg, brass trim)	14,190.
GP-183R1	6'	Hand-rubbed Sat. Ebony (tapered leg, brass trim)	14,190.
GP-183R1	6'	Polished Ebony (tapered leg, brass trim)	13,990.
GP-213R1	7'	Polished Ebony	18,790.
GP-275R1	9'	Polished Ebony	64,790.

Samick
and Conover Cable

Verticals

Model	Size	Style and Finish	List Price*
JS-042	42"	Continental Polished Ebony	3,990.
JS-042	42"	Continental Polished Mahogany/Walnut/Ivory	3,990.
JS-042	42"	Continental Satin Cherry/Walnut	4,090.
JS-143F	43"	French Provincial Satin Cherry	5,090.
JS-143M	43"	Mediterranean Satin Brown Oak	5,090.
JS-143T	43"	Satin Mahogany	5,090.
JS-115	45"	Satin Ebony	4,590.

Model	Size	Style and Finish	List Price*
JS-115	45"	Polished Ebony	4,490.
JS-115	45"	Satin Mahogany/Walnut	4,490.
JS-115	45"	Polished Mahogany/Walnut	4,590.
JS-247	46½"	Satin Ebony/Mahogany/Walnut	6,790.
JS-247	46½"	Polished Ebony/Mahogany/Walnut	6,790.
JS-121M	48"	Satin Ebony	5,290.
JS-121M	48"	Polished Ebony	5,190.
JS-121M	48"	Polished Mahogany	5,290.
JS-131	52"	Satin Ebony	5,990.
JS-131	52"	Polished Ebony	5,890.
JS-131	52"	Polished Mahogany	5,990.

Grands

Model	Size	Style and Finish	List Price*
SIG-47	4' 7"	Polished Ebony	10,090.
SIG-47	4' 7"	Polished Mahogany	10,790.
SIG-48	4' 8"	Polished Ebony	10,090.
SIG-48	4' 8"	Polished Mahogany/Walnut	10,790.
SIG-50	4' 11½"	Satin Ebony	11,790.
SIG-50	4' 11½"	Polished Ebony	11,090.
SIG-50	4' 11½"	Lacquer Satin Mahogany and Pol. Mahogany	11,790.
SIG-50	4' 11½"	Lacquer Satin Walnut and Polished Walnut	11,790.
SIG-54	5' 4"	Satin Ebony	12,490.
SIG-54	5' 4"	Polished Ebony	11,790.
SIG-54	5' 4"	Lacquer Satin Mahogany and Pol. Mahogany	12,490.
SIG-54	5' 4"	Lacquer Satin Walnut and Polished Walnut	12,490.
SIG-54 KBF	5' 3"	French Provincial Satin Mahog./Walnut/Cherry	15,590.
SIG-57	5' 7"	Satin Ebony	14,190.
SIG-57	5' 7"	Polished Ebony	13,290.
SIG-57	5' 7"	Lacquer Satin Mahogany and Pol. Mahogany	14,190.
SIG-57	5' 7"	Lacquer Satin Walnut and Polished Walnut	14,190.
SIG-57L	5' 7"	Empire Polished Ebony	14,190.
SIG-57L	5' 7"	Empire Lacquer Satin Mahog. and Pol. Mahog.	15,690.
SIG-61	6' 1"	Satin Ebony	15,390.
SIG-61	6' 1"	Polished Ebony	14,490.
SIG-61	6' 1"	Lacquer Satin Mahogany/Walnut	15,390.
SIG-61	6' 1"	Polished Mahogany/Walnut	15,390.

Sauter

Standard wood veneers are walnut, mahogany, oak, ash, and alder.

Verticals

Model	Size	Style and Finish	List Price*
122	48"	"Ragazza" Polished Ebony	30,140.
122	48"	"Ragazza" Satin Cherry	29,840.
122	48"	"Ragazza" Polished Cherry/Yew	35,240.
122	48"	"Vista" Polished Ebony	32,940.

*For explanation of terms and prices, please see pages 117–121.

Model	Size	Style and Finish	List Price*

Sauter (continued)

Model	Size	Style and Finish	List Price
122	48"	"Vista" Satin Maple	31,440.
122	48"	"Vista" Satin Cherry	32,780.
122	48"	"Master Class" Polished Ebony	38,580.
122	48"	Peter Maly "Artes" Polished Ebony	42,920.
122	48"	Peter Maly "Artes" Pol. Palisander/Macassar	44,240.
122	48"	Peter Maly "Artes" Polished White	43,720.
122	48"	Peter Maly "Pure Noble" Pol. Ebony/Veneers	40,180.
122	48"	Peter Maly "Pure Noble" Polished White/Red	41,260.
122	48"	Peter Maly "Pure Basic" Satin Ebony/Walnut	32,720.
122	48"	Peter Maly "Pure Basic" Satin White/Maple	32,720.
122	48"	Peter Maly "Rondo" Polished Ebony	35,820.
122	48"	Peter Maly "Rondo" Satin Wenge	33,140.
122	48"	Peter Maly "Vitrea" Colored Ebony with Glass	33,580.
122	48"	"Schulpiano" Satin Beech/Black Ash	26,380.
130	51"	"Master Class" Polished Ebony	43,620.
130	51"	"Competence" Polished Ebony	37,280.
130	51"	"Competence" Satin Walnut	35,420.
130	51"	"Cura" Satin Walnut	41,740.
130	51"	"Cura" Satin Cherry	43,080.

Grands

Model	Size	Style and Finish	List Price
160	5' 3"	"Alpha" Polished Ebony	77,580.
160	5' 3"	"Alpha" Satin Standard Wood Veneers	71,660.
160	5' 3"	Chippendale Satin Cherry	80,420.
160	5' 3"	Chippendale Satin Standard Wood Veneers	77,460.
160	5' 3"	"Noblesse" Satin Cherry	86,220.
160	5' 3"	"Noblesse" Polished Cherry	95,740.
160	5' 3"	"Noblesse" Satin Burl Walnut	90,040.
160	5' 3"	"Noblesse" Satin Standard Wood Veneers	83,280.
160	5' 3"	"Noblesse" Polished Standard Wood Veneers	92,660.
185	6' 1"	"Delta" Polished Ebony	84,720.
185	6' 1"	"Delta" Polished Ebony w/Burl Walnut	86,840.
185	6' 1"	"Delta" Polished Pyramid Mahogany	93,480.
185	6' 1"	"Delta" Polished Bubinga	92,780.
185	6' 1"	"Delta" Polished Rio Palisander	93,480.
185	6' 1"	"Delta" Satin Maple with Silver	79,720.
185	6' 1"	"Delta" Polished White	87,340.
185	6' 1"	"Delta" Satin Standard Wood Veneers	77,960.
185	6' 1"	Chippendale Satin Cherry	86,600.
185	6' 1"	Chippendale Satin Standard Wood Veneers	83,660.
185	6' 1"	"Noblesse" Satin Cherry	92,540.
185	6' 1"	"Noblesse" Polished Cherry	102,980.
185	6' 1"	"Noblesse" Satin Burl Walnut	96,220.
185	6' 1"	"Noblesse" Satin Standard Wood Veneers	89,720.

Model	Size	Style and Finish	List Price*
185	6' 1"	"Noblesse" Polished Standard Wood Veneers	100,480.
210	6' 11"	Peter Maly "Vivace" Polished Ebony	118,580.
210	6' 11"	Peter Maly "Vivace" Satin Wood Veneers	110,740.
210	6' 11"	Peter Maly "Vivace" Polished White	120,340.
220	7' 3"	"Omega" Polished Ebony	107,700.
220	7' 3"	"Omega" Polished Burl Walnut	119,960.
220	7' 3"	"Omega" Polished Pyramid Mahogany	118,880.
220	7' 3"	"Omega" Satin Standard Wood Veneers	103,380.
230	7' 6"	Peter Maly "Ambiente" Polished Ebony	136,160.
230	7' 6"	Peter Maly "Ambiente" Pol. Ebony w/Crystals	155,660.
275	9'	"Concert" Polished Ebony	186,040.

Schimmel

When not mentioned, satin finish available on special order at same price as high-polish finish.

Verticals

C 112 S	44"	Open-Pore Ebony/Oak/Walnut	17,780.
C 116 T	46"	Polished Ebony	16,180.
C 116 T	46"	Open-Pore Alder	16,780.
C 116 T	46"	Open-Pore Beech	15,780.
C 116 T	46"	Open-Pore Walnut	16,180.
C 116 T	46"	Satin Cherry	17,180.
C 116 T	46"	Polished Mahogany	17,180.
C 116 T	46"	Polished White	16,780.
C 120 I	47"	"International" Polished Ebony	16,780.
C 120 I	47"	"International" Polished Mahogany	18,780.
C 120 I	47"	"International" Polished White	17,380.
C 120 S	47"	Open-Pore Ebony/Oak (school studio)	17,980.
C 120 T	47"	Polished Ebony	17,580.
C 120 T	47"	Open-Pore Alder/Beech	17,580.
C 120 T	47"	Open-Pore Walnut	17,980.
C 120 T	47"	Satin Cherry	19,980.
C 120 T	47"	Polished Mahogany	19,320.
C 120 T	47"	Polished White	18,780.
C 120 TA	47"	"Akademie" Polished Ebony	18,780.
K 122 E	48"	"Elegance" Polished Ebony	24,780.
K 122 MC	48"	"Modern Cubus" Polished Ebony	25,980.
K 122 MC	48"	"Modern Cubus" Satin Swiss Pear	25,980.
K 122 MC	48"	"Modern Cubus" Polished White	26,380.
K 122 TA	48"	"Akademie" Polished Ebony	24,780.
C 124 R	49"	"Royal" Polished Ebony	22,780.
C 124 R	49"	"Royal" Polished Mahogany	25,380.
C 124 RI	49"	"Royale Intarsia Flora" Polished Mahogany	26,380.
C 124 T	49"	Polished Ebony	20,580.

*For explanation of terms and prices, please see pages 117–121.

Schimmel (continued)

Model	Size	Style and Finish	List Price*
C 124 T	49"	Polished Ebony w/Oval Decoration	21,380.
C 124 T	49"	Polished Mahogany	22,380.
C 124 T	49"	Polished Mahogany w/Oval Decoration	23,380.
C 124 T	49"	Open-Pore Walnut Antique w/Oval Decoration	22,380.
K 125 N	49"	"Noblesse" Polished Ebony	27,380.
K 125 N	49"	"Noblesse" Polished Mahogany	28,780.
K 125 P	49"	"Prestige" Polished Ebony	28,380.
K 125 P	49"	"Prestige" Polished Mahogany	29,980.
C 130 T	51"	Polished Ebony	24,780.
C 130 T	51"	Polished Ebony w/Oval Decoration	25,180.
C 130 T	51"	Open-Pore Walnut	23,180.
C 130 T	51"	Polished Mahogany/Walnut	26,580.
K 132 T	52"	Polished Ebony	29,180.
K 132 T	52"	Polished Mahogany	32,580.
K 132 W	52"	"Wilhelmina" Satin Mahogany/Walnut	38,780.

Grands

Model	Size	Style and Finish	List Price*
K 169 AN	5' 7"	"Art Nouveau" Polished Ebony	58,780.
K 169 AN	5' 7"	"Art Nouveau" Polished Mahogany/White	60,780.
K 169 BE	5' 7"	"Belle Epoque" Polished Ebony	55,780.
K 169 R	5' 7"	"Royal" Polished Ebony	52,780.
K 169 R	5' 7"	"Royal" Polished Mahogany/White	54,780.
K 169 RIF	5' 7"	"Royal Intarsie Flora" Polished Mahogany	56,780.
K 169 T	5' 7"	Polished Ebony	50,780.
K 169 T	5' 7"	Polished Mahogany/White/Burl Walnut/Ash	52,780.
K 169 T	5' 7"	Polished Flame Mahogany/Macassar	59,780.
K 169 T	5' 7"	Polished Bubinga/Bird's-Eye Maple	58,580.
K 169 TIH	5' 7"	"Intarsie Harp" Polished Ebony	56,780.
K 169 TIV	5' 7"	"Intarsie Vase" Polished Mahogany	56,780.
C 182 AN	6'	"Art Nouveau" Polished Ebony	37,980.
C 182 AN	6'	"Art Nouveau" Polished Mahogany	38,780.
C 182 T	6'	Polished Ebony	34,780.
C 182 T	6'	Polished Mahogany	35,980.
K 189 AN	6' 3"	"Art Nouveau" Polished Ebony	62,780.
K 189 AN	6' 3"	"Art Nouveau" Polished Mahogany/White	64,780.
K 189 BE	6' 3"	"Belle Epoque" Polished Ebony	59,780.
K 189 EP	6' 3"	"Empire" Satin and Polished Mahogany	66,780.
K 189 NWS	6' 3"	"Nikolaus W. Schimmel Special Edition"	64,780.
K 189 R	6' 3"	"Royal" Polished Ebony	56,780.
K 189 R	6' 3"	"Royal" Polished Mahogany/White	58,780.
K 189 RIF	6' 3"	"Royal Intarsie Flora" Polished Mahogany	60,780.
K 189 T	6' 3"	Polished Ebony	54,780.
K 189 T	6' 3"	Polished Walnut/Mahogany/White	56,780.
K 189 T	6' 3"	Polished Burl Walnut/Brown Ash	62,580.

Model	Size	Style and Finish	List Price*
K 189 T	6' 3"	Polished Flame Mahogany/Macassar	63,780.
K 189 T	6' 3"	Polished Bubinga/Bird's-Eye Maple	62,580.
K 189 T	6' 3"	Open-Pore Walnut Antique	54,780.
K 189 T	6' 3"	"Red Diamond"	62,780.
K 189 TA	6' 3"	"Akademie" Polished Ebony	54,780.
K 189 TIH	6' 3"	"Intarsie Harp" Polished Ebony	60,780.
K 189 TIV	6' 3"	"Intarsie Vase" Polished Mahogany	60,780.
K 213 AN	7'	"Art Nouveau" Polished Ebony	64,780.
K 213 AN	7'	"Art Nouveau" Polished Mahogany/White	66,780.
K 213 G	7'	*"Glas" Clear Acrylic and White*	130,780.
K 213 NWS	7'	"Nikolaus W. Schimmel Special Edition"	68,780.
K 213 OA	7'	*"Otmar Alt" Polished Ebony w/Color Motifs*	149,780.
K 213 R	7'	"Royal" Polished Ebony	59,780.
K 213 R	7'	"Royal" Polished Mahogany/White	61,780.
K 213 T	7'	Polished Ebony	57,780.
K 213 T	7'	Polished Mahogany/Walnut/White	59,780.
K 213 T	7'	Polished Flame Mahogany/Macassar	66,780.
K 213 T	7'	Polished Burl Walnut/Brown Ash	65,580.
K 213 T	7'	Polished Bubinga/Bird's-Eye Maple	65,580.
K 213 T	7'	"Red Diamond"	65,780.
K 213 TA	7'	"Akademie" Polished Ebony	57,780.
K 230 T	7' 5"	Polished Ebony	70,780.
K 256 T	8' 4"	Polished Ebony	78,780.
K 280 T	9' 2"	Polished Ebony	102,780.

Schulze Pollmann

Verticals

114/P4	45"	Polished Ebony	7,990.
114/P4	45"	Polished Mahogany/Walnut	8,190.
114/P4	45"	Polished Peacock Ebony/Walnut/Mahogany	8,590.
114/P4	45"	Chippendale Peacock Mahogany/Walnut	8,790.
118/P8	46"	Polished Ebony	13,390.
118/P8	46"	Polished Briar Walnut/Mahogany	13,990.
118/P8	46"	Polished Feather or Peacock Mahogany	13,990.
126/P6	50"	Polished Ebony	14,990.
126/P6	50"	Polished Peacock Ebony/Mahog./Walnut/Cherry	15,990.
126/P6	50"	Polished Briar Mahogany/Walnut	15,990.
126/P6	50"	Polished Feather Mahogany	15,990.

Grands

160/GK	5' 3"	Polished Ebony (spade leg)	34,790.
160/GK	5' 3"	Polished Ebony (round leg)	36,590.
160/GK	5' 3"	Polished Briar Mahogany (spade leg)	38,790.
160/GK	5' 3"	Polished Briar Mahogany (round leg)	40,790.

*For explanation of terms and prices, please see pages 117–121.

Model	Size	Style and Finish	List Price*

Schulze Pollmann (continued)

Model	Size	Style and Finish	List Price
160/GK	5' 3"	Polished Feather Mahogany (spade leg)	44,790.
160/GK	5' 3"	Polished Feather Mahogany (round leg)	46,790.
197/G5	6' 7"	Polished Ebony (spade leg)	52,790.
197/G5	6' 7"	Polished Briar Mahogany (spade leg)	56,790.
197/G5	6' 7"	Polished Feather Mahogany (spade leg)	58,790.

Seiler

Euro = $1.60

Verticals

Model	Size	Style and Finish	List Price
116	46"	"Eduard Seiler" Polished Ebony	15,900.
116	46"	"Primus" Polished Ebony	17,960.
116	46"	"Mondial" Satin Ebony/Mahogany/Walnut/Oak	19,860.
116	46"	Satin Cherry Ribbon, Intarsia	22,460.
116	46"	Chippendale Satin Walnut	22,060.
122	48"	"Primus" Polished Ebony	22,100.
122	48"	"Konsole" Polished Ebony	22,400.
122	48"	"Konsole" Satin Ebony/Mahogany/Walnut/Oak	22,700.
122	48"	"Konsole" Polished Mahogany	27,100.
122	48"	"Konsole" Polished Mahogany w/Oval Paneling	28,720.
122	48"	"Konsole" Polished Burl Rosewood/Brown Ash	28,580.
122	48"	"Vienna" Polished Mahogany w/Floral Inlays	29,900.
126	50"	"Primus" Polished Ebony	23,280.
126	50"	"Konsole" Polished Ebony	23,580.
126	50"	"Konsole" Polished Ebony w/Oval Paneling	24,320.
126	50"	"Konsole" Satin Ebony/Mahogany/Walnut/Oak	24,020.
126	50"	"Konsole" Polished Mahogany	28,280.
132	52"	"Concert" Polished Ebony	28,060.
132	52"	"Concert" Polished Ebony w/Oval Paneling	28,780.
132	52"	"Concert" Satin Mahogany/Walnut	28,940.
132	52"	"Concert" Polished Mahogany	33,340.
132	52"	"Concert" Polished Mahogany w/Oval Paneling	34,960.
132	52"	"Concert" Polished Burl Rosewood/Brown Ash	34,520.
132	52"	"Concert" Pol. Ebony w/Oval Paneling in Ebony	32,020.
132	52"	"Concert" Pol. Ebony w/Rootwd. Pilaster Strips	32,600.
132	52"	"Concert" Pol. Ebony w/Oval Pan. & Pil. Strips	33,500.

Grands

Model	Size	Style and Finish	List Price
156	5' 1"	"Vision" Polished Ebony	50,780.
168	5' 6"	"Virtuoso" Polished Ebony	57,800.
168	5' 6"	"Virtuoso" Polished Mahogany	64,200.
186	6' 1"	"Maestro" Polished Ebony	61,000.
186	6' 1"	"Maestro" Open-Pore Walnut/Mahogany	61,000.
186	6' 1"	"Maestro" Polished Mahogany	67,400.

Model	Size	Style and Finish	List Price*
186	6' 1"	"Maestro" Polished Burl Rosewood	68,200.
186	6' 1"	"Maestro" Walnut Rootwood/Pol. Pyrm. Mahog.	70,800.
186	6' 1"	Chippendale Open-Pore Walnut	67,000.
186	6' 1"	"Westminster" Polished Mahogany, Intarsia	78,800.
186	6' 1"	"Florenz" Polished Walnut/Myrtle, Intarsia	78,800.
186	6' 1"	"Florenz" Polished Mahog./Myrtle, Intarsia	78,800.
186	6' 1"	"Louvre" Polished Ebony	67,000.
186	6' 1"	"Louvre" Polished Cherry, Intarsia	78,800.
186	6' 1"	"Prado" Polished Burl Rosewood	78,800.
186	6' 1"	"Prado" Polished Brown Ash	84,800.
186	6' 1"	"Stella" Polished Flame Maple w/Marquetry	84,800.
208	6' 10"	Polished Ebony	67,200.
242	8'	Polished Ebony	88,600.
278	9'	Polished Ebony	120,700.

Sejung

Sejung makes pianos under the names Falcone, Hobart M. Cable, and Geo. Steck. The large variety of styles and finishes offered under the three brand names are very similar from one brand to the next, and in most cases the prices are the same. To save space, I have compiled one master list of models for all three brands. Although I have used the generic model prefixes "U" and "C" for the verticals and "G" for grands, each brand actually has its own prefixes: UF, CF, and GF for Falcone; FV and FG for the Falcone Georgian series; UH, CH, and GH for Hobart M. Cable; and US, CS, and GS for Geo. Steck. All the vertical piano prices shown are for models *without* a slow-close fallboard. Models with a slow-close fallboard, where available, have model numbers ending with "D" and cost $120 more than shown. All the grand piano prices shown are for models *with* a slow-close fallboard. Models without a slow-close fallboard, where available, have model numbers omitting the final "D" and cost $120 less than shown. The Falcone Georgian series has upgraded cosmetic and technical features. The Falcone Georgian verticals cost the same as the other-named verticals, but the Falcone Georgian grands cost from $140 to $400 more, depending on size. Not all models, styles, and finishes shown are available under all names.

Verticals

Model	Size	Style and Finish	List Price
U 09	43"	Continental Polished Ebony	3,790.
U 09	43"	Continental Polished Other Finishes	3,910.
U 09	43"	Continental Satin Finishes	3,850.
U 09A	43"	Continental Polished Ebony (no back posts)	3,590.
U 09A	43"	Continental Pol. Other Finishes (no back posts)	3,710.
U 09L	43"	Polished Ebony	3,850.
U 09L	43"	Polished Other Finishes	3,970.
C 12F	44"	French Provincial Satin Cherry/Brown Oak	4,190.
C 12F1	44"	French Provincial Satin Cherry/Brown Oak	4,090.
C 12IP	44"	Italian Prov. Satin Walnut/Mahogany/Cherry	4,490.
C 12M	44"	Mediterranean Satin Cherry/Brown Oak	4,190.
C 12M1	44"	Mediterranean Satin Cherry/Brown Oak/Sapele	4,090.

*For explanation of terms and prices, please see pages 117–121.

Model	Size	Style and Finish	List Price*

Sejung (continued)

Model	Size	Style and Finish	List Price*
U 12F	44"	French Provincial Polished Ebony	4,110.
U 12F	44"	French Provincial Other Polished Finishes	4,230.
U 12F	44"	French Provincial Satin Finishes	4,170.
U 12FC	44"	12F Satin with Decorated Front Panel	4,210.
U 12T	44"	Polished Ebony	3,990.
U 12T	44"	Polished Other Finishes	4,110.
U 12T	44"	Satin Finishes	4,050.
C 13F	44½"	French Provincial Satin Cherry/Mahogany	4,490.
C 13F1	44½"	Fr. Prov. Satin Cherry/Brown Oak/Mahogany	4,690.
C 13M	44½"	Designer Satin Cherry/Dark Cherry/Mahogany	4,490.
C 13M1	44½"	Designer Satin Cherry/Brown Oak/Mahogany	4,690.
C 16AT	45½"	Satin Cherry/Brown Oak	4,690.
C 16F	45½"	Fr. Provincial Satin Cherry/Brown Oak/Walnut	4,390.
C 16FP	45½"	French Provincial Satin Cherry/Brown Oak	4,450.
C 16IP	45½"	Italian Provincial Satin Cherry/Walnut	4,450.
C 16QA	45½"	Queen Anne Satin Cherry/Brown Oak/Mahogany	4,790.
U 16IC	46"	Italian Provincial Polished Ebony	4,050.
U 16IC	46"	Italian Provincial Other Polished Finishes	4,170.
U 16ST	46"	Satin Finishes (school)	4,110.
U 16STL	46"	Polished Ebony (school with lock)	4,130.
U 16STL	46"	Polished Other Finishes (school with lock)	4,250.
U 16STL	46"	Satin Finishes (school with lock)	4,190.
U 16TC	46"	Polished Ebony w/Decorated Front Panel	4,130.
U 16TC	46"	Polished Other Finishes w/Decorated Front Panel	4,250.
U 18MS	46½"	Designer Other Polished Finishes w/Front Inlay	4,230.
C 19F	47"	Country French Satin Cherry/Brown Oak/Mahog.	4,590.
C 19F1	47"	Country French Satin Cherry/Brown Oak	4,590.
C 19M	47"	Mediterranean Satin Brown Oak/Cherry/Mahog.	4,590.
C 19M1	47"	Mediterranean Satin Cherry/Oak/Brown Oak	4,590.
C 19QA	47"	Queen Anne Satin Cherry/Brown Oak	4,990.
C 47CI	47"	Modern Designer C Polished Ebony	5,490.
C 47CI	47"	Modern Designer C Other Polished Finishes	5,610.
C 47F	47"	French Provincial Satin Cherry/Mahogany	5,790.
C 47M	47"	Mediterranean Satin Mahogany	5,790.
C 47R	47"	Modern Designer R Other Polished Finishes	5,710.
C 47V	47"	Modern Designer V Polished Ebony	5,990.
U 19F	47"	French Provincial Polished Ebony	4,190.
U 19F	47"	French Provincial Polished Other Finishes	4,310.
U 19F	47"	French Provincial Satin Finishes	4,250.
U 19FC	47"	Polished Other Finishes w/Decorated Front Panel	4,390.
U 19P	47"	Designer Polished Bubinga	4,370.
U 19P	47"	Designer Other Polished Finishes	4,250.
U 19ST	47"	Polished Ebony	4,090.

Model	Size	Style and Finish	List Price*
U 19ST	47"	Polished Other Finishes	4,210.
U 19ST	47"	Satin Finishes	4,150.
U 19T	47"	Polished Ebony	4,090.
U 19T	47"	Polished Other Finishes	4,210.
U 19T	47"	Satin Finishes	4,150.
U 20T	47"	Designer Polished Ebony	4,390.
U 20T	47"	Designer Other Polished Finishes	4,510.
U 210M	47½"	Designer Special Other Polished Finishes	4,390.
U 22F	48"	French Provincial Polished Ebony	4,410.
U 22F	48"	French Provincial Polished Other Finishes	4,530.
U 22IT	48"	Italian Designer Polished Ebony	4,490.
U 22T	48"	Polished Ebony	4,290.
U 22T	48"	Polished Other Finishes	4,410.
U 22T	48"	Satin Finishes	4,350.
U 22WT	48"	Metropolitan Designer Polished Ebony	4,490.
U 23F	48"	French Provincial Polished Ebony	4,590.
U 23F	48"	French Provincial Polished Other Finishes	4,710.
U 23F	48"	French Provincial Satin Finishes	4,650.
U 23T	48"	Designer Polished Ebony	4,470.
U 23T	48"	Designer Polished Other Finishes	4,590.
U 23T	48"	Designer Satin Finishes	4,530.
U 26T	48"	Designer Polished Ebony	4,350.
U 26T	48"	Designer Satin Finishes	4,410.
U 28	48"	Designer Special Polished Bubinga	5,230.
U 28S	48"	Designer Special Polished Bubinga w/Inlay	5,370.
U 230C	48½"	Designer Medieval Special Satin Finishes	5,070.
U 25B	49½"	Designer w/HM on Front Panel Polished Ebony	4,670.
U 25S	49½"	Designer w/BLK Oval Polished Ebony	4,610.
U 25SM	49½"	Designer w/BSP Oval Polished Ebony	4,530.
U 32E	52"	Professional Designer LHM Polished Ebony	5,990.
U 32F	52"	French Provincial Polished Ebony	4,610.
U 32F	52"	French Provincial Polished Other Finishes	4,730.
U 32H	52"	Professional Designer Polished Bubinga	5,370.
U 32T	52"	Polished Ebony	4,490.
U 32T	52"	Polished Other Finishes	4,610.
U 32T	52"	Satin Finishes	4,550.

Grands

Model	Size	Style and Finish	List Price*
G 42D	4' 8"	Satin Ebony	10,110.
G 42D	4' 8"	Polished Ebony	9,910.
G 42D	4' 8"	Satin Wood Finishes	10,510.
G 42D	4' 8"	Polished Wood Finishes	10,310.
G 42D	4' 8"	Polished Bubinga	10,910.
G 42D	4' 8"	Polished Ivory/White	10,110.
G 42FD	4' 8"	French Provincial Polished Ebony	10,390.

*For explanation of terms and prices, please see pages 117–121.

Model	Size	Style and Finish	List Price*

Sejung (continued)

Model	Size	Style and Finish	List Price*
G 42FD	4' 8"	French Provincial Satin Wood Finishes	10,990.
G 42FD	4' 8"	French Provincial Polished Wood Finishes	10,790.
G 42LD	4' 8"	Louis XVI Polished Ebony	10,230.
G 52D	5'	Satin Ebony	11,110.
G 52D	5'	Polished Ebony	10,910.
G 52D	5'	Satin Wood Finishes	11,510.
G 52D	5'	Polished Wood Finishes	11,310.
G 52D	5'	Polished Bubinga	11,910.
G 52FD	5'	French Provincial Polished Ebony	11,390.
G 52FD	5'	French Provincial Satin Wood Finishes	11,990.
G 52FD	5'	French Provincial Polished Wood Finishes	11,790.
G 52FD	5'	French Provincial Polished Ivory/White	11,590.
G 52FAD	5'	FrenchAnn Polished Wood Finishes	12,110.
G 52LD	5'	Louis XVI Polished Ebony	11,230.
G 52LD	5'	Louis XVI Polished Wood Finishes	11,630.
G 62D	5' 4"	Satin Ebony	12,110.
G 62D	5' 4"	Polished Ebony	11,910.
G 62D	5' 4"	Satin Wood Finishes	12,510.
G 62D	5' 4"	Polished Wood Finishes	12,310.
G 62D	5' 4"	Polished Bubinga	12,910.
G 62D	5' 4"	Polished Ivory/White	12,110.
G 62FD	5' 4"	French Provincial Satin Ebony	12,590.
G 62FD	5' 4"	French Provincial Satin Wood Finishes	12,990.
G 62FD	5' 4"	French Provincial Polished Wood Finishes	12,790.
G 62FD	5' 4"	French Provincial Polished Ivory/White	12,590.
G 62HLED	5' 4"	Louis XVI Polished Ebony (Hexagonal)	12,630.
G 62HLED	5' 4"	Louis XVI Polished Sapele (Hexagonal)	13,630.
G 62HLED	5' 4"	Louis XVI Polished Wood Finishes (Hexagonal)	13,630.
G 62PLBD	5' 4"	Louis XVI Polished Bubinga (Octagonal)	13,630.
G 62QAD	5' 4"	Queen Anne Polished Wood Finishes	13,110.
G 72D	5' 8"	Satin Ebony	13,110.
G 72D	5' 8"	Polished Ebony	12,910.
G 72D	5' 8"	Satin Wood Finishes	13,510.
G 72D	5' 8"	Polished Wood Finishes	13,310.
G 72D	5' 8"	Polished Bubinga	13,910.
G 72D	5' 8"	Polished Ivory/White	13,110.
G 72FD	5' 8"	French Provincial Polished Ebony	13,390.
G 72FD	5' 8"	French Provincial Satin Wood Finishes	13,990.
G 72FD	5' 8"	French Provincial Polished Wood Finishes	13,790.
G 72FD	5' 8"	French Provincial Polished Ivory/White	13,590.
G 72FFD	5' 8"	Rococo Polished Ivory/White	13,910.
G 72HLD	5' 8"	Louis XVI Satin Wood Finish (Hexagonal)	14,110.
G 72HLD	5' 8"	Louis XVI Polished Bubinga (Hexagonal)	15,710.

Model	Size	Style and Finish	List Price*
G 72LD	5' 8"	Louis XVI Polished Ebony	13,230.
G 72LD	5' 8"	Louis XVI Satin Wood Finishes	13,830.
G 72LD	5' 8"	Louis XVI Polished Wood Finishes	13,630.
G 72PLD	5' 8"	Louis XVI Polished Wood Finishes (Octagonal)	13,910.
G 72PLSD	5' 8"	Louis XVI Polished Wood Finishes (Octagongal)	14,410.
G 72PLSD	5' 8"	Louis XVI Polished Sapele (Octagonal)	15,010.
G 72QAD	5' 8"	Queen Anne Satin Wood Finishes	14,230.
G 87BCD	6' 2"	Polished Bubinga w/Rim Band/Beveled Lid	15,230.
G 87D	6' 2"	Satin Ebony	14,110.
G 87D	6' 2"	Polished Ebony	13,910.
G 87D	6' 2"	Polished Wood Finishes	14,310.
G 87D	6' 2"	Polished Bubinga	14,910.
G 87FD	6' 2"	French Provincial Polished Ebony	14,390.
G 87FD	6' 2"	French Provincial Satin Wood Finishes	14,990.
G 87FD	6' 2"	French Provincial Polished Wood Finishes	14,790.
G 87FFBD	6' 2"	Rococo Polished Wood Finishes	15,230.
G 87HLBCD	6' 2"	Louis XVI Polished Beech Ebony (Hexagonal)	16,630.
G 87HLD	6' 2"	Louis XVI Satin Wood Finish (Hexagonal)	15,110.
G 87LD	6' 2"	Louis XVI Satin Ebony	14,430.
G 87LD	6' 2"	Louis XVI Polished Ebony	14,230.
G 87LD	6' 2"	Louis XVI Satin Wood Finishes	14,830.
G 87LD	6' 2"	Louis XVI Polished Wood Finishes	14,630.
G 87LD	6' 2"	Louis XVI Polished Ivory/White	14,430.
G 87PLD	6' 2"	Louis XVI Satin Wood Finishes (Octagonal)	15,110.
G 87PLSD	6' 2"	Louis XVI Polished Wood Finishes (Octagonal)	15,510.
G 208D	6' 10"	Satin Ebony	17,010.
G 208D	6' 10"	Polished Ebony	16,790.
G 208D	6' 10"	Satin Wood Finishes	17,390.
G 208D	6' 10"	Polished Wood Finishes	16,790.
G 208HLD	6' 10"	Louis XVI Satin Wood Finish (Hexagonal)	17,990.
G 208HLBCD	6' 10"	Louis XVI Satin Wood Finish (Hexagonal)	18,310.
G 208HLBCD	6' 10"	Louis XVI Polished Wood Finish (Hexagonal)	18,110.
G 228D	7' 6"	Polished Ebony	20,790.
G 278D	9' 2"	Polished Ebony	44,790.

Sohmer (Persis International)

Verticals

S-126	50"	Polished Ebony	11,780.
S-126	50"	Polished Mahogany	12,180.

Grands

S-160	5' 3"	Polished Ebony	23,180.
S-160	5' 3"	Polished Mahogany	23,980.
S-180	5' 10"	Polished Ebony	26,180.

*For explanation of terms and prices, please see pages 117–121.

Model	Size	Style and Finish	List Price*

Sohmer (continued)

Model	Size	Style and Finish	List Price*
S-180	5' 10"	Polished Mahogany	26,980.
S-218	7' 2"	Polished Ebony	35,780.

Sohmer & Co. (SMC)

Verticals

Model	Size	Style and Finish	List Price*
43F	43"	French Provincial Satin Cherry	4,990.
43T	43"	Satin Mahogany/Walnut	4,990.
47S	46½"	Satin Ebony	6,790.
47S	46½"	Polished Ebony	6,790.
47S	46½"	Satin Mahogany/Walnut	6,790.
47S	46½"	Polished Mahogany/Walnut	6,790.
48P	48"	Polished Ebony	5,390.

Grands

Model	Size	Style and Finish	List Price*
50T	5'	Polished Ebony	13,900.
50T	5'	Satin Mahogany/Walnut/Cherry	14,600.
50F	5'	French Provincial Semi-Gloss Mahog./Cherry	20,800.
63E	5' 4"	Empire Semi-Gloss Mahog./Walnut/Cherry	23,000.
63F (Ind.)	5' 4"	French Provincial Semi-Gloss Cherry	19,390.
63F	5' 4"	French Provincial Semi-Gloss Mahog/Walnut	21,500.
63H	5' 4"	Hepplewhite Semi-Gloss Mahog./Walnut/Cherry	20,000.
63T	5' 4"	Satin Ebony	17,400.
63T	5' 4"	Polished Ebony	16,800.
63T	5' 4"	Semi-Gloss Mahogany/Walnut/Cherry	19,000.
77E	5' 9"	Empire Semi-Gloss Mahogany/Walnut/Cherry	23,500.
77E (Ind.)	5' 9"	Empire Semi-Gloss Cherry	21,600.
77F	5' 9"	Fr. Prov. Semi-Gloss Mahogany/Walnut/Cherry	22,100.
77F (Ind.)	5' 9"	Fr. Prov. Semi-Gloss Cherry	20,200.
77H	5' 9"	Hepplewhite S-G Mahogany/Walnut/Cherry	20,400.
77H (Ind.)	5' 9"	Hepplewhite Semi-Gloss Cherry	18,790.
77T	5' 9"	Satin Ebony	18,100.
77T	5' 9"	Polished Ebony	17,400.
77T (Ind.)	5' 9"	Polished Ebony	15,390.
77T	5' 9"	Semi-Gloss Mahogany/Walnut/Cherry	19,500.
90H	6' 2"	Hepplewhite S-G Mahogany/Walnut/Cherry	20,900.
90T	6' 2"	Satin Ebony	18,600.
90T	6' 2"	Polished Ebony	17,800.
90T	6' 2"	Semi-Gloss Mahogany	20,000.
95T	6' 8"	Satin Ebony	28,800.
95T	6' 8"	Polished Ebony	27,800.
95T	6' 8"	Semi-Gloss Mahogany/Walnut/Cherry	29,800.

Model	Size	Style and Finish	List Price*

Steck, Geo. — see "Sejung"

Steigerman

"Premium Series" model numbers begin with "SP."

Verticals

Model	Size	Style and Finish	List Price*
SU108	42"	Continental Polished Ebony	3,800.
SU108	42"	Continental Polished Dark Walnut/Mahogany	3,950.
C43	43"	Satin Oak/Cherry/Walnut/Mahogany	4,300.
SU110	43"	Polished Ebony, w/toe blocks	4,000.
SU110	43"	Polished Mahogany/Walnut, w/toe blocks	4,150.
C45	45"	Satin Oak/Cherry/Walnut/Mahogany	4,500.
SU115	45"	Polished Ebony	4,100.
SU115	45"	Polished Mahogany/Walnut	4,250.
P116	45"	Satin Light Walnut, institutional	4,400.
SPU115	45½"	Polished Ebony	5,400.
SPU115	45½"	Polished Mahogany/Walnut	5,550.
SU117	46"	Polished Mahogany, curved leg	3,750.
XU118	46½"	Polished Ebony/Dark Walnut	3,750.
SU120	47"	Polished Ebony	4,300.
SU120	47"	Polished Dark Mahogany	4,450.
SPU123	48½"	Polished Ebony	7,560.
SPU123	48½"	Polished Mahogany/Walnut	7,660.
SPU131	52"	Polished Ebony	7,850.
SPU131	52"	Polished Mahogany	8,000.
SPU132HA	52"	Polished Ebony	4,592.
All models		Color instead of Polished Ebony, add'l	150.

Grands

Model	Size	Style and Finish	List Price*
XG143	4' 8"	Polished Ebony	9,600.
XG148	4' 10"	Polished Ebony	10,800.
SPG151	5'	Polished Ebony	13,300.
SPG151	5'	Polished Mahogany/Walnut	13,700.
SPG151C	5'	Polished Ebony	14,000.
SPG151C	5'	Polished Mahogany/Walnut	14,400.
XG158S	5' 2"	Polished Ebony	11,400.
SPG161	5' 4"	Polished Ebony	14,970.
SPG161	5' 4"	Polished Mahogany/Walnut	15,350.
SPG161G	5' 4"	Polished Ebony	16,000.
XG168S	5' 6"	Polished Ebony	12,400.
SPG178	5' 10"	Polished Ebony	16,470.
SPG178	5' 10"	Polished Mahogany/Walnut	16,870.
XG185S	6'	Polished Ebony	14,400.
SPG198	6' 5"	Polished Ebony	19,500.
All models		Color instead of Polished Ebony, add'l	400.
All models		Slow-Close Fallboard, add'l	110.

*For explanation of terms and prices, please see pages 117–121.

Steinberg, Gerh.

Verticals

Model	Size	Style and Finish	List Price*
HM-109	43"	Continental Polished Ebony	5,590.
HM-109	43"	Continental Pol. Mahogany/Walnut/Oak/White	5,790.
HM-109	43"	Continental Satin Finish	5,790.
HM-109	43"	Polished Ebony	5,790.
HM-109	43"	Polished Mahogany/Walnut/Oak/White	5,990.
HM-109	43"	Satin Finish	5,990.
HM-109	43"	Queen Anne Polished Ebony	5,990.
HM-109	43"	Queen Anne Polished Mahogany/Walnut	6,190.
HM-109	43"	Queen Anne Satin Walnut	6,190.
HM-116	46"	Deco Leg Polished Ebony	6,190.
HM-116	46"	Deco Leg Polished Ebony w/Walnut Trim	6,350.
HM-116	46"	Deco Leg Polished Mahogany/Oak/White	6,590.
HM-116	46"	Queen Anne Polished Ebony	6,350.
HM-116	46"	Queen Anne Polished Mahogany/Walnut	6,650.
HM-117	46"	Decorator Cabinet (square leg) Satin Mahogany	7,850.
EV-123	48"	Polished Ebony	6,580.
EV-123	48"	Polished Ebony w/Pommele Center	6,650.
EV-123	48"	Polished Mahogany/Walnut/Oak/White	6,730.
EV-123	48"	Satin Finish	6,730.
EV-123	48"	Queen Anne Polished Ebony	6,730.
EV-123	48"	Queen Anne Polished Mahogany/Walnut	6,950.
EV-125	49"	Polished Ebony	6,950.
EV-125	49"	Polished Ebony w/Pommele Center	7,090.
EV-125	49"	Polished Mahogany/Walnut/White	7,280.
EV-125	49"	Queen Anne Polished Ebony	7,180.
EV-125	49"	Queen Anne Polished Mahogany/Walnut	7,370.
EV-125	49"	Queen Anne Pol. Mahogany/Walnut w/molding	7,580.

Grands

Model	Size	Style and Finish	List Price*
S-159	5' 3"	Polished Ebony	18,320.
S-159	5' 3"	Polished Mahogany/Walnut/Oak/White	19,000.
S-159	5' 3"	Satin Finish	19,000.
S-159	5' 3"	Polished Ebony (round leg)	18,650.
S-159	5' 3"	Polished Mahogany/Walnut (round leg)	19,340.
S-159	5' 3"	Satin Finish (round leg)	19,340.
S-159	5' 3"	Queen Anne Polished Ebony	18,650.
S-159	5' 3"	Queen Anne Polished Mahogany/Walnut	19,340.
S-159	5' 3"	Queen Anne Satin Finish	19,340.
S-159	5' 3"	Designer Satin Ebony w/Bubinga Fallboard/Lid	19,690.
S-186	6' 1"	Polished Ebony	20,380.
S-186	6' 1"	Polished Mahogany/Walnut/Oak/White	21,260.
S-186	6' 1"	Satin Finish	21,260.
S-186	6' 1"	Polished Ebony (round leg)	20,720.

Model	Size	Style and Finish	List Price*
S-186	6' 1"	Polished Mahogany/Walnut (round leg)	21,590.
S-186	6' 1"	Satin Finish (round leg)	21,590.
S-186	6' 1"	Queen Anne Polished Ebony	20,720.
S-186	6' 1"	Queen Anne Polished Mahogany/Walnut	21,590.
S-186	6' 1"	Queen Anne Satin Finish	21,590.
S-186	6' 1"	Designer Satin Ebony w/Bubinga Fallboard/Lid	21,760.

Steinberg, Wilh.

Verticals

IQ 14	45"	Continental Polished Ebony	14,190.
IQ 16	46"	Polished Ebony	15,190.
IQ 16	46"	Satin Beech/Oak/Alder	15,190.
IQ 16	46"	Satin Walnut/Mahogany	15,390.
IQ 16	46"	Satin Cherry	15,590.
IQ 16	46"	Satin Cherry with Yew	16,990.
IQ 24	48½"	Polished Ebony	16,990.
IQ 24	48½"	Satin Beech/Oak/Alder	16,990.
IQ 24	48½"	Satin Walnut/Mahogany	17,590.
IQ 24	48½"	Satin Cherry	17,990.
IQ 24	48½"	Satin Cherry with Yew	18,790.
IQ 24	48½"	"Amadeus" Polished Ebony	18,190.
IQ 24	48½"	"Amadeus" Satin Walnut/Mahogany	18,590.
IQ 28	51"	Polished Ebony	20,390.
IQ 28	51"	Satin Walnut/Mahogany	20,790.
IQ 28	51"	Satin Cherry	21,790.
IQ 28	51"	Satin Cherry with Yew	22,390.
IQ 28	51"	"Amadeus" Polished Ebony	22,790.
IQ 28	51"	"Amadeus" Satin Cherry	22,790.
IQ 28	51"	"Passione" Polished Ebony	24,390.
IQ 28	51"	"Passione" Satin Walnut/Mahogany	24,790.

Grands

IQ 77	5' 8"	Polished Ebony	50,790.
IQ 77	5' 8"	Satin Walnut/Mahogany	54,790.
IQ 77	5' 8"	Satin Cherry	55,390.
IQ 99	6' 4"	Polished Ebony	60,590.
IQ 99	6' 4"	Satin Walnut/Mahogany	68,790.
IQ 99	6' 4"	Satin Cherry	69,790.

Steingraeber & Söhne

This list includes only those models most likely to be offered to U.S. customers. Other models, styles, and finishes are available. Euro = 1.40

Verticals

122 S	48"	Satin Ebony	30,954.

*For explanation of terms and prices, please see pages 117–121.

Model	Size	Style and Finish	List Price*

Steingraeber & Söhne (continued)

Model	Size	Style and Finish	List Price*
122 S	48"	Polished Ebony	34,420.
122 S	48"	Polished Sapele Mahogany	36,868.
130 PS/S	51"	Satin Ebony	46,068.
130 PS/S	51"	Polished Ebony	46,068.
130 PS/S	51"	Polished Ebony w/Twist & Change Panels	49,778.
130 PS/S	51"	Polished Sapele Mahogany	47,988.
130 PS/S	51"	Satin Special Veneers	47,860.
130 PS/S	51"	Polished Special Veneers	53,956.
130 PS/R	51"	Satin Ebony with SFM Action	47,358.
130 PS/R	51"	Polished Ebony with SFM Action	47,358.
130 PS/R	51"	Polished Ebony w/Twist & Change Pan. w/SFM	51,068.
130 PS/R	51"	Polished Sapele Mahogany with SFM Action	49,278.
130 PS/R	51"	Polished Special Veneers with SFM Action	55,246.
130 K	51"	"Classic" Satin Ebony	46,068.
130 K	51"	"Classic" Polished Ebony	46,068.
130 K	51"	"Classic" Polished Ebony w/Twist & Change	49,778.
130 K	51"	"Classic" Polished Sapele Mahogany	47,988.
130 K	51"	"Classic" Satin Special Veneers	47,860.
130 K	51"	"Classic" Polished Special Veneers	53,956.
138 K	54"	"Classic" Satin Ebony	50,828.
138 K	54"	"Classic" Polished Ebony	50,828.
138 K	54"	"Classic" Polished Ebony w/Twist & Change	54,570.
138 K	54"	"Classic" Polished Sapele Mahogany	55,164.
138 K	54"	"Classic" Satin Special Veneers	55,058.
138 K	54"	"Classic" Polished Special Veneers	61,226.

Grands

Model	Size	Style and Finish	List Price*
168 N	5' 7"	Polished Ebony	83,850.
168 N	5' 7"	Satin Special Veneers	111,082.
168 N	5' 7"	Polished Special Veneers	122,096.
168 K	5' 7"	"Classicism" Polished Ebony	95,438.
168 K	5' 7"	"Classicism" Satin Special Veneers	123,178.
168 K	5' 7"	"Classicism" Polished Special Veneers	134,870.
168 S	5' 7"	"Studio" Polished Ebony	78,308.
205 N	6' 9"	Polished Ebony	108,858.
205 N	6' 9"	Satin Special Veneers	136,450.
205 N	6' 9"	Polished Special Veneers	148,024.
205 K	6' 9"	"Classicism" Polished Ebony	120,698.
205 K	6' 9"	"Classicism" Satin Special Veneers	148,162.
205 K	6' 9"	"Classicism" Polished Special Veneers	159,758.
205 S	6' 9"	"Studio" Polished Ebony	105,572.
D-232	7' 7"	"Semi-Concert" Polished Ebony	144,810.
E-272	8' 11"	Polished Ebony	199,052.
E-272	8' 11"	Polished Special Veneers	237,456.

Steinway & Sons

These are the prices at the Steinway retail store in New York City, often used as a "benchmark" for Steinway prices throughout the country. Model K-52 in ebony; model 1098 in ebony, mahogany, and walnut; and grand models in ebony, mahogany, and walnut include adjustable artist bench. Other models include regular wood bench. Ebony models are in a satin finish; all other models are in a semi-gloss finish called "satin lustre."

Verticals

Model	Size	Style and Finish	List Price
4510	45"	Sheraton Satin Ebony	21,500.
4510	45"	Sheraton Mahogany	23,900.
4510	45"	Sheraton Walnut	24,900.
4510	45"	Sheraton Dark Cherry	26,600.
4510	45"	Sheraton Macassar Ebony	31,600.
4510	45"	Sheraton Marbelized	30,400.
1098	46½"	Satin Ebony	20,100.
1098	46½"	Mahogany	22,100.
1098	46½"	Walnut	22,900.
1098	46½"	Dark Cherry	23,900.
1098	46½"	Marbelized	28,200.
K-52	52"	Satin Ebony	26,400.
K-52	52"	Mahogany	29,900.
K-52	52"	Walnut	30,900.
K-52	52"	East Indian Rosewood	38,600.
K-52	52"	Marbelized	36,600.

Grands

Model	Size	Style and Finish	List Price
S	5' 1"	Satin Ebony	43,800.
S	5' 1"	Mahogany	49,100.
S	5' 1"	Walnut	51,100.
S	5' 1"	Figured Sapele	53,700.
S	5' 1"	Dark Cherry	54,200.
S	5' 1"	Kewazinga Bubinga	55,900.
S	5' 1"	Santos Rosewood	62,100.
S	5' 1"	East Indian Rosewood	62,800.
S	5' 1"	African Pommele	63,200.
S	5' 1"	Macassar Ebony	69,100.
S	5' 1"	Marbelized	62,100.
S	5' 1"	Chinoiserie	60,100.
S	5' 1"	Hepplewhite Dark Cherry	56,900.
M	5' 7"	Satin Ebony	50,300.
M	5' 7"	Mahogany	56,300.
M	5' 7"	Walnut	58,400.
M	5' 7"	Figured Sapele	60,200.
M	5' 7"	Dark Cherry	61,800.

*For explanation of terms and prices, please see pages 117–121.

Model	Size	Style and Finish	List Price*

Steinway & Sons (continued)

Model	Size	Style and Finish	List Price*
M	5' 7"	Kewazinga Bubinga	63,200.
M	5' 7"	Santos Rosewood	69,100.
M	5' 7"	East Indian Rosewood	70,100.
M	5' 7"	African Pommele	70,700.
M	5' 7"	Macassar Ebony	77,600.
M	5' 7"	Marbelized	69,800.
M	5' 7"	Chinoiserie	66,400.
M	5' 7"	Hepplewhite Dark Cherry	64,600.
M 1014A	5' 7"	Chippendale Mahogany	70,600.
M 1014A	5' 7"	Chippendale Walnut	72,300.
M 501A	5' 7"	Louis XV Walnut	90,900.
M 501A	5' 7"	Louis XV East Indian Rosewood	105,900.
O	5' 10½"	Satin Ebony	56,800.
O	5' 10½"	Mahogany	63,300.
O	5' 10½"	Walnut	65,600.
O	5' 10½"	Figured Sapele	67,900.
O	5' 10½"	Dark Cherry	68,800.
O	5' 10½"	Kewazinga Bubinga	70,900.
O	5' 10½"	Santos Rosewood	77,900.
O	5' 10½"	East Indian Rosewood	79,300.
O	5' 10½"	African Pommele	79,600.
O	5' 10½"	Macassar Ebony	87,900.
O	5' 10½"	Marbelized	78,900.
O	5' 10½"	Chinoiserie	73,100.
O	5' 10½"	Hepplewhite Dark Cherry	72,300.
A	6' 2"	Satin Ebony	65,400.
A	6' 2"	Mahogany	72,300.
A	6' 2"	Walnut	74,600.
A	6' 2"	Figured Sapele	77,400.
A	6' 2"	Dark Cherry	78,600.
A	6' 2"	Kewazinga Bubinga	80,900.
A	6' 2"	Santos Rosewood	88,600.
A	6' 2"	East Indian Rosewood	89,100.
A	6' 2"	African Pommele	90,200.
A	6' 2"	Macassar Ebony	99,800.
A	6' 2"	Marbelized	88,700.
A	6' 2"	Chinoiserie	84,400.
B	6' 10½"	Satin Ebony	73,600.
B	6' 10½"	Mahogany	81,100.
B	6' 10½"	Walnut	83,600.
B	6' 10½"	Figured Sapele	86,900.
B	6' 10½"	Dark Cherry	88,100.
B	6' 10½"	Kewazinga Bubinga	90,700.

Model	Size	Style and Finish	List Price*
B	6' 10½"	Santos Rosewood	99,400.
B	6' 10½"	East Indian Rosewood	100,300.
B	6' 10½"	African Pommele	100,600.
B	6' 10½"	Macassar Ebony	111,400.
B	6' 10½"	Marbelized	97,900.
B	6' 10½"	Chinoiserie	92,600.
B	6' 10½"	Hepplewhite Dark Cherry	93,100.
D	8' 11¾"	Satin Ebony	111,400.
D	8' 11¾"	Mahogany	124,100.
D	8' 11¾"	Walnut	127,100.
D	8' 11¾"	Figured Sapele	133,700.
D	8' 11¾"	Dark Cherry	137,200.
D	8' 11¾"	Kewazinga Bubinga	139,100.
D	8' 11¾"	Santos Rosewood	152,600.
D	8' 11¾"	East Indian Rosewood	153,700.
D	8' 11¾"	African Pommele	154,400.
D	8' 11¾"	Macassar Ebony	170,400.
D	8' 11¾"	Chinoiserie	133,100.
D	8' 11¾"	Hepplewhite Dark Cherry	143,900.

Grands (Hamburg)

I frequently get requests for prices of pianos made in Steinway's branch factory in Hamburg, Germany. Officially, these pianos are not sold in North America, but it is possible to order one through an American Steinway dealer, or to go to Europe and purchase one there. The following list shows approximately how much it would cost to purchase a Hamburg Steinway in Europe and have it shipped to the United States. The list was derived by taking the published retail price in Europe, subtracting the value-added tax not applicable to foreign purchasers, converting to U.S. dollars (the rate used here is 1 Euro = $1.55, but is obviously subject to change), and adding approximate charges for duty, air freight, crating, insurance, brokerage fees, and delivery. Only prices for grands in polished ebony are shown here. *Caution:* This list is published for general informational purposes only. The price that Steinway would charge for a piano ordered through an American Steinway dealer may be different. (Also, the cost of a trip to Europe to purchase the piano is not included!)

S-155	5' 1"	Polished Ebony	74,800.
M-170	5' 7"	Polished Ebony	81,900.
O-180	5' 10½"	Polished Ebony	86,800.
A-188	6' 2"	Polished Ebony	92,600.
B-211	6' 11"	Polished Ebony	107,600.
C-227	7' 5½"	Polished Ebony	126,200.
D-274	8' 11¾"	Polished Ebony	162,300.

*For explanation of terms and prices, please see pages 117–121.

Model	Size	Style and Finish	List Price*

Story & Clark

All Story & Clark pianos include PNOscan, USB, and MIDI connectivity.

Verticals

Model	Size	Style and Finish	List Price
110	44"	Continental Polished Ebony/Mahogany	4,190.
110	44"	"Huntington" Oak/Mahogany	4,790.
110	44"	"Calais" Cherry	4,790.
118	46"	"Academy" Satin or Polished Ebony	5,390.
118	46"	"Academy" Oak	5,390.
121	47"	"Cosmopolitan" Polished Ebony	7,390.
All verticals		With Pianomation Petine Installed, add'l	4,990.

Grands

Model	Size	Style and Finish	List Price
145	4' 9"	"Prelude" Polished Ebony	8,590.
145	4' 9"	"Prelude" Polished Mahogany	8,990.
150, 151	4' 11"	"Manhattan" S-G Ebony w/Birdseye Maple Acc.	13,990.
152	4' 11"	"Manhattan" Semi-Gloss Ebony, No Accents	13,990.
155	5' 1"	"Academy" Satin Ebony	9,990.
155	5' 1"	"Academy" Pol. Ebony/Mahogany/Br. Ribbon	9,990.
155	5' 1"	"Academy" Polished White	9,790.
155	5' 1"	French Provincial Polished Ebony	10,790.
155	5' 1"	French Provincial Polished or Satin Mahogany	11,590.
163	5' 4"	"Cosmopolitan" Polished Ebony	14,190.
163	5' 4"	"Melrose" Polished Ebony	14,790.
163	5' 4"	"Melrose" Polished Mahogany	16,390.
163	5' 4"	"Park West" Satin Ebony	14,790.
163	5' 4"	"Park West" Polished Ebony	13,990.
163	5' 4"	"Fairfax" Polished Ebony	14,790.
172	5' 7"	"Artist Conservatory" Polished Ebony	9,790.
172	5' 7"	"Artist Conservatory" Polished Mahogany	10,390.
172	5' 7"	"Artist Conservatory" Polished Brown Ribbon	10,390.
177	5' 9"	"Fairfax" Polished Ebony	15,790.
177	5' 9"	"Versailles" Satin Lacquer Cherry	18,390.
177	5' 9"	"Versailles" Satin Antique Ivory	18,390.
177	5' 9"	"Park West" Polished Ebony	14,990.
185	6' 1"	"Artist Professional" Polished Ebony	10,990.
186	6' 2"	"Islander" British Colonial Satin Teak/Walnut	18,190.
186	6' 2"	"Park West" Polished Ebony	15,790.
205	6' 8"	"Artist Semi-Concert" Polished Ebony	15,390.
215	7'	"Park West" Satin Ebony	17,390.
All grands		With Pianomation Petine Installed, add'l	4,990.

Model	Size	Style and Finish	List Price*

Suzuki

The models and prices below are the ones listed on Suzuki's Web site.

Verticals

Model	Size	Style and Finish	List Price
T-43C	43"	Continental Polished Ebony	2,587.
T-43C	43"	Continental Polished Mahogany	2,697.
T-43	43"	Polished Ebony	2,687.
T-43	43"	Polished Mahogany	2,797.
T-45	45"	Polished Ebony	2,887.
T-45	45"	Polished Mahogany	2,997.
T-48	48"	Polished Ebony	3,087.
T-48	48"	Polished Mahogany	3,197.

Grands

Model	Size	Style and Finish	List Price
F-410	4' 10"	Polished Ebony	5,887.
F-410	4' 10"	Polished Mahogany	6,097.
F-52	5' 2"	Polished Ebony	6,487.
F-52	5' 2"	Polished Mahogany	6,697.
F-58	5' 8"	Polished Ebony	7,487.
F-58	5' 8"	Polished Mahogany	7,697.
F-62	6' 2"	Polished Ebony	8,487.

Vogel

Verticals

Model	Size	Style and Finish	List Price
V-115 M	45"	Continental Polished Ebony	11,980.
V-115 M	45"	Continental Wood Finish	12,980.
V-115 T	45"	Polished Ebony	11,980.
V-115 T	45"	Polished Mahogany/White	12,980.
V-121 T	48"	Polished Ebony	13,580.
V-121 T	48"	Polished Mahogany	14,780.

Grands

Model	Size	Style and Finish	List Price
V-160 C	5' 3"	Chippendale Polished Ebony	32,580.
V-160 C	5' 3"	Chippendale Polished Mahogany/Walnut/White	32,580.
V-160 R	5' 3"	"Royal" Polished Ebony	31,180.
V-160 R	5' 3"	"Royal" Polished Mahogany/Walnut/White	32,580.
V-160 RIO	5' 3"	"Royal" Polished Mahogany Intarsia Oval	37,380.
V-160 RM	5' 3"	"Royal" Polished Flame Mahogany Coffer	35,380.
V-160 T	5' 3"	Polished Ebony	27,380.
V-160 T	5' 3"	Polished Mahogany/Walnut/White	28,780.
V-160 TI	5' 3"	Polished Mahogany Intarsia	37,380.
V-177 C	5' 11"	Chippendale Polished Ebony	33,580.
V-177 C	5' 11"	Chippendale Polished Mahogany/Walnut/White	33,580.
V-177 R	5' 11"	"Royal" Polished Ebony	32,180.
V-177 R	5' 11"	"Royal" Polished Mahogany/Walnut/White	33,580.

*For explanation of terms and prices, please see pages 117–121.

Model	Size	Style and Finish	List Price*

Vogel (continued)

V-177 RI	5' 11"	"Royal" Polished Mahogany Intarsia	38,380.
V-177 RM	5' 11"	"Royal" Polished Flame Mahogany Coffer	36,180.
V-177 T	5' 11"	Polished Ebony	28,380.
V-177 T	5' 11"	Polished Mahogany/Walnut/White	29,780.
V-177 TI	5' 11"	Polished Mahogany Intarsia	38,380.

Vose & Sons

Verticals

113	45"	Polished Ebony	4,390.
113	45"	Polished Mahogany	4,490.

Grands

147	4' 10"	Polished Ebony	9,990.
147	4' 10"	Polished Mahogany	10,390.

Walter, Charles R.

Verticals

1520	43"	Satin Ebony	11,720.
1520	43"	Semi-Gloss Ebony	11,820.
1520	43"	Polished Ebony	11,960.
1520	43"	Satin Walnut	11,400.
1520	43"	Satin Cherry	11,370.
1520	43"	Satin Oak	11,040.
1520	43"	Satin Mahogany	11,580.
1520	43"	Italian Provincial Satin Ebony	11,720.
1520	43"	Italian Provincial Semi-Gloss Ebony	11,820.
1520	43"	Italian Provincial Polished Ebony	11,960.
1520	43"	Italian Provincial Satin Walnut	11,420.
1520	43"	Italian Provincial Satin Mahogany	11,600.
1520	43"	Italian Provincial Satin Oak	11,050.
1520	43"	Country Classic Satin Cherry	11,280.
1520	43"	Country Classic Satin Oak	11,100.
1520	43"	French Provincial Satin Oak	11,420.
1520	43"	French Prov. Satin Cherry/Walnut/Mahogany	11,720.
1520	43"	Riviera Satin Oak	11,010.
1520	43"	Queen Anne Satin Oak	11,500.
1520	43"	Queen Anne Satin Mahogany/Cherry	11,720.
1500	45"	Satin Ebony	10,700.
1500	45"	Semi-Gloss Ebony	10,880.
1500	45"	Polished Ebony	10,990.
1500	45"	Satin Oak	10,250.
1500	45"	Satin Walnut	10,800.

Model	Size	Style and Finish	List Price*
1500	45"	Satin Mahogany	10,940.
1500	45"	Gothic Satin Oak/Cherry	10,910.
All Verticals		Chinese-made action instead of Renner, less	1,200.

Grands

Model	Size	Style and Finish	List Price*
W-175	5' 9"	Satin Ebony	43,010.
W-175	5' 9"	Semi-Polished and Polished Ebony	44,120.
W-175	5' 9"	Satin Mahogany/Walnut/Cherry	44,930.
W-175	5' 9"	Semi-Polished & Pol. Mahogany/Walnut/Cherry	46,070.
W-175	5' 9"	Open-Pore Walnut	43,850.
W-175	5' 9"	Satin Oak	41,340.
W-175	5' 9"	Chippendale Satin Mahogany/Cherry	46,340.
W-175	5' 9"	Chip. Semi-Polished & Pol. Mahogany/Cherry	47,440.
W-190	6' 4"	Satin Ebony	44,130.
W-190	6' 4"	Semi-Polished and Polished Ebony	45,240.
W-190	6' 4"	Satin Mahogany/Walnut/Cherry	46,050.
W-190	6' 4"	Semi-Polished & Pol. Mahogany/Walnut/Cherry	47,190.
W-190	6' 4"	Open-Pore Walnut	44,970.
W-190	6' 4"	Satin Oak	42,460.
W-190	6' 4"	Chippendale Satin Mahogany/Cherry	47,460.
W-190	6' 4"	Chip. Semi-Polished & Pol. Mahogany/Cherry	48,560.

Weber

"Legend" Verticals

Model	Size	Style and Finish	List Price*
WLE 410	43"	Continental Polished Ebony/Ivory	3,575.
WLE 410	43"	Continental Polished Mahogany	3,575.
WLE 410L	43"	Polished Ebony/Mahogany/Ivory	3,655.
WLF 430	43"	French Provincial Satin Cherry	3,990.
WLF 430	43"	Mediterranean Satin Oak	3,990.
WLF 430	43"	Queen Anne Satin Cherry/Oak	3,990.
WLF 430	43"	Satin Mahogany	3,990.
WLE 460S	46½"	Satin Oak/Walnut	5,995.
WLE 480S	48"	Polished Ebony/Mahogany	5,350.
WLE 520S	52"	Polished Ebony/Mahogany	6,070.

"Sovereign" Verticals

Model	Size	Style and Finish	List Price*
WSF 44	43½"	French Provincial Satin Cherry	7,240.
WSF 44	43½"	Mediterranean Satin Oak	7,240.
WSF 44	43½"	Queen Anne Satin Cherry/Oak	7,240.
WSE 470	47"	Satin and Polished Ebony or Mahogany	7,445.
WSE 480	48"	Satin and Polished Ebony or Mahogany	7,655.
WSE 52	52"	Polished Ebony	9,910.

"Albert Weber Platinum" Verticals

Model	Size	Style and Finish	List Price*
AW 48	48"	Polished Ebony	10,150.
AW 48	48"	Satin Mahogany/Cherry/Bubinga/Rosewood	10,150.

*For explanation of terms and prices, please see pages 117–121.

Model	Size	Style and Finish	List Price*

Weber (continued)

Model	Size	Style and Finish	List Price*
AW 121S	48"	Polished Ebony/Mahogany	11,110.
AW 52	52"	Polished Ebony	12,550.
AW 52	52"	Satin Bubinga/Rosewood	12,550.

"Legend" Grands
WLG 50S	4' 11"	Polished Ebony/Mahogany/Walnut	11,375.
WLG 50C	4' 11"	French Prov. Satin Mahogany/Walnut/Cherry	12,070.
WLG 50SL	4' 11"	Polished Ebony/Mahogany/Walnut	11,455.
WLG 51S	5' 2"	Polished Ebony/Mahogany/Walnut	12,640.
WLG 57S	5' 9"	Polished Ebony/Mahogany/Walnut	14,150.
WLG 60S	6' 1"	Polished Ebony/Mahogany/Walnut	15,160.

"Sovereign" Grands
WSG 50	5' 1"	Polished Ebony	13,910.
WSE 51	5' 1"	Satin and Polished Ebony	16,805.
WSE 51	5' 1"	Polished Mahogany	16,805.
WSE 51D	5' 1"	Queen Anne Satin Cherry/Mahogany	19,720.
WSG 57	5' 9"	Satin and Polished Ebony	18,055.
WSG 57	5' 9"	Polished Mahogany	18,055.
WSG 60	6' 1"	Satin and Polished Ebony	22,630.
WSG 60	6' 1"	Polished Mahogany	22,630.

"Albert Weber Platinum" Grands
AW 57	5' 9"	Satin and Polished Ebony	27,670.
AW 57	5' 9"	Polished Mahogany	27,670.
AW 60	6' 1"	Satin and Polished Ebony	29,350.
AW 60	6' 1"	Polished Mahogany	29,350.
AW 69	6' 10"	Satin and Polished Ebony	35,110.
AW 76	7' 6"	Satin and Polished Ebony	48,550.
AW 90	9'	Polished Ebony	60,800.

Weinbach

Grands
Estate 50	5'	Polished Ebony	11,790.
Estate 50	5'	Polished Walnut/Mahogany	12,390.
Estate 50 DC	5'	Demi-Chippendale Polished Ebony	12,790.
Estate 50 DC	5'	Demi-Chippendale Polished Walnut/Mahogany	13,390.
Manor 55	5' 5"	Polished Ebony	12,990.
Manor 55	5' 5"	Polished Walnut/Mahogany	13,590.
Manor 55 DC	5' 5"	Demi-Chippendale Polished Ebony	13,990.
Manor 55 DC	5' 5"	Demi-Chippendale Polished Walnut/Mahogany	14,590.
Chateau 60	6'	Polished Ebony	14,790.
Chateau 60	6'	Polished Walnut/Mahogany	15,390.

Model	Size	Style and Finish	List Price*

Wyman

Verticals

Model	Size	Style and Finish	List Price*
WV108	42½"	Continental Polished Ebony	3,690.
WV108	42½"	Continental Polished Mahogany/Cherry/White	3,750.
WV110	43"	Polished Ebony	4,090.
WV110	43"	Polished Mahogany/Cherry/White	4,150.
WV110	43"	American Country Satin Gallery Oak	4,690.
WV110	43"	Satin Sable Brown Mahogany	4,690.
WV110	43"	French Provincial Satin Sable Cherry	4,790.
WV110	43"	Country French Satin Oak	4,790.
WV115	45"	Polished Ebony	4,290.
WV115	45"	Polished Mahogany/Cherry/White	4,350.
WV118	46"	Polished Ebony	4,890.
WV118	46"	Satin Walnut	4,950.
WV118DL	46"	Polished Ebony w/Chrome Trim (double leg)	4,990.
WV120	48"	Polished Ebony	4,690.
WV120	48"	Polished Mahogany/Cherry/White	4,750.
WV127	50"	Polished Ebony w/Mahog. Trim (straight leg)	6,790.
WV127	50"	Polished Ebony w/Mahog. Trim (curved leg)	6,850.
WV132	52"	Polished Ebony	5,790.

Grands

Model	Size	Style and Finish	List Price*
WG145	4' 9"	Polished Ebony	8,590.
WG145	4' 9"	Polished Mahogany/Cherry/White	8,990.
WG160	5' 3"	Polished Ebony	10,390.
WG160	5' 3"	Polished Mahogany/Cherry/White	10,790.
GP160	5' 3"	Polished Ebony	9,950.
GP160	5' 3"	Polished Mahogany/Cherry/White	10,550.
WG170	5' 7"	Polished Ebony	11,590.
WG170	5' 7"	Polished Mahogany/Cherry/White	11,990.
GP175	5' 8"	Polished Ebony	11,950.
GP175	5' 8"	Polished Mahogany/Cherry/White	12,550.
WG185	6' 1"	Polished Ebony	13,590.
WG185	6' 1"	Polished Mahogany/Cherry/White	13,990.
GP190	6' 3"	Polished Ebony	13,950.
GP190	6' 3"	Polished Mahogany/Cherry/White	14,550.
GP215	7'	Polished Ebony	20,750.
GP215	7'	Polished Mahogany/Cherry/White	21,350.
All models		Satin Ebony, Mahogany, Cherry Finishes, add'l	300.
All models		CD Player System, add'l	4,500.

*For explanation of terms and prices, please see pages 117–121.

Model	Size	Style and Finish	List Price*

Yamaha
including Disklavier and Silent Piano (formerly MIDIPiano)

Verticals

Model	Size	Style and Finish	List Price*
M460	44"	Satin Cherry/Brown Cherry	4,590.
M560	44"	Hancock Satin Brown Cherry	4,990.
M560	44"	Sheraton Satin Mahogany	4,990.
M560	44"	Queen Anne Satin Cherry	4,990.
P22	45"	Satin Ebony/Walnut/Oak	5,990.
P660	45"	Sheraton Satin Brown Mahogany	6,390.
P660	45"	Queen Anne Satin Brown Cherry	6,390.
T118	47"	Polished Ebony	5,190.
T118	47"	Polished Mahogany/Walnut	5,590.
T121	48"	Polished Ebony	7,390.
U1	48"	Satin Ebony	9,250.
U1	48"	Polished Ebony	8,990.
U1	48"	Satin American Walnut	9,790.
U1	48"	Polished American Walnut/Mahogany	10,390.
U1	48"	Polished White	10,490.
YUS1	48"	Satin Ebony	11,250.
YUS1	48"	Polished Ebony	10,990.
YUS1	48"	Satin American Walnut	11,790.
YUS1	48"	Polished American Walnut/Mahogany	13,390.
U3	52"	Polished Ebony	12,490.
U3	52"	Satin American Walnut	12,690.
U3	52"	Polished Mahogany	13,690.
YUS3	52"	Polished Ebony	13,590.
YUS3	52"	Polished Mahogany	15,790.
YUS5	52"	Polished Ebony	15,790.

Disklavier Verticals

Model	Size	Style and Finish	List Price*
DU1A	48"	Satin Ebony	17,050.
DU1A	48"	Polished Ebony	16,790.
DU1A	48"	Satin American Walnut	17,590.
DU1A	48"	Polished Mahogany	18,190.
DU1A	48"	Polished White	18,290.
DYUS1A	48"	Polished Ebony	18,790.
DYUS1A	48"	Satin American Walnut	19,590.
DYUS1A	48"	Polished Mahogany	21,190.

Silent Piano Verticals

Model	Size	Style and Finish	List Price*
U1SG	48"	Polished Ebony	11,700.
U1SG	48"	Polished White	13,990.
YUS1SG	48"	Polished Ebony	13,700.
U3SG	52"	Polished Ebony	15,200.
YUS3SG	52"	Polished Ebony	16,300.

Model	Size	Style and Finish	List Price*
YUS5SG	52"	Polished Ebony	17,780.
Grands			
GB1	4' 11"	Polished Ebony	11,790.
GB1	4' 11"	Polished American Walnut/Mahogany	13,390.
GB1	4' 11"	French Provincial	13,790.
GB1	4' 11"	Georgian	13,790.
GC1	5' 3"	Satin Ebony	18,390.
GC1	5' 3"	Polished Ebony	17,790.
GC1	5' 3"	Satin American Walnut	19,890.
GC1	5' 3"	Polished Mahogany/American Walnut	19,890.
GC1	5' 3"	Polished Ivory/White	19,390.
C1	5' 3"	Satin Ebony	23,390.
C1	5' 3"	Polished Ebony	22,990.
C1	5' 3"	Satin American Walnut	25,790.
C1	5' 3"	Polished American Walnut	26,790.
C1	5' 3"	Satin and Polished Mahogany	26,790.
C1	5' 3"	Polished White	25,990.
C2	5' 8"	Satin Ebony	26,590.
C2	5' 8"	Polished Ebony	25,990.
C2	5' 8"	Satin American Walnut	29,190.
C2	5' 8"	Polished American Walnut/Mahogany	30,590.
C2	5' 8"	Satin Light American Oak	29,590.
C2	5' 8"	Polished White	29,190.
C3	6' 1"	Satin Ebony	35,790.
C3	6' 1"	Polished Ebony	34,790.
C3	6' 1"	Satin American Walnut	38,790.
C3	6' 1"	Polished Mahogany/American Walnut	40,790.
C3	6' 1"	Polished White	38,790.
S4B	6' 3"	Polished Ebony	62,190.
C5	6' 7"	Satin Ebony	38,590.
C5	6' 7"	Polished Ebony	37,990.
C5	6' 7"	Polished Mahogany	47,990.
C6	6' 11"	Satin Ebony	42,790.
C6	6' 11"	Polished Ebony	42,190.
C6	6' 11"	Polished Mahogany	50,590.
S6B	6' 11"	Polished Ebony	70,390.
C7	7' 6"	Satin Ebony	48,590.
C7	7' 6"	Polished Ebony	48,190.
C7	7' 6"	Polished Mahogany	54,790.
CFIIIS	9'	Satin Ebony	127,790.
CFIIIS	9'	Polished Ebony	126,190.
Disklavier Grands			
DGB1CD	4' 11"	Polished Ebony (playback only)	20,590.
DGB1CD	4' 11"	Polished Mahogany/Walnut (playback only)	22,390.

*For explanation of terms and prices, please see pages 117–121.

Model	Size	Style and Finish	List Price*
Yamaha (continued)			
DGC1B	5' 3"	Satin Ebony	27,990.
DGC1B	5' 3"	Polished Ebony	27,390.
DGC1B	5' 3"	Polished Mahogany/Walnut	29,590.
DGC1M4	5' 3"	Satin Ebony	36,990.
DGC1M4	5' 3"	Polished Ebony	36,390.
DGC1M4	5' 3"	Satin American Walnut	38,190.
DGC1M4	5' 3"	Polished American Walnut/Mahogany	38,190.
DGC1M4	5' 3"	Polished Ivory/White	38,190.
DC1M4	5' 3"	Satin Ebony	42,090.
DC1M4	5' 3"	Polished Ebony	41,690.
DC1M4	5' 3"	Satin American Walnut	42,590.
DC1M4	5' 3"	Polished American Walnut	45,590.
DC1M4	5' 3"	Satin and Polished Mahogany	45,590.
DC1M4	5' 3"	Polished White	42,590.
DC2B	5' 8"	Polished Ebony	36,090.
DC2B	5' 8"	Polished Mahogany/American Walnut	40,690.
DC2M4	5' 8"	Satin Ebony	45,190.
DC2M4	5' 8"	Polished Ebony	44,590.
DC2M4	5' 8"	Satin American Walnut	47,790.
DC2M4	5' 8"	Polished American Walnut/Mahogany	49,190.
DC2M4	5' 8"	Satin Mahogany	49,190.
DC2M4	5' 8"	Polished White	47,790.
DC3M4	6' 1"	Satin Ebony	55,390.
DC3M4	6' 1"	Polished Ebony	54,550.
DC3M4	6' 1"	Satin American Walnut	58,650.
DC3M4	6' 1"	Polished American Walnut/Mahogany	60,390.
DC3M4	6' 1"	Polished White	58,650.
DC5M4	6' 7"	Satin Ebony	58,090.
DC5M4	6' 7"	Polished Ebony	57,490.
DC5M4	6' 7"	Polished Mahogany	67,590.
DC6M4	6' 11"	Satin Ebony	62,290.
DC6M4	6' 11"	Polished Ebony	61,690.
DC6M4	6' 11"	Polished Mahogany	70,090.
DC7M4	7' 6"	Satin Ebony	68,190.
DC7M4	7' 6"	Polished Ebony	67,790.
DC7M4	7' 6"	Polished Mahogany	74,790.
DC7M4	7' 6"	Polished White	69,790.
Disklavier Pro Grands			
DC3M4PRO	6' 1"	Polished Ebony	58,750.
DS4M4PROB	6' 3"	Polished Ebony	87,990.
DC5M4PRO	6' 7"	Polished Ebony	61,690.
DC6M4PRO	6' 11"	Polished Ebony	65,890.
DS6M4PROB	6' 11"	Polished Ebony	96,090.

Model	Size	Style and Finish	List Price*
DC7M4PRO	7' 6"	Polished Ebony	71,990.
DCFIIISM4PRO	9'	Polished Ebony	158,390.

Silent Piano Grands

Model	Size	Style and Finish	List Price*
C1S	5' 3"	Polished Ebony	26,390.
C2S	5' 8"	Polished Ebony	28,990.
C3S	6' 1"	Polished Ebony	37,190.
C5S	6' 7"	Polished Ebony	39,590.
C6S	6' 11"	Polished Ebony	43,390.
C7S	7' 6"	Polished Ebony	48,790.

Young Chang

Verticals

Model	Size	Style and Finish	List Price*
AF-108S	42½"	Satin Mahogany	3,990.
AF-108S	42½"	French Provincial Satin Cherry	3,990.
AF-108S	42½"	Satin Queen Anne Oak/Cherry	3,990.
AF-108S	42½"	Mediterranean Satin Oak	3,990.
T-109	43"	Polished Ebony/Mahogany/Ivory	3,575.
PF-110	43½"	Satin Mahogany	7,240.
PF-110	43½"	Satin Queen Anne Oak/Cherry	7,240.
PF-110	43½"	Mediterranean Satin Oak	7,240.
PF-110	43½"	French Provincial Satin Cherry	7,240.
T-110	43½"	Polished Ebony/Mahogany/Ivory	3,655.
T-116E	46½"	Polished Ebony	4,480.
T-116S	46½"	Satin Ebony	5,995.
T-116S	46½"	Satin Walnut/Oak	5,995.
PE-121	48"	Satin and Polished Ebony	7,655.
PE-121	48"	Polished Mahogany	7,655.
PE-121S	48"	Polished Ebony/Mahogany	11,110.
T-121	48"	Polished Ebony/Mahogany	5,350.
YP-48	48"	Polished Ebony	10,150.
YP-48	48"	Satin Mahogany/Bubinga/Rosewood	10,150.
YP-49	49"	Polished Ebony w/Chrome	11,590.
PE-131	52"	Polished Ebony	9,910.
T-131	52"	Polished Ebony/Mahogany	6,070.
YP-52	52"	Satin and Polished Ebony	12,550.
YP-52	52"	Satin Bubinga/Rosewood	12,550.

Grands

Model	Size	Style and Finish	List Price*
GS-150C	5'	Satin Mahogany/Walnut/	12,070.
GS-150	5'	Polished Ebony/Mahogany/Walnut	11,375.
GS-150L	5'	Polished Ebony/Mahogany/Walnut	11,455.
PG-150	5'	Polished Ebony	14,155.
GS-157	5' 1"	Polished Ebony/Mahogany/Walnut	12,070.
PG-157	5' 1"	Satin and Polished Ebony	16,805.

*For explanation of terms and prices, please see pages 117–121.

Young Chang (continued)

Model	Size	Style and Finish	List Price*
PG-157	5' 1"	Polished Mahogany	16,805.
PG-157D	5' 1"	Queen Anne Satin Mahogany	20,760.
PG-157D	5' 1"	Queen Anne Satin Cherry	20,760.
GS-175	5' 9"	Polished Ebony/Mahogany/Walnut	14,150.
PG-175	5' 9"	Satin and Polished Ebony	18,055.
PG-175	5' 9"	Polished Mahogany	18,055.
YP-175	5' 9"	Satin and Polished Ebony	27,670.
YP-175	5' 9"	Polished Mahogany	27,670.
GS-185	6' 1"	Polished Ebony/Mahogany/Walnut	15,160.
PG-185	6' 1"	Satin and Polished Ebony	22,630.
PG-185	6' 1"	Polished Mahogany	22,630.
YP-185	6' 1"	Satin Ebony	29,350.
YP-185	6' 1"	Polished Ebony/Mahogany	29,350.
YP-185	6' 1"	Polished Bubinga/Rosewood	29,350.
YP-185	6' 1"	Polished African Pommele	29,350.
YP-208	6' 10"	Satin and Polished Ebony	35,110.
YP-228	7' 6"	Satin and Polished Ebony	48,550.
YP-275	9'	Polished Ebony	60,800.